THE HAPPIPRENEUR

Taryn Lee Johnston &
Tony Robinson OBE

This second edition published: December 2021

By Chronos Publishing

ISBN: 978-1-914529-31-3

Paperback Edition

This book is a memoir, reflecting the author's present recollections of experiences over time. Some names and characteristics have been changed, some events have been compressed, and some dialogue has been recreated. Memory can be a fickle thing, so the Author trusts that any minor errors in times, dates and details of particular events will be understood.

Some names and identifying details have been changed to protect the privacy of individuals.

Cover photography Alex Holt Photography

Courtesy of Alison Chesworth, EKM

Cover Design by Danji's Designs

Dedication

This book is dedicated to every small business owner, those that try, day after day, win some and fail often.

It's for those that never sell out their integrity, despite the offer on the table.

Foreword by Tim Campbell MBE

I have known Tony for over ten years having met him at a SFEDI awards night. Tony is effervescent - a walking magician in terms of enthusiasm and energy when it comes to helping others. He is the most authentic and genuine of men and I am delighted to introduce this book.

Every business owner will tell you about the bad advice they have received or companies that haven't paid and any entrepreneur that's looking for the Holy Grail, a business book that stops this, will be looking for a long time - the best lessons are those learned by hard work and by making mistakes. Having been ripped off once, you won't be again. However, this book does tell you the truth and will hopefully give you enough solid advice that you'll make fewer, costly mistakes.

Tony is always the most charismatic man in the room. He's very flamboyant with his clothes and always the hat and this is how it should be in business. It's about standing out and being different. The bit that makes successful people distinctive is individuality. In an industry that's driven by appearance and persona, some may look on Tony as a bit of a mad man, but the people who are 'out there' are the ones that are going to make a difference to the world.

All of the most successful entrepreneurs I have ever met have an ability to disarm you in one way or another, that's their superpower. The power of being an individual is disarming.

This book is about a legacy.

The thing about legacy, it's about planting a seed in the garden and not knowing what will grow or being around to see what grows. Tony has the ability, without knowing it, to have left an amazing legacy of confident entrepreneurs, those who are out there now, doing things because of his intervention. He's not a proud man but he should be, that like a doctor or a teacher, he's left the world in a better place because of his actions. He might not achieve the goals that he aspires to right now, it might be a way off from what he hoped to have done in the time he had, but sometimes when you're running forward as Steve Jobs said, "*you can't join the dots looking forward*" but you often don't get a chance to stop for a second, look behind you and see how all the dots have joined up together; Tony's dots add up to an amazing picture of a confident entrepreneur.

He is a person with integrity, one who thinks of others before himself. He has created a vision; one that has infected people with his same kind of energy, and I think that's an achievement to be proud of. In a world where there is a lot of greed, where people are doing things just for themselves, without any consideration for others or how it will impact them, Tony stands for the micro-man.

Tony may not see himself as an entrepreneur, but I personally think that the term 'entrepreneur' is one that has been so overused that it no longer has the same respect that it deserves and many people are using it as a job title.

For me, entrepreneur is a mindset, it's a way of looking at challenges how you identify risk, it's a way that you build and create from things that weren't there, where you can see around the corner when others can't see in front of their face! Those things for me, as an entrepreneur, are what Tony has been able to do successfully. It doesn't matter if he did it once or 20 times, the fact is he's done it. He is the guy that has been able to go to individuals and say "listen, this is how we want to run things, this is the way we want to go, come with me and follow in this direction" and people trust him, they might not see where he's going but they trust him enough to say "*ok, I'm on the journey*".

Tony is an entrepreneur in its truest sense, as they're not about money in the bank, or building companies; my mum was an entrepreneur, one who took her skills and utilised those to make clothes, make cakes and to do the things that were necessary to generate an income for her family. She'd never be on the Forbes 100 list nor get an award from the Queen for being an entrepreneur. There are people like her, out there everywhere, doing what it takes, under the radar without thinking about accolades. These are the entrepreneurs, fighting daily to make ends meet, finding new and innovative ways to change their world and leading by example.

I would challenge Tony and his modest view of himself and say that actually, he should own "entrepreneur". Since in a world of very limited role models, Tony is someone worth looking up to. Someone who isn't motivated by financial returns. A person they can look towards and say *'that's the kind of person I want to be.'*

This book will give you a true sense of the man, his business advice will not steer you wrong and if you're lucky enough to have Tony in your corner, then you know, you're going to succeed.

Table of Contents

Introduction

I first met Tony in 2013. He was looking for help with '*Freedom from Bosses Forever*' and my then business partner had most of the contact, but I recall thinking what a "nice chap" Tony was. It was only after the shocking realisation that my business partner had been, let's say 'not entirely honest' and had almost ruined my business, that I discovered what a truly decent human being Tony was.

Our paths didn't cross for some time after that, although I remained aware of him online through various social media platforms and always did what I could to support his endeavours. He in turn always repaid the favour, often going above and beyond.

In 2018 Tony reached out and asked if I'd be interested in writing his biography. I of course jumped at the chance, in part hoping to repay the kindness he'd shown me back in 2013, but also because I'd come to realise what he stood for and the importance of his message.

Of course, anyone who knows Tony will also understand how perturbed I was when he suggested that rather than just being about his life, the book should also offer business help and support, and be somewhat of an expose′ for unscrupulous business practices

AND have input from fellow businesspeople… phew!

I've got to be honest, it stumped me for a while as I racked my brains on how to accomplish it all. I'd like to say, it came to me in a moment of inspiration and maybe it did, but I know it dawned on me that the book needed a core. A core that reflected what encapsulates Tony.

Integrity.

Defined as *the quality of being honest and having strong moral principles.*

I've come to know the man that he is incredibly well. I've dusted out as many of his closets as I could find and asked him some "*oh my goodness how can I answer that*" type questions. I believe he's never once been dishonest and admits his mistakes fully and with gusto!

The information I have found out about certain business practices is in the public domain, you only need take off the rose tinted glasses and Google further than page one to discover the things that I write about in here. I'm not revealing dark hidden secrets or- telling you more than your common sense would tell you… if you asked it! However, I'm sure that there will be those who disagree with me, devoted followers and "cult" members, yet to wake up to the reality in front of them. For those readers I can only hope that the moment of truth isn't too painful when it happens.

If you're hoping that I managed to dig up some dirt

or that I found out Tony is not as authentic as he appears, then you're in for a disappointment. I'm yet to find a single person who would tell me that Tony is not the man he portrays himself as and believe me I looked! He genuinely is in equal parts lovely, bonkers and dedicated to helping micro-business (0-9 employees) owners!

This is a book predominantly about business, but I hope it is a great read too.

It is the story of one man's life and what he has learned about business ownership. It is about living a happy rather than a wealthy life.

What he has learned will be useful for prospective and existing business owners and those wanting to help people make ends meet. Entrepreneurs and intrapreneurs will enjoy the essential truths about enterprise.

His story explains why he campaigns to make life better for micro-business owners and what he wants the Establishment to do to level the playing field.

I hope that you enjoy reading it as much as we have enjoyed bringing it to you.

Part 1

Riches to Rags - the making of a Happipreneur

"For many years now I have had a quaint idea that all humans - yes, the whole six billion of them on the planet - are out of their fucking minds"

Albert Ellis

I
The End or the Beginning?

I met Tony in Hull, it's late summer and we decided to go for lunch in a little Italian. The food was nice but the conversation better.

I asked Tony where it all started and what was the catalyst for becoming the champion of small businesses?

It's interesting to note that his first anecdote and the place he wanted me to start as far away as possible from where he is now.

It's Friday 22nd August 1986. Early evening. Tony is expecting a couple of hours in the pub, a few drinks celebrating the end of a hard week at work and the end of an era in terms of career.

Instead, he is whisked off to a local hall, where inside are his work colleagues, friends and family. All of whom have colluded against him.

No, it's not an intervention… it's *This Is Your Life*.

Everyone has joined to celebrate the life of the man they have come to love and admire and who has resigned as the CEO of a multi-million-dollar company.

By most people's standards this isn't a normal leaving party, but as you come to know Tony, you'll understand why they've gone to the trouble.

You'd be forgiven for thinking that the BBC were involved, as it's been arranged to that level of detail and care. Tony tells me he was overwhelmed by the gesture, but when asked to elaborate on why they'd go to this trouble he said that his team had become like family. That over the five years they'd been together, he and they had done so much. They'd held charity events, fun days and raised a great deal of money for various institutions.

What may come as more of a shock, is that the company was Amway UK. For anyone in the 1980's this was a big name, but one associated with pyramid selling tactics, scandal and uncomfortable dinner parties as friends tried to hook you in.

Initially for me, it was hard to connect Tony with a company such as this. My memory of Amway was sketchy at best, but I knew people who'd been involved, and I allied the name with other multi-level marketing (MLM) companies such as The Cambridge Diet & Herbal Life.

Amway is still the largest Direct Selling company in the world today and the Devos family which co-own it with the Van Andel family are one of the richest and most influential families in America. They have consistently been the largest family donor to the Republican Party and Betsy De Vos, the wife of Tony's boss at Amway, is Secretary of State for Education for Donald Trump.

However, in getting to know Tony, I see Amway as one of the pivotal moments in his business career. A moment where that internal moral compass pointed in the wrong direction and when he finally realised it, he simply couldn't continue along that path. The leaving party is an example of how he inspires others irrespective of the circumstances.

This is key to understanding the man.

At the very height of his career, where his salary could have been considered obscene, where he was in fact 'living the dream', flying around the world in jet planes, meeting the presidential and influential movers and shakers, Tony pulled on the brakes. Metaphorically said, "*I'm sorry, but I cannot, with a clear conscience, continue working for a company whose business practices conflict with what I know to be right.*"

Yet in an amazing moment of irony, it was the same moral compass that could not allow Tony to walk away immediately. Rather, he gave his boss Dick Devos, who he really liked, and the son of the co-founder, another year of his time to find and induct a suitable replacement.

We'll come back to Amway later as it and others form what I call the 'bad for business' way of working.

For now, I want to set the scene. It's the 80's. A time of 'loads-a-money', brick mobile phones, yuppies and the desire to become as successful as possible, no matter the expense of anyone else.

It's Dynasty and Dallas, glamour and fortune. And Tony was in the thick of it.

Ask yourself, would you, in Tony's position have

allowed your ethics to derail your achieved status and success?

One day you're mixing with the cream of society, the next you're on your own, trying to create a business from scratch. Well not on your own, because luckily for you, there is a business partner who has your back and more often than not your front and side too! Tony's support was a woman called Clare Francis.

Tony left Amway in 1986 and along with Clare created The Business Advisory Bureau Limited.

"The best years of your life are the ones in which you decide your problems are your own.

You do not blame them on your mother, the ecology, or the President.

You realize that you control your own destiny."

Albert Ellis

II
Nature vs Nurture

Tony didn't start out with aspirations to become a high-level CEO. Born in 1952 and lucky to have a father who was a successful salesperson he first lived in a modest home in a pleasant road in Hessle in Hull. Tony grew up an only child, and he admits to looking back on his childhood with rose-tinted glasses, seeing it as a happy time, filled with friends.

He was lucky enough to have two friends on Pulcroft Road who he still sees today, Bruce Cuming and David Johnson. He was Bruce's best man, one of five times he's been a best man, and they have one of those enduring friendships that time nor tide cannot weather.

Unlike the rest of Tony's family living in the centre of Hull, just a few miles away in pre-fabs and council properties, they owned their own house.

When Tony was ten years old, the Robinsons with the addition of his Grandma and Uncle Ron, his mother's brother, moved about half a mile from Pulcroft Road to a large semi-detached house with a big garden in Marlborough Avenue, Hessle. Tony admits by this time the Robinson household was considered wealthy and very 'posh' by the rest of the family,

From Tony being eleven to eighteen, his father - assisted by his mother, a sales rep and two part time staff - ran his own business from Marlborough Avenue. Tony's father's lungs were failing, and he had to work from home. That he couldn't walk more than a few steps before losing his breath was down to a combination of forty cigarettes a day and the sawdust from the box mill he'd previously been Managing Director of.

Tony's family now owning their own business, albeit for health reasons, put them 'in the same boat' as most of their friends, including the Cumings and his father's brother, John, who was one of Hull's most successful entrepreneurs. He was one of the largest fish merchants on Hull Fish Docks, but also had other business interests in Yorkshire and Scotland and even co-owned a large pleasure boat in Bridlington.

Before leaving the box mill, Charles Robinson, Tony's father, had negotiated with the five biggest box mills in Hull that he would be the sales agency for them to keep their factories full of orders. His commission would be around two point five percent on each order. With five times the manufacturing capacity than each factory on its own, he backed himself to get major national orders from Metal Box, Batchelors, Birds Eye, Schweppes and other big names. In other words, apart from the more local customers that each factory had, Tony's father, had changed five competitors into something of a cartel.

None of the major buyers knew CTR Associates was a small enterprise and home based. Tony remembers that once a buyer from the South West insisted on meeting his parents and his father arranged for a helicopter to land in the grounds of the Grange Hotel and Country Club, where the buyer was duly given a wonderful meal. Such was the importance in those days of appearing to be a serious and successful business. I find this really interesting as later you'll see a similar behaviour from people in a different time, it's all about looking the part, thankfully Tony's father could support the image with the back-up of a strong albeit unconventional business.

Tony remembers that his father visited a tailor each year to select the cloth and buy two new suits. He wore these suits every weekday for the year. He was always immaculately dressed, and Tony has on his desk a photo of him on the phone at home in white shirt, tie, braces, cufflinks and so forth - his daily attire. Tony, like it or not, was learning a great deal about business from an early age.

Tony's mother Edna, who Tony's wife Eileen says often 'put on a posh voice' in company, like "*Mrs Bouquet*" from the popular TV series, was a brilliant 'front of house'. She knew the trade, was a qualified shorthand secretary and had assisted her husband at the box mill. Edna could charm her way through the gatekeepers to get to speak to the Chief Buyer of these major companies and then hand the phone over to her husband to do the selling - the opportunity to quote for an order of fruit boxes, stillages or pallets.

Edna was quite a large lady and always said that

they wouldn't have much business if the buyers could see her as they imagined her to be much younger and slimmer. Tony coined or may have heard the phrase 'life is a continual diet' from his mother's lifelong battle with her weight.

Starting again after the war, many of Tony's parents' friends started their own business as the best way of making money and to rebuild their lives. At this time Tony remembers that everyone looked after each other, this was just the way it was.

Whether it was swapping or giving food or lending money, you did what you could as a community together. He remembers free fish every Friday, free sacks of potatoes, toiletries and incredibly cheap (Tony was learning about retail mark ups) spectacles. You would buy locally and support local businesses, something we both feel is so important and how business should be today.

I asked him whether this had helped him when it came to creating his own business and on reflection he tells me, it most likely did. There was always talk of business at home. At the time, it seemed incredibly boring as it would to any child. He helped in the office from thirteen years of age, answering the phone, calculating prices for quotations, doing mailshots and taking cheques to the bank. He had to pass his driving test quickly to help the business too - more of that later.

These life lessons stay with us though and like inheriting a love of reading or being interested in the arts, Tony's mind was sharpened from an early age on how to be successful in business. He just didn't know it yet.

But I'm getting ahead of myself as a lot of the life-defining moments for Tony happened before the family moved to Marlborough Avenue and his father started his own business.

From an early age Tony would visit the box mill on Hull Road in Hessle. The conditions there were terrible because of the noise and sawdust. It was quite a frightening environment for a small child, particularly someone as uncoordinated as Tony.

Tony was perhaps a cuckoo child, he was never quite like either of his parents, although introverted like his mother, he was far from his father who was an extroverted, gregarious man.

His father was a businessman first and foremost, a man who liked to be liked, one of the traits Tony would tell you is a weakness of his own, he was very generous and very popular. He would be the first to buy big rounds of drinks in his bowling club or local pub. He was a successful salesman, which is what had allowed him to build a prosperous career in the metal and timber box industries. He had incredible mental arithmetic skills and always had an eye for a great and innovative deal to benefit his customers and his employers.

Tony remembers that when his father started his own business one of the first things he did was to do a deal to get Portuguese pine wood imported from Lisbon and into the factories. It was of equivalent quality to Swedish pine wood, but it meant lower prices to the customer and therefore more sales for his father. He was always testing out new opportunities for business, such as putting together investors to build an indoor bowling green or to manufacture polystyrene freezer boxes for fruit and veg. Those days of innovation and opportunities were rife, you just had to have the right mind. Today we have lots of people with the right minds, the opportunities are harder to come by.

At home however Charles Thomas Robinson was an angry man, whose rage was often directed at Tony's mother. He was a bully domestically and not a man who understood children. Like many from that era children were not beings that you played with, they were just something that you tolerated until they became of use or at least able to converse with.

Tony recalled holidays in Swanage where his father booked a beach hut for two weeks and then surveyed the beach for kids for his son to play with for the two weeks. Within a short period of time his father had organised a football or cricket match with several children already playing on the beach. Now you might think that this was a great thing for a father to do, however Tony knew that it was a way to introduce him to new 'friends' so that he'd always have people around to entertain him for the holiday and his father could read his paper in peace or go for a drink.

Tony's father was very sick, although he never took a day off, with worsening emphysema. It was this illness and perhaps the drugs, that made him so angry and he was quick to take that anger out on his family. It was only after his death that Tony was able to feel truly independent, prior to this he felt that he was invisible. Again, it's clear to see here the drive that Tony inherited. Not taking time off when needed is one of the main things you'll see those self-employed doing. That lack of realisation until it's too late, that if you don't take care of 'you', there is no business.

I was shocked to hear Tony tell me that he often wished that his 'Auntie' Marie, Bruce's Mum, and his Uncle Ron, a Hull docker, were his parents as he felt much more at home with them. Auntie Marie would make him laugh and was lovely to be around and his Uncle Ron who later lived with them, had time for him and was a gentle and practical man.

Tony's mum was intelligent, it was her that took care of the admin and ensured that things ran smoothly. However, she didn't fully understand her son or really connect with him. Tony recalls his mother as always laughing with her friends - she usually had a different friend she did something with - theatre, a slimming class, cinema or a card game - on every weekday night. However, it was only really with his Auntie Marie that the fun and laughter included him. He was very happy, though, as he was always outside, after school, playing sports with friends.

Aged eight Tony contracted polio, although at that time the doctors and consultants had no idea what it was. This was a significant moment that was to change his life. I imagine that almost dying does that to a person. He was terribly ill for a full year. He would suffer from fevers so severe that he almost wished that he would not wake up, many times there was uncertainty that he would.

Frequent trips to hospital for tests left him worse with asthma attacks and eventually his GP arranged for specialists to see him at home. During this time, Tony was able to hide from his father, of whom he was terrified, but some friends and his cousins would be allowed short visits to his room.

Eventually an operation to remove perfectly healthy tonsils and clear the adenoids flushed out the mystery germ and the recovery was almost instant. He'd been bed ridden for a year and needed to learn how to walk again. He still walks on his toes today and is renowned for his clumsiness.

Two decades later, when he was doing post graduate studies in HR management, Tony found out he was in the lowest three percent of the population for spatial awareness. It probably wasn't his illness as a child that had made him clumsy, with little perspective or no directional sense, but a condition on the autism spectrum now called dyspraxia.

Anyone who knows Tony does not ask him for directions or expect him to be able to follow them. He can get lost within a few hundred metres of his home! Whether this condition was worsened by the polio he is unsure. The illness also left him with a weakness in the lungs and asthma, that he still suffers from today.

Unable to go to school his mother took over his education and would often read to him for hours and set him exercises that she got from the school. His mother had brought up her two younger brothers, including Uncle Ron, after the death of her mother.

Tony believes she was a superb teacher and he's certain the reason he always thought he'd be top of the class in anything to do with reading, writing or arithmetic was because of her teaching getting him in advance of class work. He also credits his creativity today to her and the time they spent together.

He says that although fatter from a year in bed, all he wanted to do was to get back to playing sport. Once able to return to his junior school he became what you can only call a 'swot' and was Head Boy at eleven years old. He loved to learn and had a quick mind, but at school in those days you also needed to be tough.

Playmates like Bruce helped with the toughening up process, but he remembers how difficult it was to look tough with an overprotective mother. Once, he was escorted by his mother to the opposite side of Hessle to apologise to an adversary and their parents for a fight in the school playground. Not a cool look!

Tony admits to two 'of many big headed' traits from his school years - junior and secondary - which exist today. The first was that he always wanted to be popular with everyone - classmates, teachers, friends and family.

The second was that he always expected to earn the right to be asked by teachers or classmates to be the leader or captain of the group or sports team. This included expecting to be top of the class in any reading, writing and arithmetic subject - homework, classwork and exams.

Getting back to being top of the class, cricket captain and Head Boy after his year in bed, gave him this level of confidence. Those who know him are not surprised that he expected to be near the bottom in anything that involved co-ordination, movement, perspective, drawing, making things or speaking another language. He finds it difficult enough to speak English.

He says he was 'scarred for life' by not being able to progress from the cubs to the scouts because he couldn't do leapfrog. I think he's joking, but it wouldn't surprise me if it were true!

Both these traits - popularity and wanting to be the leader - can be a strength and a weakness, particularly in business. He admits he isn't ruthless and, unusually, says he's always tried hard to be the same person with the same values and behaviours in education, sport, work and home. He doesn't like it that many of his successful business friends adopt a different persona at work than they have among family and friends.

After Hessle C of E Junior School he was accepted into Beverley Grammar School. Tony looks back at his secondary school days with a great fondness and it's evident that he was fortunate to have gone to an all-boys grammar that produced excellent students.

His year's roll of honour includes his classmate, Sir Jim Ratcliffe, one of the UK's richest businessmen, and the 'Gangs of New York' and 'Peak Practice' actor, Chris Burgess who became Vice Principal of Guild

Hall School of Drama and, again, who Tony still sees today.

His friend Digby Bates, who later became a circuit judge, the 'hanging judge' as Tony refers to him, and was Tony's best man, were two of the last five pupils from Hessle that attended Beverley Grammar school, an hour's bus journey away. Tony made many school friends and there are regular re-unions to this day. Those sorts of enduring friendships tell you a lot about the time and how important it is to Tony to keep grounded to his roots.

That's not to say it was an easy school. Like so many back then, teachers had a power that often they abused, with bullying and discipline that was eradicated in years to come. The did however, produce winners. Whether it was in sport, drama or academia, Beverley Grammar School turned out students that would go on to do great things.

The high academic, performance arts and sporting standard is hardly surprising as it is the oldest state school in the country and in the top five oldest schools. St John of Beverley was their founder. It prides itself on producing people at the top of their field. The current British number one tennis player, Kyle Edmund is from BGS and there have been internationals at various sports, like Neil Mallender at cricket.

Coincidentally, Tony's Pulcroft Road friend, David Johnson, who became first violin in one of Germany's great orchestras, regularly collaborates with David Chew OBE who went to Beverley Grammar School.

David Chew is, one of the UK's great cellists and is equally famous in South America where he lives. Tony enjoyed seeing them both in concert recently in Scarborough.

Tony credits Beverley Grammar School as having given him the tools he would need later in life to go on to succeed when challenged. For Tony, starting at the school, one of the biggest things he needed to learn fast was how to mix with other children from often totally different backgrounds to his classmates in Hessle. He thought some may be brighter than him too. He also needed to learn how to be assertive in his early years at the school in order to be heard and given opportunities both academic and sporting.

From the ages of nine to sixteen, Tony was very much the 'goody two shoes' with his main ambition to become a professional cricketer for Yorkshire. Having overcome Polio, he was determined to prove himself and pushed hard to excel academically and in sports, particularly cricket, football, table tennis and tennis.

What's interesting and quite sad here is that his father was a great sportsman and yet he never taught Tony how to play, nor did Tony invite him to his matches to watch. When I commented on this, he told me that he knew his father would criticise and that he would be so nervous about him being there that he'd play badly. He was pleased that his father saw him get his first fifty in men's cricket for Hull YPI, although he only found out that his father had been there a day or so later.

As a parent I find both sides to this really very sad, it was a way in which they could have bonded and grown together and yet years of bullying and anger had made the gulf so wide that not even a mutual love of sport could bridge it.

Business was never Tony's dream. Far from it as he wanted to be a professional cricketer, an actor or writer, anything but a businessman. More than anything, Tony's hunger to play professional cricket was a long shot, as he wasn't a 'natural' at any sport, but still tenable.

He was school captain every year, represented East Yorkshire, played men's league cricket from 15 and became known as an opener in the Geoffrey Boycott mould. Boring for spectators and teammates but incredibly hard to get out. Tony's eldest child, Carl, has a middle name of Geoffrey and Eileen was booked into an East Yorkshire maternity hospital even though they were living in Hemel Hempstead. Eileen never made it, but it shows the importance of Yorkshire County Cricket to Tony, as at that time only those born in the county could play for the county.

Whilst he never went on to achieve this cricket dream, he attributes part of his desire to excel at everything he does to the determination to play and practice drilled into him during his time at school. He has won a mountain of trophies in cricket, tennis, table tennis and football and even today admits to 'loving' awards, including his three or four half marathon and marathon 'finishers' medals each summer. He was at a 'winning trophies' kind of school.

The school had expectations and woe betide you if you didn't meet their standards. Discipline was hard and dished out with brutal efficiency.

As a result of this Tony gained thirteen O' Levels. He would have had fifteen he tells me but an inability to draw and a dislike of cutting up animals cost him an O Level in biology and a dodgy German teacher lost him that one too.

He continued into the sixth form at Beverley Grammar School and was a School Officer and then a Prefect, but admits he stopped working as hard academically as the three Gs; girls, guitar and gigs, plus sport and the stage, both at school and at the East Riding County Youth Theatre, became more interesting than English, History and Economics A levels. Tony kept a school report from this time, his first one with any negatives on it, with the headmaster stating, '*Spotlight off - study light on*'.

Isn't that a great comment? I can almost see the stubborn Tony digging his heels in more after reading that. Mind you, it could be used for many of us business owners today, distracted by social media when we should be working - 'social oxygen off - business focus on'! Teaching marketing, that phenomenon of social oxygen is one that always gains attention, the need to have your phone with you in order to feel connected, get your dopamine rush from likes and to be validated by your loyal following.

In the March of his final year Tony's father died. He

could have got a letter from the school to explain why the family turmoil led to him messing up his exams, by not revising. He passed three A' Levels but the grades were B, D and E, rather than meeting the B & C offers he'd received to read English and Philosophy at Warwick and Anglia Universities. By the time of his exams he'd pretty much fallen out of love with the school.

During an A' level exam, a teacher asked him to move his car in a side street near the school and this was the final straw. His friends at the time had also pretty much fallen out with the school by then too.

Chris Burgess went on to become a famous actor, Steve Halliwell a top rock musician and Nick Levitt is tour director for the biggest rock bands in the world.

Steve and Nick left school to join Hull Truck theatre group. Tony would have loved to have joined them, but knew he didn't have their skills. Tony admits to a stubborn streak which means he never asks for favours nor expects any.

Driving his own car to school for most of the sixth form was very unusual in those days, as well as showing how well off the Robinsons of Hessle were, it rankled with teachers. Tony had to learn how to drive so that he could help with the business in his school holidays by dropping samples and quotations to prospective new customers in Yorkshire and Lincolnshire.

His father had saved a nearly new Ford Anglia for Tony that had been provided to a sales rep he'd sacked. Tony took the test and passed after just twelve lessons - that is only twelve hours of driving. He believes he has two claims to fame about passing his test before he could drive properly.

Firstly, he had two endorsements on his new full licence at the age of seventeen years three months. One of the endorsements was for having nine people in the car. His father went to court to speak up for Tony, but didn't say anything when the police statement quoted Tony as having said "*We didn't count them*".

His second claim to fame was that he'd never driven at night until the day he passed his test. I've explained about his dyspraxia and he doesn't drive today, but on that first night he ran the car off the road and into a ditch. He says his mates who were in the car have never let him drive them anywhere again. Clare Francis and Tina Boden his business partners today, did not allow him to drive them anywhere either.

After the death of his father, Tony threw himself into drama and still held on to his beloved cricket despite the school making him only joint captain.

Girlfriends, theatre productions, pubs, a 'hopeless band', gigs including all night festivals were all enjoyable distractions from study during his A-level years.

Well, it was the time of free love and the pill and Tony delights in recounting the bands he was lucky enough to see. For a rock chick like myself it's amazing to hear about Free & Jethro Tull and of course the seven days spent at the Isle of Wight Festival, watching The Who, Hendrix and Joni Mitchell.

It's easy to forget the sheer scale of the last great festival in 1970 at the Isle of Wight - 600,000 - four times the size of Glastonbury but only one stage, no big screens and no mobile phones. There were only a handful of over thirties, including all the organisers, at the festival. I could digress here and write an entire section on music such is Tony's love, but perhaps that's another book.

It was the year of hippies, staying with strangers and taking over their houses for the weekend, culminating with an end of weekend clean up and picking up petals! Perhaps that's why it was called flower power!

Tony wasn't into pot, apart from his pipe being regularly filled and passed around at the Isle of Wight, but did drink - a lot. His 'look' that included cardigans, long hair, beard and smoking a pipe from his infamous collection... It's an image I'll leave you with.

Having listened to him, it's more than apparent that Tony is steadfast in his belief that it was his time at Beverley Grammar that set him and so many of his classmates up with the knowledge of how to succeed in business. He had learned the key enterprise skills he needed by the age of sixteen - discipline and practice. These are skills that can be taught in school today.

Tony is convinced that most people have their key skills, attitudes and behaviours defined by the age of eighteen in boys and sixteen in girls. He believes that he chose a route to happiness and fulfilment rather than a route to wealth and status as his raison d'étre because of everything he'd learned by the time he left Beverley Grammar School.

He says he'd been to a lot of funerals, including his

Gran who died at their house and then his Father, at whose hospital bedside he and his Mum were at, to know that life is short. Rather like millennials today, there was a massive generation gap and a rage against the establishment. Tony's generation had their own poets in Dylan, Cohen and Lennon and many felt it was their duty to be different and make a positive difference.

Tony knows exactly how he felt at the time because he was a prolific writer from the age of fourteen - fiction, poetry and two plays - and although a lot of his poems when he was seventeen and eighteen are about his ex-fiancée Gill, there were many that suggested the status quo was not acceptable and that the corruption of society and minds had to be challenged. Freedom to control your own destiny was a recurring theme and, later in life, Tony would say that therefore starting and running your own business is the very best career option.

Three women had shaped his happiness and fulfilment ambition and values. His girlfriend Gill, who didn't have much money at all, Tony felt guilty about his relative wealth and that he had so many clothes - but was brilliant, caring and lived in the happiest family Tony has ever seen.

His mother, who had given him the love of literature and the theatre - all kinds, including ballet and opera - which in turn led him to believe that as a writer and performer he had skills which were transferable to any career choice.

Judith (Jude) Hawkshaw, who he met at the County Youth theatre and became his lifelong friend and mentor, who told him 'what's what' and would never allow him to do wrong to others. Jude was changing the world for the better at sixteen - helping people less fortunate than her. His recent poem 'One Saint Jude' says it all about her influence.

What I find interesting is that reading between the lines, it was a hard childhood and yet Tony doesn't see this. By today's standards the pressure was immense to succeed, he was one of only five children from Hessle given the opportunity to attend the grammar school and so had to prove in a way his worthiness to be there.

He lived under a cloud of fear and repression, a family lacking in the ability to show love and yet has evolved from this as a man with an immense heart. For someone so anti-business he certainly went on to make it his own.

Tony has coined the term 'Happipreneur' partly to describe what he and millions of others around the world do and partly as a piss-take of all the posers that are fake entrepreneurs. He also doesn't really like inflated generic titles to describe business owners such as 'solopreneurs' - self-employed would be better.

Happipreneurs make ends meet while leading a happy and 'be useful' life. Tony's riches to rags story is the difference between what the media would class as an entrepreneur lifestyle and what he would class as a Happipreneur lifestyle. He would also say you can be rich as a Happipreneur it's just that he isn't.

His riches phase (as you'll read more about later) included a big detached house with big gardens in a village, top of the range executive car, private health care, flying first class around the world, the finest food and having spacious suites in the best hotels. The much longer rags phase has included a semi-detached house in a town street with a small back yard, no car and using his free bus pass to get back from his runs to Filey and Whitby for a pint, fish pie and mushy peas.

But what on earth made him think he could be happy at a 'less grand' lifestyle compared even to his parents? He thanks Judith (Jude) Hawkshaw and his Uncle Ron. Tony didn't see them as mentors. He's found that very few business owners owe their success, or in his case failure, to having mentors. What he does say is that they both led happy, 'be useful' lifestyles and he learned from them until Jude died on the operating table and Uncle Ron committed suicide. Both deaths occurred nearly a decade ago.

About halfway between Tony's school in Beverley and home in Hessle is Willerby. Many times during the week from age 15, Tony would get off the school bus there. At weekends he would often hitch a lift or if no-one stopped, would walk it. This was his young hippy time of girls, gigs and guitar - and underage drinking. Most of his friends lived in touching distance of Willerby.

Jude was one such friend. If it got very late after drinks and going around to someone's house, Tony would ask to sleep on the floor. This usually required waiting until his potential host's parent or parents had gone to bed and he'd sneak back in the back door. He remembers many a time being told to 'get out' when discovered.

Jude's house was different, her Mum and Dad, always said "*Yes - stay on our sofa*" and so Jude and Tony's friendship developed. Jude was quite large, not easily impressed, smart and very direct. The first time he realised that was when she gave him some 'advice' couched as "*you will do this*" on how to behave with his potential girlfriends.

Tony rather liked Janet Prince, who was, and is today, a superb actor and was a friend of Jude's. Janet had allowed him to stay on her floor so he thought Janet might like him too. Jude's 'You've no chance!' meant not only 'do not bother my friend' but also 'don't make a fool of yourself'. So began the regular 'putting me right' sessions with Jude. There was no chance that Tony would be allowed to forget his responsibilities to families and friends, nor adopt any airs and graces during his rich phase. Jude became Carl's Godmother and attended Tony's OBE celebration.

Nearly every Christmas, Tony and Eileen would go to Hull to see Jude and her mother and, of course, Uncle Ron too. In later years Tony and Eileen would visit Jude in the lovely house she built in Ipswich and Jude would stay at Tony and Eileen's for the Scarborough Jazz Festival. It wasn't their chats that Tony learned most from, it was Jude's actions that he described as both inspiring and saintly.

From first meeting her until shortly before her death, Jude was always ferociously independent and determined to always do what was right, however difficult or unpopular that was. Being useful was everything, money was always secondary. As well as practical help for the disadvantaged she brought respite and joy into their lives too. Eventually, she was recognised with an MBE for her pioneering work in social housing, particularly for the elderly and people with disabilities, but her lifelong work in helping people that needed a hand-up started from school when she was bullied for always wheeling her friend in a wheelchair around.

After school, Jude travelled extensively and spent many years abroad, as did Tony's daughter Sinead. When she returned to the UK to look at careers and qualifications, and see her Mum more regularly, she took on one of the most dangerous jobs she could, providing 48-hours safe houses for homeless drug addicts and alcoholics in Doncaster and then Whitley Bay.

On several occasions, her life was in danger and many times she was battling her employers. As a campaigner for other's rights, she was legendary. Never once did she worry about the consequences to her earning a living or to personal relationships - she never married. Jude is a hero to Tony, and although she was only self-employed at the end of her life, Tony believes she was a Happipreneur all her life and, as they say in Yorkshire, 'kept him on the straight and narrow'.

Uncle Ron didn't marry either and after leaving Tony's home spent over 30 years living in the largest block of council flats in Hull. He was a docker who retired early because of bad health, had few friends in his early life and no friends in his later life and committed suicide. That doesn't sound like a happy and useful life does it? To understand why Uncle Ron is also a hero and role model to Tony is to understand how important he thinks integrity, family, being useful to others and self-sufficiency are to living a happy life.

Jude was a Christian, so like his wife Eileen, there is a particular meaning to life. Tony believes in many stoic values, which have been adopted in many faiths, but he doesn't believe in God. His Uncle Ron didn't believe in God either and Tony as the executor of his Uncle's will had to ensure two things. Firstly, that his crematorium send-off was the cheapest possible with no service. Secondly, that a substantial amount of money he had saved through his lifetime was split equally ten ways between his brother's family and Tony's family.

Uncle Ron created his own meaning out of life and controlled the only things any of us can control - thoughts and, more importantly, actions. While he was mobile, he helped everyone in the family by driving them to appointments and doing odd jobs in their houses, prefabs and flats and gardening was his speciality. He never accepted payment. He was a font of wisdom, almost encyclopaedic knowledge about the world we live in, even though he'd rarely been abroad.

However, he never offered his knowledge or advice unless you asked for it. He, like Jude, provided a place of safe refuge for anyone in the family, including Tony's Mum, that was having a hard time. He was the definition of happy with his 'lot', he lost many of his friends in the bombing of Hull and he'd expected to die of a serious illness in his mid-thirties. He was the definition of *'Be Useful'* to his family and friends. He handled awful setbacks with his health and he even handled having accidentally killed a man with his fork-lift truck, without resorting to drinking or drugs. He never drank.

Tony doesn't think Uncle Ron ever read philosophy, he got most of his knowledge from magazines and newspapers, but if he had done would have understood stoicism and particularly 'life is short - remember we all die', 'all we can control are our actions', 'love dealing with stuff however horrible' and the concept of 'virtue'. This last one is what differentiates Uncle Ron from most other dockers and, certainly, from most entrepreneurs. Uncle Ron was never on the fiddle, he was never taking advantage of anyone or any situation. He was always trying to do the right thing and, like Jude, wouldn't be coerced by peer pressure - even fellow trade union members, if he thought something was wrong.

Most dockers used their work clothes allowance to buy the cheapest they could and spend the rest on golf hats, shirts and socks - Ron wouldn't. He'd have been a lousy MP most of them fiddle up to £20,000 a year and give their secretarial allowance to a member of their family. He never took the freebies on offer from the container lorries and 'damaged goods' in the hold at the Docks.

So honest was he that they eventually gave him a job working for Customs.

When he became less mobile, he ate and drank frugally, in his flat and saved his pension money so that when his health deteriorated to the point where he would commit suicide - he'd told Tony he would do that one day - there would be a tidy sum of money to be equally dispersed among all his remaining family members.

Despite having low incomes at many times during their life both Saint Jude and Uncle Ron always found a way of making ends meet and sharing with their family any money they had. They avoided the loan sharks and the scammers. I started the book talking about integrity, being useful and living a happy life. Saint Jude and Uncle Ron were the main influence on Tony for this. They also stopped him getting too big headed, reminded him of his responsibilities and that in the scheme of things, materialism isn't a good look.

Q&A Time

Q: Do any famous entrepreneurs you've met remind you of your Dad?

A: Lord Sugar reminds me of my Dad as a businessman. Both could be blunt and intimidating, yet loved by the people closest to them for their humour and loyalty.

Neither had a long, formal education yet they had bucket loads of business nous. They'd fill a room with their presence. Dad sold wooden, rather than electronic products, was from Yorkshire, taller, fair haired, a Methodist and was never on the telly. They could be twins!

Q: ***How did you meet Lord Sugar?***

A: Back in the day, when he was Chairman of *Spurs* and in the process of signing *Jurgen Klinsmann,* he rang me in our little offices near Milton Keynes. He commanded me to meet with him at *Amstrad* HQ, in Brentwood. My sole input to the one-minute phone conversation was 'Yes'.

He wanted us to help him market and 'direct sell' a new product, called the Index Phone. We failed in the three-month project but were paid promptly. I doubt if he remembers me. I only met him a few times, but I learned a lot about how he operates from one of his Directors, the late *Jim Rice.* Lord Sugar made me laugh, was very straightforward and I became a fan.

Q: ***What do you mean by a 'fan'?***

A: This was before 'The Apprentice' and becoming 'SurAlan' but the media couldn't get enough of him - he was a celebrity entrepreneur. What I liked, before I even met him, was the total absence of glitz, glamour and spin. Many famous American entrepreneurs were talkers not 'doers'. I was proud that here was a British 'doer' who had started from nothing, to build an electronics manufacturing business that was world famous.

He used to write regularly about business in the Sunday newspapers, yet donated his fee to charity. I thought that was class and I just felt that most of what he said was more useful than anything I'd learned about in business school.

Many of his political and sport opinions I disagree with, but I remain a fan. I read about, watch and listen to him whenever I can.

I've had chats about him with *Tim Campbell MBE,* the first The Apprentice Winner, who has supported our events for many years. Tim worked with Lord Sugar at Amstrad for two years. Tim is a fan. *Adam Corbally* was a The Apprentice finalist and hosted our most recent annual #MicroBizMatters Day and he's a fan too.

Q: ***What have you learned from Lord Sugar?***

A: I don't want to be sued so let me make clear this is *my* interpretation from things he's said, and I've read. Here are eight things that I think have worked for him, work for me and should work for others starting their own business:

1. Distrustful isn't a bad place to start - many people will oversell or even con you into parting with your time and money.

2. Be prepared to be on your own - no-one can build a business on their own but when things go pear shaped, and they will, you may find you can't rely on any of your business colleagues for support.

3. Stick to everything you agree and meet all your commitments. Lord Sugar made some amazing deals with manufacturers and retailers because he was trusted. #PayIn30Days is good business sense.

4. Repeat business is the best business. Obvious, I know but any success Clare and I ever had in business was from loving our existing customers - going the extra mile. How do you think Lord Sugar heard of us?

5. You know best how to run your own business - after 18 months you'll know more about your products/services and customers than the gurus, experts, coaches, trainers and mentors.

6. All you need is paper and a pencil and a lot of hard work - sales and profit come from learning what works in your business *by doing*. Test trading or trading is more important than planning until you've got a viable business. Many

   start-ups over complicate everything with accounting, productivity, social media and communications apps when they should be winning customers.

7. Positive cashflow is vital and allows you to grow organically - no debt. In the early days Lord Sugar would try to sell all he needed by Wednesday to cover all the week's costs so that all the margin from sales on a Thursday and Friday went straight to assets.

8. Owner led businesses are usually better at making decisions, negotiating great deals, providing a happy workplace and satisfying customers than their corporate equivalents.

"An ounce of practice is generally worth more than a ton of theory"

EF Schumacher

III
Be Your Own Boss Skills

When starting out on this book, Tony sent me quite a lot of audio recordings as we weren't able to get together as often as we'd have liked. However, as with most business ventures, it was the face to face conversations from which I have gained the most. Listening to Tony's recordings, he's very factual and completely honest, but you need a little not-so-subtle probing to get to the nitty gritty!

After school, aged nineteen Tony went off to Middlesex Polytechnic (now Middlesex University) in Hendon, London, where he studied for a degree in English and American Literature and Philosophy. Well, I say studied, he actually partied, drank, played a lot more sport, travelled to Leeds in his reading weeks to see his girlfriend, Gill and really didn't try that hard.

Tony met Gill at seventeen while he was at Beverley Grammar School, Gill became Deputy Head Girl of Beverley High School. They got engaged and Gill even moved from Leeds Polytechnic, where she was studying Speech Therapy, to London in the second year of their respective courses, so they could be together.

Tony's was a new degree and as such not well organised. The schedule was poorly planned and relied on students reading all of the classics in their reading weeks. If you've ever tried reading five Dickens novels in a week you'll know that this is not an easy task.

Tony recalls that had it not been for one particular lecturer, he'd have most likely dropped out.

That lecturer was Jonathan Sacks, who became Chief Rabbi and is now Lord Sacks. A little over four years older than Tony, he'd not long graduated from Cambridge with a First in Philosophy. It was his enthusiasm and talent for sharing his love of the subject, ethics, that captured Tony. To this day it is a subject that he thoroughly enjoys. He regards himself as a stoic. He doesn't see philosophy as wishy washy, but something that enables you to see a far greater picture and evaluate your place in that picture. Tony never missed one of these lectures and tutorials, although the same can't be said for the rest of the English and American Literature syllabus.

One of the things that Tony feels set him up for his future came from these Philosophy lectures and the understanding of how, if you take away your own baggage of 'beliefs' on a subject, you can view it very differently.

Another message, and I think this ties in with integrity, was learning that to get on in life, there's a lot of truth in the old George Burns joke "*if you could fake honesty you could fake anything*". At the time this statement was quite an eye opener, but it has stayed with him and, I believe, enabled him to see past a lot of the glitter and showmanship of top-level business.

Tony did indeed complete the course, although it was touch and go, he still felt (although unspoken) a lingering guilt at leaving his mother in Hull to manage the company, not that he wanted any part of it, nor did he want to be trapped in it, but it was hard on the family and after a while new business stopped coming in, old contracts tailed off, finally causing the business to close. On reflection this lesson would be another that he would take into his business life, the knowledge of what it takes to run a family enterprise and the characters/skills required to make it a success.

Tony knew he had the business skills to succeed in the family business and seeing their family fortune disappear year by year, could not have been easy. But his freedom to achieve everything in his own right was all consuming. He wasn't sure how he'd earn a living but he felt confident that he always would.

Managing to come out with a third class, BA Honours without studying tells you a little of the ability he has, despite the lack of anything resembling the determination to succeed that dogged his earlier years. Perhaps I'm being a little unfair, there were no Firsts handed out that year and the highest grade earned was a 2:1 but most were 2:2 and 3rds. His wife, Eileen, who was on the same degree went back the next year and resat her exams.

The one room bedsits in 94 Sunningfields Road in Hendon, North London - baby belling cooker, bed and sink - became a very important part of Tony's life during the three years of his degree and four years beyond.

It was there that Gill moved to from Headingley in Leeds to continue her speech therapy studies. It wasn't ideal living with too many people. Too much damp and not enough facilities. Today we might see it as strange, but Tony and Gill still hid their living together from their parents, so as not to cause upset.

There were a few awkward moments in these early years in London, including a bi-sexual flatmate who wanted time with both Tony and Gill. As Tony was purely heterosexual, he had to turn the flatmate down and shortly after the chap moved out.

Tony was deeply in love with his fiancée Gill, but after a year of living together she realised that their relationship was not to be and ended things between them. He was devastated. He said the weekend they went back to East Yorkshire to tell their parents the wedding would not be taking place was just "*the pits*".

On deeper probing he tells me that he did have quite a low boredom threshold and, I think, a roving eye. Whatever the reason they went their separate ways and Tony decided he wasn't ready for a 'normal' relationship as he saw it, he wanted to see a little bit more of life and to be free.

A year or so after the split, Eileen, his future wife, and him moved into another room in Sunningfields Road. Tony tells me that they were friends long before they became romantically involved and it's that friendship, he believes that has kept them together all these years.

Eileen and Tony had known each other for nearly seven years before they married and, in that time, became best friends.

Eileen's story is also one worth telling. She was an orphan from an early age after her grandfather died. He was bringing her up in Moville, at the tip of Northern Ireland, but in the Republic. After his death she moved twenty miles along the coast to be brought up in Derry, where she lived in the infamous Nazareth House Orphanage.

Now closed, the child abuse is well documented and the Nuns and Priests associated with it have been given a harsh reputation. It is testament to Eileen that she was one of the first children from there to go to a Grammar School and then to go to a university to gain a degree. She not only got away from the area as the troubles really hit, but also made such a success of her life without any financial or family support at all.

A winner of Opportunity Knocks not only once but five times, Eileen was an accomplished piano and accordion player. Eileen took a year off school to tour with the Nazareth House Ceilidh band and to babysit for Phil Coulter, Derry's most famous musician, Eurovision song contest winner and writer of its most famous song - 'The Town I Loved So Well'. It is Eileen's love of family and her steadfastness in the role of family matriarch that has enabled Tony to go off on so many of his ventures. Of course, I am getting ahead of myself here and at this moment in time, Tony is still trying to find where life is going to take him.

Before both Gill and Eileen, Tony had his first love, he was fifteen. Combining a love of music and his burgeoning feelings for the young lady in question, he took her to see Mick Ronson in a band called 'The Rats'. Mick Ronson would later be known as David Bowie's lead guitar player in Ziggy Stardust and the Spiders from Mars. However, Tony's love interest was not to be as she actually left him at the concert and went off with the band!

The path of love wasn't to run smooth there and generally for him for many years after. Tony was always quite popular with men too. After all it was the free-loving 70's, although as previously mentioned, those infatuations were definitely not for him.

Perhaps it was simply a sign of the times or maybe the freedom he felt by the release of his father's death, but this time in Tony's life was mainly about fun. He played a great deal of sport at Middlesex Poly. His cricket went downhill once he stopped travelling back to Hull to play and he knew that the key to his success had been practice and game time which he was now not having. He thinks his tennis, table tennis and football improved. He enjoyed even more gigs and many a 'lock in' in the local pub, the Chequers. It was as though the studious child of the grammar school had disappeared.

Certainly, the only evidence of the enterprise skills he'd learned were that he continued to help his mother from a distance, with some of the key family business decisions and he blagged his way into several student jobs and roles which helped him earn some money. In many ways he was quite enterprising in using books of criticism enabling him to write mandatory essays rather than reading the novels or attending the lectures. Anything he really wanted to learn, like Philosophy, he still succeeded by using his ability to practice and practice.

He did have to learn a great deal about the world of work in student holiday jobs in order to make ends meet and he and Eileen ended up with their room in 94 Sunningfields Road as a freebie for their performing the duties of caretakers in the house they lived in.

This entailed reporting maintenance tasks to the agent and collecting overdue rents - there were many. The most important task, which brought Tony's negotiating skills to the fore, was to empty the electricity meters and give the money direct to the landlord. This task was made difficult by the fact that most tenants had wired their meters to bypass the coin slot. Tony had to give them notice of when he'd knock on the door to empty the meter in order to give them time to put a fair number of coins in the receptacle.

To me this further highlights his integrity. He knew that he had a job to do and therefore had to have money to give the landlord, but as a struggling student could understand his fellow tenants and so gave them the opportunity to pay up. He could have been a complete git and let the landlord know what was going on, but he liked to be liked after all so maybe that wasn't ever going to be on the cards!

Q&A Time

Q: You've been starting and running your own businesses for over 30 years do you regret thinking business sucked when you were a student?

A: No regrets. I still think most big business sucks! I've been working with Government for even longer and that sucks too. You can have a great job within these massive organisations but most of the jobs are not fulfilling.

Even highly paid managers can have crap, stressful jobs. 40% of big business workers are under pressure and unhappy. There are no #Happipreneurs there!

Q: Is it a leadership problem?

A: It's the organisation's purpose that is the problem - they get the leaders the purpose deserves. At the top of both Government and Big Business, are millionaires looking to become richer and more powerful at the expense of the rest of us. Business owner-led organisations, even big ones, are different. Most of these are OK. But FTSE 100 Businesses and Government have been my clients and, while I like many of the people working for them, I don't like what they do. Particularly, I don't like what they do to the most vulnerable as suppliers, customers and employees. I don't like what their cumulative bullying does to 600,000 start-ups a year and 5.6 million micro-business owners. After all, I am the Micro-business Champion - I get to see their worst side every day.

Q: Such as?

A: Freedman economics focused on 'maximising shareholder value'. This is almost inhumane, as was proven by UK and USA big business and Government during the pandemic (at time of writing Spring 2020 we're in lockdown). The UK and USA leadership in Government and Big Business were interested in the economy first and, as Schumacher predicted, public welfare second. They should have followed the South Korea model and saved lives first by not importing the virus and then testing and tracking everyone. NHS staff and care workers were gamed - no excuses for this.

Like all Labour Party members, I'd campaigned for 'Save our NHS' for many years before the pandemic. I started campaigning for #PayIn30Days over two decades ago. But the cost of Government ignoring our pleas were many deaths and killer debts.

Q. But what about small and micro-business, like your parents?

A: It was only about twenty years ago that I really recognised the difference between running your own business and business in general. I always understood that controlling your own destiny is priceless, but I hadn't really understood all the benefits to me of being a micro-business owner.

My focus wasn't business, it was on being a professional in HRD and Marketing - providing products and services to help our clients. Clare and I had created a business so that we could do that. It was a way of earning a living that fitted what we are qualified in, are good at and we were free from bosses forever. We only wanted to make ends meet and so even when we had seven staff and 20 associates, I thought we weren't really a proper business, not like my father's. I never wanted one of those.

Q. So are you saying that if you'd known as a student what you know now you might have started a business earlier than you did?

A: Definitely. I'd have had many low-cost side hustles and test trades by the time I was 25 and I'll bet one of them would have worked. I'm really pleased that students now understand you can do what you love in your own enterprise and make a positive difference too. Young people can test trade as students and become Happipreneurs never having to work for the man.

Some like my friend, the late Stefan Topfer and one of our #MicroBizMatters young entrepreneur friends, Chris Percival, became millionaires from businesses they started at university. For me, enterprise skills are exciting - business studies are boring.

I meet many students through being Patron of the John Cracknell Youth Enterprise Bank and being Chair of Yorkshire in Business, and it seems normal for them to want to run their own business to pursue their interest in music, art, writing, design, food, clothes, games, sport, pets, tech, beauty, health, fitness and so forth. It's fabulous but it wasn't the same when I was a student.

"We are quite competent enough to produce sufficient supplies of necessities so that no-one will live in misery"

EF Schumacher

Image Set A:

1. Tony's Mum & Dad with self-employed friends - a fish merchant and a chemist
2. Tony's Mum and Dad married October 1946
3. Tony with Grandma & Mum in Scarborough
4. Dad buying Portuguese Pine in Estoril Casino, Portugal 1966
5. Head Boy Hessle CofE Junior School 1963
6. Dave Leigh & Tony winning a Hull West Park doubles trophy.
7. Beverley Grammar School Football Team
8. Captain Beverley Grammar School Cricket - 1967
9. Beverley Grammar School Honours Board cricket captains 1971
10. Chris (Richard lll) & Tony (Buckingham) - rehearsal
11. Oh What A Lovely War rehearsal 1970
12. One of many holidays with mates at Butlins, Filey in the summer 1969
13. With Sir Jim Ratcliffe & BGS Schoolmates on a cycling holiday 1970
14. Isle of Wight close to the stage 1970
15. Middlesex Polytechnic Table tennis Team
16. Chris Burgess and Barrie Wyse music and drama teacher 2004 BGS reunion
17. 40 Years On - They all joined BGS in 1964 This is the 2004 year reunion
18. 2019 BGS Classmates - less and less each year

A. RUDLAND J.
D.SANDERS 1969
K.OXTOBY 1970
A.C.ROBINSON/I.HARDY 1971
R.M.KELLY 1972
A.GOFF 1973
T.A.SWANN 1974
J.R.HANWELL 197
J.P.WILSON 197
S.BELLIS 197
N.A.MALLENDER 197
N.A.MALLENDER 197
C. LOWE 19

OF WIGHT
FESTIVAL OF MUSIC 1970

IV
Working for The Man - Making Ends Meet

That's not to say that he didn't work or learn different skills. In the ten years between 1971 and 1981 Tony was to discover hardship - certainly relative to his days in East Yorkshire. He learnt about the urgency of life in London.

Reflecting on his childhood, Tony concluded that he had been coddled. Whilst perhaps not a traditional upbringing, Tony had access to everything he needed. The families had all worked together to ensure that no one went without and business had been good.

Even at university it was easier to a certain degree as he had a grant, but the grant was not enough to live on, and many students took as many jobs as they could. Tony still believes this is better than Student Loans (and Start Up Loans) as they can leave someone in debt for the rest of their life.

There was no fallback money from home as the orders declined and Tony's mother sold the small number of shares Tony's father had left her. Eventually his Mum downsized to live off the proceeds. In the ten years from leaving home to starting at Amway, Tony had four and a half years at Middlesex Polytechnic - on a degree, then a post graduate diploma in HR management - and needed holiday jobs throughout that time.

The other five and a half years he was employed by NCR Limited.

Now he was to see what it was like for those without that support and how people functioned when not part of a close-knit community.

Living in London rounded off Tony's life education and toughened him up. He says it was invaluable in terms of forming his and Eileen's views on how to make ends meet, loyalty, trust, equality, diversity and what he calls 'the value of a pound'. He said he'd understood how to make deals from being 17 when his Dad and Mum had to leave the office and left him with instructions on which orders he was allowed to negotiate on - what the fallback price was and which he should refer to one or other of the Managing Directors of a box mill. The timing was all-important - the deal would be lost if it wasn't settled in the day.

He was also used by his father in the negotiating process. So, he'd drive a sample to a big food producer in Lincolnshire and his father would ring the chief buyer and say my son's in your reception with a sample of the box I can make for you for £x, if I have a minimum order of £x today. Tony said his father never told him what his plan was so he got incredibly nervous thinking he'd have to do the selling. He didn't like that.

The most humiliating of these excursions was when he was first sent to Hull Fish docks with a sample. He got all dressed up smart and hadn't realised that the fishdocks are like an ice rink. Leather shoes are not what filleters and fish merchants wear. He falls down regularly even on non-slippery surfaces so you can imagine how many times he fell on the fish docks…

However, he said it was only in London that he realised how real life isn't what appears in the media and most people's lives and businesses are ups and downs, never a straight line. Most of the wheeling and dealing, informal lending and tiding people over until payday took place in the pubs. He got to understand the 'cash in hand', favours and bungs, time is money, avoidance of debt, the value of who you know and how much is a good deal and how much is a bad deal. This is what he calls the 'value of a pound'.

He learned the 'value of a pound' from some very colourful characters. Gill's cousin had a pub in the East End and visiting them for a weekend meant working in the pub too. There was a mixture of villains that built up huge debt 'on the slate' mixing with TV stars like Monica Rose from Opportunity Knocks which Eileen had starred on a few years before. Tony remembers the shock Gill, he and Gill's cousin and spouse felt when they found out their bar manager had been creaming off some of the takings for years and had scarpered - nowhere to be found in London.

Big John had a newspaper and flower stall at Golders Green station. It was the perfect front for selling knocked off goods - shirts, perfume even TVs, to his regulars. He had a lot of 'cash in hand' and liked to spend it on a Saturday night with Tony. He wasn't the kind of person you could say, "*Sorry, I'm busy this Saturday*" to. Tony says he understands the trepidation of people going out drinking knowing it's very difficult to say, *"I'll just have a diet coke."* He doesn't complain when he meets old friends today and they say to him, *"My wife has told me not to drink much tonight as you always make me ill."*

Big John could drink a lot and he loved the Saturday midnight movie at the cinema in Hendon Central. Tony said a miracle would happen every Saturday night into Sunday morning. Big John would fall asleep as the titles rolled and would stay asleep, snoring loudly, (nobody dared nudge Big John to get him to stop) and then miraculously awake at the end of the film as the credits rolled. He never saw a film, but Tony never asked him why he loved going to the midnight cinema.

No one really likes to think about it, but let me ask you, what would you be prepared to do in order to put food on the table or support your family? Would you buy goods 'off the back of a lorry' or maybe even participate in acquiring those goods? These were the people that Tony was to come into contact with. He and Eileen worked at number of holiday jobs, many unpleasant and hard graft, but they were never afraid of work. What Tony was sometimes afraid of, were the people around him.

This was a time before credit cards and the only way people could borrow money was if they had a slate at the local pub. Often run by unscrupulous people it was not an easy way to live. Should you renege on payments, the consequences would be harsh and often painful. We think now about Pay Day lenders, whilst the bailiffs may be intimidating, they are still bound by law, those that knocked on your door from the loan sharks had no qualms about roughing people up and sending a 'message' at the end of a fist. There is still some of that happening today. There will always be those who prosper of others' misfortunes, but I can almost respect the 'honesty' of these people as opposed to the 4,214% API on the Pay Day loans.

These 'sharks' of today make it too easy for the most vulnerable in society to borrow more money than they can ever afford to pay back, it is, in our opinion, a despicable way to do business.

Tony founded and captained the Vikings cricket team and they had amazing characters and top-class cricketers from around the world. Most had been students at one time at Middlesex University. Eileen was the scorer and loved the fact it was so multicultural. You weren't allowed to be in the Vikings cricket team without facial hair but they made an exception for an East African called John Foong.

This report at Edmonton Cricket Club explains why: "*John's fifth ball swung sharply away from the bat and was edged into the hands of Norman Tong in the slips, and by this time, the excitement among the team members had to be experienced to be believed' John Foong had five wickets in five consecutive balls.*" He also went onto win the Vikings batting prize for that season.

The same newspaper report said, "*Mention is also due to Tony Robinson captain of this motley crew, who in his third season continued to give purpose and direction to the club both on the field and in social activities.*" Tony and Eileen would say these years living, working and playing sport in London were a crash course in understanding different cultures, values and religions.

About a third of the club didn't drink alcohol, but still attended all the after-match parties and social events. Eileen pretty much hates Scarborough and Hull because of racist people. Tony says that it's amazing she hasn't been punched, as after the Brexit referendum when people were shouting *"You can all f***ing go home now*" to any people of colour Eileen, all 5 foot and seven stone of her would tell them off. It's one of the reasons Eileen loved working in the Hull University Library in Scarborough. It was multicultural.

Tony is very public too in standing up for all minority ethnic groups, LGBT and women. He says today, that his and Eileen's views on this are still a problem for most of his friends and business associates.

The Chequers pub in Hendon was the epicentre of Tony and Eileen's education at the University of Life. Although they've always led independent lives with independent social agendas, (they hardly ever watched television together for example) at some point during an evening they'd both end up together, still younger than Tony and Eileen are now.

Two old gentlemen were in the Chequers most nights. Norman was a lorry driver, who like Tony's Uncle Ron, a docker, proves that exceptional levels of wisdom, knowledge, intelligence and practical know-how are not the province of people in white-collar jobs. The other old gentleman was self-employed and one of the top commercial photographers in Britain. He was also on the board of the professional body.

Tony admired both of them, particularly for their independent styles and the fact they were so interesting and knowledgeable. He learned so much and realised the importance of being free from bosses, rules and regulations in order to be happy.

The barman of the Chequers, Pedro, was a captain at Mill Hill Village Cricket club and persuaded Tony and Nick to start playing league cricket again. That introduced them both to the storytelling of David English in the clubhouse. Tony isn't a friend of Dr David English CBE, known as 'The Loon' but Pedro was. So close a friend that Pedro was at the funeral of David English's father. Famously when the hearse broke down, Pedro went to pick up his father in the coffin and deliver it to the church in his Hendo Borough Council Mobile Library van. Anyway, Pedro being a friend of David English, now known as the Godfather of English cricket, meant that Tony and Nick could listen to the funniest stories of the greatest independent maverick in the world.

Who is David English? He's raised millions of pounds for charity. He's written songs with the Bee

Gees, Eric Clapton, Elton John and George Harrison. As president of RSO records he helped create the most successful independent records label in the world (they once had an unprecedented five singles in the American Top 10 in one week).

As a budding film actor, he taught Robert Redford the intricacies of cricket on the set of 'A Bridge too Far' (as well as tormenting Anthony Hopkins with terrible jokes). As a pal of English cricket legend, Ian Botham he joined Beefy on his leukaemia charity walks and hosted the renowned Sir Ian Botham and Sir Viv Richards roadshows.

As the founder of the Bunbury Cricket Club, who else could persuade Bill Wyman to bat against the bowling of Gary Lineker, whilst Phil Collins wicket-keeps? Bunbury Cricket Festival and Bunburys TV series he has achieved legendary status in the cricket world. Most of England's greatest cricketers have been spotted at the Bunbury Festival for under 15s.

Like Lord Sugar, Penn and Teller, Mike Winnet (the Contrepreneur), Diogenes the Dog and many others, David English will not realise what an effect he had on Tony's life and his subsequent approach to business.

"*The stories were funny, hilarious often, and utterly enthralling. A large group of us, whenever he was in the bar would listen for hours. I spent a late evening until 5am session in South Africa in 2003 with Phil Tufnell, England cricketer, 'I'm a celebrity get me out of here' winner, Strictly contestant and team captain on*

A Question of Sport, many years later and he is a very funny man and a superb court jester but David English is truly a different class.

He made me want to be independent, a bit of a maverick, a one-off, who knew lots of interesting people. Why? I love to entertain, and I love laughter and I figured you don't get much of either if you keep your head down and stick to the rules. There's nothing wrong with living a steady and responsible life, but if you're going to be a professional speaker and writer who makes people laugh you need to be thinking and doing some crazy things with other very interesting and talented people. The first person I met that would fit my definition of a #Happipreneur was David English. He's made some money, but I genuinely believe he's not been motivated by money. He has been motivated to be useful and he's made a positive difference to thousands of lives through his own force of personality, friendships and love of life."

Tony is not convinced that our personalities and values change much through life, even with near death experiences. He doesn't believe that Boris Johnson will believe in economics as if people mattered, as a result of his brush with death during the pandemic.

What Tony does believe is that we can learn new skills and improve our skills; and we can change the environment we work and play in so that our personality and skills shine.

Tony has used role models to learn how to constantly shine through many changes in circumstance.

David English is one. He studied Brian Close for cricket captaincy, Lord Sugar for business owner skills, Serena Williams for micro-business leadership, Dickens for creativity and multiple income streams and Charlie Mullins for business growth without banks and investors. If he was delivering professional services again, he would choose Janice B Gordon as his role model - and not just for brilliant, colourful self-made clothes. Then his key, whether it be speaking on stage, deal-making or building your personal brand, is to practice, practice and practice.

By now Tony and Eileen were living together and whilst she was still at university, having needed an additional year to finish her degree, Tony had to find well paid work. Eileen was to reciprocate earning the bulk of the money when Tony did his post graduate HR diploma and Eileen's salary as a qualified librarian at the Consumers Association was what put the food on the table. This shows that even in those days they were a very strong team who looked out for each other.

They moved from Hendon to Finsbury Park and he remembers being associated with many a dangerous person, but none you would exactly call friends. What he did know though, was that if one of them wanted you to do something, you did it! You also did it without question.

That's not to say he was involved in any illegal activities, but often found himself keeping people company when he didn't really want to be there. Often Eileen would be forced to make it home as quickly as they could for fear of dodgy people hanging around the tube station. None of this type of living was known to Tony.

He wasn't what you would call street smart and it was a long way from Hull.

He was popular everywhere he went and the group hospital laundry he worked for in summer jobs, with its foul linen bonus, even offered him a supervisor's job for when he finished his degree.

Looking at that time, Tony can relate the hardships to those he sees now of people setting up their own business. How vulnerable you are when you don't have money and how hard you have to work to make ends meet.

Debt makes you do difficult things, but also makes you grateful for the opportunities you get. Tony and Eileen both remember the highlight of their time in Finsbury Park as the day Eileen found a ten-pound note in an overcoat that neither knew they had. It meant the first proper meal for a week and bottles of ale to celebrate. When Tony first met Eileen, she could out drink him with Guinness and a whisky chaser. Things might be different now, but it's the little memories like these that Tony recounts with pleasure.

Tony's need for one well paid job and a career after finishing his degree led to him hounding the local temp agencies to find something. He was still uncertain about what he wanted to do, still convinced as only young academics can be that he would be 'discovered'. Whether this was through acting, singing the blues or playing cricket, Tony didn't really mind.

In his heart I believe he is still Byron with his love of poetry and his eccentric streak that calls for stage and lilting moments.

However, the spotlight didn't call. What did was a lovely lady at one of the agencies who must have seen something in him. She re-wrote his CV to make less about his time at university and build more on his knowledge and work at the family business. This change was to get Tony a 'temp' job at NCR Limited - formerly the National Cash Register Company, a computers and terminals company and one of the oldest and largest US multinationals. He bought her a huge box of chocolates as a thank you.

Something else about Tony: if you help him, he never forgets and will do everything in his power to tell other people and to show you his appreciation.

At that time, in the IT industry, there was IBM and what Tony says were called the 'seven dwarves'. NCR Limited was the next largest to IBM in the UK and the company he joined had 6,000 employees at that time in over 60 locations and that did not include, perhaps up to 5,000 at its manufacturing plants in Dundee.

NCR Limited is the only one of the seven dwarves still going strong today and most ATMs (cash dispensers) in the world are manufactured by NCR.

The temp job was in the Organisation and Methods (System Analysis) Department which does seem odd as Tony can't draw or really read diagrams and here he was in a department that required such a skill. He was the youngest in the department, but this worked as they all liked him and he settled in. The temporary job quickly becoming permanent.

He made a deal to help the others with their report writing if they'd do his flow diagrams for him.

It worked out well and he enjoyed the fact that, although he was based at offices in Brent Cross, the projects he was worked on could be at many sites in the UK.

Tony cannot just do an office job. In fact he's not an ideal employee, because he can't stand to be supervised or have his time controlled. He needs the freedom of travelling to different locations and has done this all his working life.

He played table tennis in the same team as his manager and this helped to secure a good working relationship and fast salary increases. In only a short period of time he was being trusted to attend senior meetings and being entertained by contractors, including Xerox. One occasion leading to an extended lunch and finishing with a bottle of expensive brandy.

Tony, in retrospect, says that he owes a massive debt to his parents in giving him the social skills to 'get on' in business. He'd travelled to London to the theatre from the age of 11, been to many 'posh dos', and knew all the CEOs of the five box mills that his father worked with. The side of business he was seeing at NCR Limited was definitely more entertaining than his student holiday jobs. It wasn't just for fun though. Tony had a skill that he hadn't until then been aware of; negotiation - making great deals on behalf of the company.

This skill led to him running his own special projects within the department. After two years of being there Tony had become the 'Bright Ideas Officer'; something he created from a suggestions scheme that few of the 6000 employees were participating in. His writing skills were in good use then too as he published a Bright Ideas magazine. Many hundreds of thousands were saved and made by bright ideas from employees after further enabling the company suggestion box.

His work took him to many locations at NCR Limited, with different working conditions dependant on the type of work there, such as engineering, manufacturing, sales showrooms or administrative. As the work he was doing was all about efficiency and productivity it brought him face to face with the biggest issue facing employees in large companies at that time - increased technology meant insecurity leading to loss of jobs. His work also brought him face to face with trade unions which were resisting change for the same reasons.

In 1974 there had been a huge swathe of redundancies, primarily in Dundee with manufacturing plants, but also across the UK in the field engineering divisions. This had left a lot of feelings of uncertainty throughout the workplace. NCR was a company with a great reputation of providing for and looking after its staff, even today it is voted one of the best companies to work for in the world. Yet despite this, people remained afraid of losing their jobs.

Tony was starting to see his ambitious streak come into play. It had previously only been seen in sport but now, despite still being introverted, he wanted to get on and climb the ladder. He wondered if there was a career for him in industrial relations.

Whilst working his first two years at NCR Limited, he had obtained, through day release and evening classes, a diploma in Administrative Management, but he wanted to do more. He decided to go back to Middlesex Polytechnic to do a full-time diploma in Human Resource Management. A bold choice for a man who had hardly tried the first time at university. He spoke to NCR and they unofficially agreed that he could work full time there for the HR department during holidays and if he passed his diploma, there might be a job for him that was Industrial Relations related. Eureka!

By now Eileen had her post graduate library qualification and had a fantastic job working for Which? Magazine. They were back in Hendon, this time in much better accommodation - a large flat with two bedrooms and a lounge/kitchen area and sharing with just one other, in 96 not 94 Sunningfields Road and they knew that they could afford it.

If NCR did give Tony a job in Personnel in the summer holidays, all would be well. Tony went back to Middlesex Polytechnic (University) which had the best post grad HR diploma in London. NCR were true to their word and this time Tony studied hard to realise his ambition.

This is another turning point for it was here that

whilst studying economics as part of the course, he was introduced to '*Small Is Beautiful*' by E. F. Schumacher, written in 1973. Tony feels that this is one of the most influential books ever in the world and it was to have a huge impact on his life. Perhaps more in later life, but it has stayed with him since 1976.

'*Small is Beautiful'* was published in 1973 near the end of E. F. Schumacher's life. Not that he would have known he would die 4 years later. We never know how long we've got, although being a similar age Tony says it's the reason he doesn't buy green bananas!

Schumacher promoted '*for the many not the few'*. Schumacher recognised entrepreneurship and socialist values could co-exist, saying, *"In small scale enterprise, private ownership is natural, fruitful and just"*.

At the time Tony wasn't to know how much he would take this to heart, but the book made a huge impression on him.

Yet again Tony was blessed with a fantastic lecturer, a left-wing guy who explained monopolistic companies and how big pharma and big energy can rig the markets to better themselves and not the people. As Schumacher suggests large scale enterprise does nothing for public welfare.

Without sounding like Citizen Smith (I am showing my age here!), it was at a time when strikes were thick and fast, so much so that many students were actually locked in, not out of university and Tony himself never received his degree ceremony due to strike action. Power to the people was a common phrase.

Sitting through a cloud of smoke (everyone smoked in those days and lecture halls were reminiscent of Victorian London with its smog) Tony listened avidly to lecturers that bummed cigarettes from their students and talked about Unions.

Tony had already decided that he needed to excel in the employment law side of his diploma if he wanted to get a major Industrial Relations role. He wanted to get into negotiations with trade unions, everything else in HR - recruitment, psychology, training and especially, health and safety was secondary but he wanted to be top of the class again.

Tony felt he could do some good. I'll refer back to the integrity angle of the book, Tony didn't want to negotiate for the man, no, he wanted to keep people in jobs.

Win-win negotiations means that the employer and the trade union get something out of the deal. Both parties often need saving from themselves and that's where the professional negotiators on behalf of the employer and the union come in.

Apart from the negotiating skill, knowledge of employment law and salary and benefits policy plus a head for calculating figures, the priceless trait of a negotiator, is trust. Professional negotiators at that time built personal reputations based out of skill and reliance. Especially when there was a go slow, walk out or strike, the professional negotiator was the centre of attention.

Tony has three skills by now - negotiating,

performing and writing - all three were good to go for a role in Industrial Relations - and he could now make a positive difference.

Tony's post graduate diploma in HR finished in December 1977 and this time he had distinctions. On January 21st, 1978 Tony and Eileen, both 25, were married and this is an enterprising story in itself.

Tony and Eileen organised and funded the wedding themselves as Tony's Mum no longer had spare cash and Eileen was an orphan. This aside, it wasn't going to be done on a budget, it was going to be a beautiful affair, one that would include all of their friends and family. If they were doing this, then it would be perfect and the dream wedding that Eileen wanted. As Eileen is a Catholic, they chose the Catholic Church in Hessle as the venue and Phil Coulter's brother, a priest and well-known theologian would take the service. Bruce's father, Bill would give Eileen away. Tony paid for his Best Man, Digby, the solicitor and ushers, including the actor, Chris, his tennis doubles partner Dave, as well as Cousin Colin, their morning suits, top hats and accessories. Eileen did similar for her friends as bridesmaids.

Their wedding was a great example of their teamwork, put together with military precision and they still believe to this day it is the finest wedding they've ever been to. As they were paying for it themselves, remember they had one parent between them, they decided to make it an amazing affair, but only for 60 people.

They also only had a small number of relatives by

then, in fact Eileen had none - Bruce‘s Dad gave her away and they figured that limiting the numbers would give them the opportunity to create a truly memorable event for all their guests. Remember, Tony loves putting on unusual events.

The wedding though, was one of the very few incidents were Tony really did get into trouble for his drinking and entertaining. Preceding the wedding Tony had 3 stag nights, one in Hendon, well why not? They closed a room at the Chequers for the evening and he had two smaller affairs in central London and Hessle.

One couple were invited from London to Hull, representing each of their groups of friends. So, one each from Which and NCR Limited, one from all the sports teams, the Chequers, their degree courses, housemates and so forth.

The regularly brought up incident was at Tony's first stag night in the Chequers. At least sixty of Tony's friends, work colleagues and sports colleagues were present. At about midnight, while Tony was doing his Little Walter impression singing 'My Babe' on top of a table in only his briefs, Eileen and her friends walked into the room. They'd been for a meal and Tony said something, which Eileen says was not very nice. He didn't tell me what it was, so we'll have to leave it to the imagination!

Eileen didn't call it off so I'm hoping it wasn't too bad.

As Tony says, everyone knows what will happen at

a Wedding or any formal event, but if you are to exceed all expectations you have to relentlessly pursue getting the very best and most talented supplier for each element. Tony and Clare later put their success in running major events down to just this philosophy. A ‘package’, even an expensive package, just won’t do.

Eileen‘s winter white dress had a beautiful white fur hood. She was truly beautiful, and Tony felt that he was a very lucky man to be marrying his best friend.

The reception was in a posh venue, the French Restaurant at the Willerby Manor Hotel and there would be a slap-up meal with a choice of sumptuous starters, then roast beef with Yorkshire puddings followed by profiteroles with hot chocolate sauce - Tony is big on chocolate. It’s hard to imagine Tony going for the bells and whistles in this way, but he knew that it would make Eileen happy and they correctly believed they would only marry once, so it was best to do it right.

The speeches would be amazing - Tony, Digby and Uncle Bill - and the ‘costumes’ as Tony puts it, of the bride, her bridesmaid, the groom, best man and Uncle Bill would be second to none.

They chose a mass of table accessories, wrote and printed programmes - something of a speciality for

Tony for the next 30 years - (and **this** is the killer) chose the most talented of contractors. They’d been to a lot of weddings by this time in their lives and they contacted the best independent photographer, florist, dressmaker, morning suit hirer, tailor, Rolls Royce hirer, top hat supplier, hairdresser and cakemaker they could find.

They arranged for Hull and Hessle friends and family to take in at least a couple of their friends travelling to the wedding. There was a pre-wedding rolling feast of stews at Tony's Hessle home for everyone arriving the night before. I can imagine that it was a time of immense happiness and fun with people getting together, catching up and helping to celebrate.

Jude co-ordinated a late evening drinks at the Grange Hotel and Country Club where Eileen and Tony spent their honeymoon night. There may have been Tony and friends on guitar, many times, but no disco. Who needs that when you can have an impromptu jam surrounded by so many talented friends and family? This was Tony in his element, performing and loving being centre of attention. The performer in Tony (and Digby) was at its peak. Tony and Digby had done a lot of public speaking at work and as students. Tony had successfully completed best man duties at weddings before his own and Digby had won numerous prizes, mainly beer, at Newcastle University and then at Lincoln's Inn for his talks and jokes.

Much of Digby's material was not suitable for a family audience but he could tone it down. They knew each other's faults well and so they had a lot of good material to take the mickey out of each other and of course, they had recent memories to share from the stag dos. Digby is a much-missed, wonderful storyteller with plenty of great jokes embedded into his tall tales. The year before he died, he gave what is regarded as the best speech at Beverley Grammar School Old Boys Christmas Dinner.

Eileen and Tony were completely broke for two years thereafter and their honeymoon was limited to ringing up B&Bs the night before on a hastily arranged tour of the Yorkshire Moors. But it was worth it.

Despite the expense, the wedding was a great success and their attention to detail in providing the most fabulously different winter nuptials in the world paid off.

Tony's abiding memory is of some of his Aunts raiding other tables and stuffing their handbags with the free cigars, cigarettes, chocolate mints and profiteroles.

After completing his studies, NCR made good on their word and he joined them after his honeymoon, in the position of Personnel Manager, based at their Boreham Wood Print Works. It was in this role that all of the skills he developed living within the rougher side of jobs and communities in London, came into play.

The print industry at that time had the strongest and most powerful unions in Britain. The Unions ruled so much so that the Fathers and Mothers of the Chapel (shop stewards) had more power and influence over employees than the supervisors and managers. If, as a manager you weren't liked, you weren't allowed on the shop floor and woe betide any man walking into the women's floor - they would be taking their lives into their hands and be met with a barrage of heckling that would do sailors proud!

It's funny that today we're very concerned about equal rights and harassment, but women gave as good as they got in those days. Women owned those floors; it was their domain. Men were often scared to set foot in there. Overall it was a difficult environment to work in. As Personnel Manager, the other managers who were all print related people - ex union members who had been promoted - were very suspicious of a young guy coming to negotiate on their behalf with trade unions on salaries, benefits and most importantly, the introduction of new technology.

Like starting at Beverley Grammar School, Tony had to assert himself quickly or he would be left in an office, one he'd been given a long way from the shop floor and other managers and there would be no knock on the door or phone ringing. A feature of Tony's career has been finding creative solutions - often off the wall - to problems. His Bright Ideas scheme was like that and his founding of SFEDI, #MicroBizMatters Day and his #PayIn30Days campaign are more recent examples.

He couldn't walk through the Print Works and stop to talk to people and ask questions during the day - if the managers didn't stop him, the SOGAT Women certainly would. So he decided to work 9 am to 9 pm every day. Everyone knew he was only paid 9-5 like the rest of them but at night when the security guards took over from the receptionists and all the managers had left, he found he could walk through the print works and chat.

Word soon got around that he was OK and more importantly, what he was trying to do.

That meant that the Fathers and Mothers of the Chapel started to come to his office during the day.

Admittedly, sometimes they were just trying to catch him out, but eventually they knew he understood employment law, company and trade union policies better than most of their managers. See again, this trait of practicing and learning to get better at something than anyone else! Also, the nod towards integrity. Trying to ensure that he was on the right side and going out of the way to help people who were, initially hostile and suspicious.

Eventually he won around all of the managers too at a time of some major national strikes, where all employees were locked out, Tony managed to negotiate deals with full time trade union officials, which got much needed new technology into the print works with no job losses and NCR Borehamwood kept working. Even when much of their competition was closed.

Tony got himself onto the British Printing Industries Federation Employment Law Council in London, so everyone was quite proud of him. They must have been happy with him as he even proposed and accepted to get rid of the managers' dining room so that all employees would eat and drink together in a much better facility. Tony is big on equality. This was unheard of. Today we're all about inclusion and ensuring that there is good communication. We have open plan offices and open-door policies, but this was not a thing back then, there was still a clear division of them against us left over from the 50's and 60's. To make something like this happen was actually pretty radical.

There were also daily grievances that required his presence and it was here that Tony relied on the tactics he'd learned playing cricket and captaining teams. Talking of cricket and equality, after Tony's degree he founded, captained and opened the batting for Middlesex Polytechnic Vikings Cricket Team, with his friend Nick Keyte, who he was best man for. Eileen was their scorer and they borrowed a ground off the Poly and had some serious county standard talent.

Not only were they usually unbeaten each year, but they were renowned for the finest teas in London. All the players and their partners took turns, but the best was always an Indian Sikh with his curries. This is how cricket should be and is a great example of how people can come together from all walks of life to initially play sport, but at the same time network, provide impromptu business advice as well as socially engage. There's often been the understanding that a lot of top business deals are made, not in the boardroom, but on the golf club or in the bar. This is absolutely true, but it doesn't need to just be top CEO's that work this way. We do business with people that we like and know, so meeting regularly at sporting events is a great way to build business contacts and more importantly, business knowledge.

After two years at NCR Borehamwood Print Works Tony became the youngest Industrial Relations

Manager of a major company in the UK, based at NCR Limited Head Office in Marylebone. He and Nick moved to play cricket with Mill Hill Village.

This was his dream job as it gave him the freedom to be a law unto himself. You need to understand the set up. NCR had two industrial relations managers, Tony and Steve Abel. Steve became a great friend. Tony and Steve loved comparing notes, out of hours, on their work with different trade unions. They also talked a lot of politics as they had different experiences and views (and there's a lot of politics in Trade Union relations). They'd both had some interesting jobs and met some really interesting people, Steve perhaps more than Tony, from when he was involved in writing speeches for Liberal Party leading politicians, including the infamous, Cyril Smith.

In this company of about six thousand employees there were about twenty trade unions which meant twenty annual negotiating rounds for wages, salaries and benefits. Tony and Steve, with the help of a personnel officer to do all the paperwork and research back at Head Office, split the workload between them - Tony keeping the print unions and adding some more from different departments and locations. Tony's Personnel Officer Chrissie, was the reason he retained a reputation for professionalism. Tony always wanted to influence people with know-how and evidence rather than spin.

However, Steve and he had a fairly maverick way of approaching their jobs as co-Industrial Relations

Managers, which could have led to them getting into trouble. There are always some executives in organisations that hate the idea of people working from home and believe that you're not working if you're not behind your desk. Steve and Tony were often not behind their desks. They were travelling the country working with trade unions and sometimes they were in the pub during working hours.

Chrissie was not just a great personnel manager she was also a great problem solver and would say to someone who asked, '*When will Tony be back?*' '*I don't know but I'll be talking to him soon, what is it that you want?*' If Chrissie could not answer their question there and then, by the time he spoke to her Chrissie had found out the answer to their problem and passed it on to him. He'd be able to ring the enquirer with all the answers and still stay in the pub with Steve. Their professionalism, thanks to Chrissie, was preserved.

During annual negotiations and other disputes which occurred during the year, every eye in management, directors and shareholders was on Tony and Steve. They even had to brief the board on progress. After all, the cost of the negotiations in salary and benefits, increase or lost time due to industrial action had a major impact on the bottom line. During a negotiation or dispute, naturally they had to work all hours, through the night if necessary. After all, time was money.

The great thing was, they were both totally self-managing. As always, Tony had a great boss and if they made the deals didn't ask too many questions about what time they'd got into the office, where they were in the country or what they were doing. The answer to what they were doing was drinking.

Steve had worked for a Trade Union and then writing speeches for the Liberal Party leaders before he joined NCR and was used to working erratic hours and the night life. Tony had never found getting up in a morning easy even though he always did.

This was the perfect job and the phrase 'one for the road' was their given saying as they rang their wives to tell them that is what they were having. Often the road would run out and they'd kip at hotels or colleagues' places in central London rather than pay for taxis to their respective homes and face the long commute the next morning. Tony would ring Eileen to say he was staying in central London with Steve 'One for the road' Abel or other friends rather than coming home.

Eileen would never tell him off and neither would she be bothered. It's not as though there was a meal waiting for him or something they were going to do together.

On average, until the last few years, Tony has spent about a third of the year away from home in hotels. Even when away from home for three or four successive nights he is unlikely to ring home. Eileen is just as bad or good, depending on your perspective. If Eileen is away on holiday with Sinead or a friend, she won't ring Tony either.

Sadly, after eighteen months of great fun and success there was a re-organisation in the HR Department and the structure changed so that Tony was promoted to Personnel Operations Manager, with site personnel managers reporting to him, including Cathy and Stuart who he'd helped recruit from Middlesex Poly HR diploma course.

This meant he had a team in Marylebone, at Borehamwood and Brent Cross and had to be in the office every day dealing with recruitment, training and even the dreaded, health and safety. For the first and only time in his employed career he felt shackled and bored - catching himself falling asleep at one point. He did manage to pull his usual trick of developing something that would give him an opportunity to perform, an employment law seminar he gave to managers and supervisors at regional offices around the country.

This grand tour stopped the boredom for a while and with Tony, travelling anywhere can be an adventure. In Manchester one morning he was arrested for getting lost as usual, but he hadn't even left the hotel! Take a wrong turn he went down the fire escape and out the fire exit. Tony was going to feed some coins into the parking meter, but security felt he was trying to escape without paying his bill. It's happened many times since. It's to do with his spatial awareness, or lack thereof, I've seen him turn the opposite way to directions given only moments before!

Boredom as Personnel Operations Manager, despite

an excellent salary and perks, made Tony for the first time realise that he would need to be running his own show as quickly as possible. He'd always had great bosses but there would come a time when the almost yearly promotions would stop or, as now, the work would become tedious. He was determined to pursue happiness and fulfilment and falling asleep at his desk wasn't in the script.

There are moments in everyone's lives that accumulate over time and mould you into the person you will later become. It's my belief that the hardships in London, the fear and uncertainty of industry and the political unrest of the 80's all banded together to strengthen Tony's spirit and give him the understanding of people that he has today.

While at NCR two factors of corporate life hit him hard between the eyes. The first was how few managers were able to avoid redundancy after the age of about 45, and it was getting younger.

The second was how professionals would benchmark themselves against similar positions in other similar companies. They would look at salary and perks and there was an understanding of the hierarchy within the industry, you knew how to climb the professional ladder and which company meant you were climbing up and what was a step down.

Executive careers were and are, largely sector based and the way people progress their careers is rarely by talent but by politics. Tony had been promoted on ability in specific professional areas, but he was a maverick and most people were promoted because of 'fitting in', being team players and worst of all being a 'safe pair of hands'. He knew that a professional career in the sector was time limited, but he also felt his was personality limited too. Tony would often sit in pubs surrounded by friends that weren't employed, that were running their own businesses and compare stories. He wasn't thinking of immediate self-employment, but he was now fascinated by the difference between the two worlds.

He also knew it was an inevitability that he would need the freedom of running his own business at a time of his own choosing rather than being pushed. He was desperately sad about redundant executives at NCR taking on franchises and self-employed businesses that they had little talent or love for, but at a certain age, and it was getting younger all the time, you were past your sell by date for an executive corporate career.

Tony was bored and knew that he needed to be an HR Director, as his last senior position before doing his own thing. He felt time was running out. For someone as ambitious as Tony, Director level was a must at 30 and he was 29 now. His Director Paul was only 35 so that position wasn't going to open up any time soon at NCR. He was well known to the head-hunters by now and when Hay came calling with the offer of a position as Corporate Services Manager (and Director) at Amway UK Limited, he threw his name in the hat. After a lengthy recruitment process including the usual battery of psychological tests (the ones with diagrams in them do his head in) and unusually a formal meal with the other Amway UK Directors, he was offered the job with a fabulous salary and perks.

Before leaving NCR, after 3 months' notice, Chrissie organised the most wonderful series of leaving parties in different locations. He still has the cards with all the signatures to this day. Did I tell you he's obsessive at collecting stuff too - books, theatre and sports programmes, vinyl, CDs, DVDs, hats and leaving cards?

The last surprise party was at the NCR HQ in Marylebone Road where they closed the 3rd floor to create an area where everyone could attend for late afternoon refreshments.

Tony was very sad to leave. Eileen was also very sad for him to leave and in her normal blunt way had said, "*You're stupid!*"

The reason for this was that she'd attended, with Tony, an Amway Convention at the Birmingham Odeon in September 1981. After only twenty minutes of flag waving and motivational hype Eileen turned to Tony and said,

"It's a cult. Contact NCR and tell them you're coming back."

Q&A Time

Q. Do you think getting all those postgraduate business qualifications, particularly in HRM and HRD, has helped you in your own business?

A: Not at all. Clare and I learned more from our respective fathers that ran their own business. The business qualifications and professional institute memberships helped me to climb the corporate career ladder. Then when we started our business the qualifications plus positions we'd held gave us credibility in the professional services we were offering. That's all.

Q. Was it a waste of time then?

A: No. I love learning and still do. After the disaster of my degree, which put me off reading novels for about ten years, it was great to be learning stuff that would get me the job I wanted to do. Although I'm a #Happipreneur now, I've always been very competitive and I knew that there was no hope of getting into senior HR positions, and I wanted to be in Industrial Relations, without being qualified.

Q. Was Human Resource Management what you expected?

A: There's a lot more sex in it than I expected.

Q. Sex?

A: Well, if you've read City Boy or City Girl about the 2008 financial crash, you'll realise that the biggest corporations and the City of London, Government even, are often like a sleazy gentlemen's club. The high performers get a lot of extracurricular perks that the top brass turn a blind eye to.

Frankly, they don't know what their high performers are up to, but as long as they're making the big deals they protect them. It's still going on 30 years after I was in HR. There is a reason they keep down the number of women in senior positions.

The higher these men get in these London HQs, the more they expect to get out of their business travel and expenses allowance. There are a lot of Harvey Weinstein's out there. 'Work hard - Party hard' was the mantra. Then there are various times of the year when there is a sexual tsunami - sales conventions and Christmas parties, for example.

The more senior you are in HR, the more you have to deal with the fall-out. It's not all sex but it is all dodgy deals and relationships. Even Government, that bastion of propriety, spends, I think, about £28 million a year in settlements and non-disclosure agreements. Hopefully this is on the decrease.

Q. So have you been involved in these extra-curricular activities?

A: That's the problem about being in HR - you're meant to set an example. So, although, I've been to all the finest clubs in London, it was purely for research purposes!!! I've always been taken to places like the Stork Club, Stringfellows and Tramps - you usually have to leave your American Express Gold Card behind the bar and I've never had one - champagne is over £100 a bottle.

Seriously, though there's a lot I hated in senior HR, and later in PR, about being the 'legal' cleaner up. I loved Industrial Relations and Remuneration and Benefits but not much else.

Top HR people are a bit like the solicitors that top professional footballers have to call, if they've transgressed. Sexual shenanigans inside the organisation are the worst and I've always hated it that the senior male executive is always the one to stay in the organisation and the more junior female employee is the one who leaves, with compensation. I hope that's changed now.

I also hope everyone you've interviewed will say I'm inclusive and determined about equality, but I've been given many jobs to do that are discriminatory. Most I've refused to do and that's why I'm no good with bosses.

Q: What has been useful in your building your own businesses from your HR training?

A: The interpersonal skills and leadership training I received was awesome. I agree with Chester L Karrass, the doyen of negotiating, who says "*In business, you don't get what you deserve, you get what you negotiate.*". I don't think in Clare and my business we tendered for anything, but we picked up huge contracts by building relationships and negotiating deals.

I ended up providing training on negotiation to some of the top executives in the biggest companies and in the civil service. I owe most of any success I've had to my negotiating skills and NCR Limited taught me that. I also had loads of practice as Industrial Relations

Manager. Remember, I'm talking about win-win negotiating - it makes for happy customers, happy suppliers and happy employees. It's the best problem solving and opportunity gaining skill I know. It should be in every Happipreneur's armoury.

Q: Did you stay in touch with Steve?

A: After we both left NCR Ltd we did actually meet up again once, when I was speaking at a CBI event for the Sales Qualifications Board, which I'd co-founded with Clare and Richard Berry, Director General of the DSA. Steve came over to speak to me and naturally, we went for 'one for the road' - the chemistry was still there.

"Even injustice has its good points. It gives me the challenge of being as happy as I can be in an unfair world"

Albert Ellis

V
Selling Unachievable Dreams - The Amway Years

This chapter is a scoop for this book as Tony has kept his own counsel about the bad side of the global MLM sector, and his role in it, for three and a half decades. I had to convince him to share this as he was reluctant, Amway (short for The American Way) is not known for its understanding of anyone not singing along to their playbook, he worried that speaking out could have ramifications.

However, he figured that UK legislation, the technology and the people are so different now that he is not harming anyone he met during his five happy years at Amway UK, by revealing how prospective independent business owners can guard against losing money, time and in some cases, health, family and friends in the pursuit of wealth.

On the positive side there are also many useful lessons he learned about successful entrepreneurship and the benefits of a business of your own that he has used in his campaigns to make lives better for prospective and existing business owners.

Hold on to your hats - Tony's is a fedora.

To whet your appetite for the revelations, here's a recent post from David Brear, a prolific blogger and investigator on *MLM The American Dream Made Nightmare*. Tony has learned a lot from David's investigations and blog since 2012 and they have communicated with each other.

A concerned Blog reader has written to me to ask:

***Q**: Why have lawyers, economists and other academics not denounced MLM as dangerous nonsense?*

***A**: Of course, over the decades, there have been a significant number of lawyers, economists and other academics who have had their noses deep in the stinking 'MLM' trough.*

*Meanwhile, despite a growing mountain of quantifiable evidence proving beyond all reasonable doubt that effectively every ill-informed person who has signed up for a so-called 'MLM income opportunity' has (by design) failed to generate an overall **net**-profit/income, the latest media warnings regarding the 'MLM' phenomenon still cannot accept the glaring reality that this is another form of pernicious (blame-the-victim) cultic racketeering and, instead, repeat elements of thought-stopping 'MLM business' jargon (without detailed qualification or heavy irony). Furthermore, certain independent academic observers are quoted who have found the evidence, but who apparently still imagine that (what is commonly referred to as) the 'MLM business model,' can be reformed.*

David Brear, as you can see, does not pull any

punches. But let's get back to Tony's story.

Leaving NCR was hard, not because Tony didn't want to go, simply because of the people he had met along the way. It seems that even then he touched people and let them know that he genuinely cared and was interested in them and was already angling to get some of his NCR colleagues, particularly Chrissie, into his new team at Amway. Tony has nearly always recruited on attitude and trust.

The times he's recruited on skill and qualifications - as HR specialists are meant to do - have always been a disaster. Like his cricket teams he'd been used to selecting every member of his work team and letting them develop their role in the team. He wasn't keen to 'inherit' a team - another reason why self-employment is better for Tony and, he believes, better for many people. Work must be fun because life must be fun, so the people you work with must be fun too - simple as!

Tony was immensely flattered to have been offered the Amway opportunity. Not just because of the salary, car and perks, but because it was the direction he knew he needed to go if he was to complete his career ladder climb to the highest level. There was also a nod to Tony's narcissism, which he fully admits to being one of his flaws. It was a huge ego boost for someone his age to have been given this role and for him to have succeeded in view of the competition and all of the entry interviews and tests.

Hay at that time were the premier executive search organisation in the UK, so he knew that having won the Amway job he'd be in the top echelon of most hireable HR executives for the future. He hoped this would be his last job before doing his own thing, but he liked being headhunted. He would be the youngest at Director level at Amway UK and probably, at Amway internationally. He was certain he'd be the only one with a beard - his 'look' was still not on trend!

By now, Tony was not only completely far away from his original disinterest in the family business, but still poles apart from where he is today. It's as though this was the middle ground of the man he could be and the man he wanted to be.

At the time Amway had 200 staff in the UK and over 50,000 distributors with a sales turnover of about £20 million. Distributors are now known as independent business owners. Having been founded in 1959 Amway Corporation was the second largest, to Avon, direct selling company in the world.

They were massive in the USA and Australasia, but had taken some time to get going in many European countries, including the UK. Tony was joining Amway UK when business was booming. The next two years were to be the peak of their sales in the UK, but, of course, Tony did not know that.

One of his first tasks was to co-ordinate the building of a new multimillion HQ and hi-tech pick pack facility (think Amazon) in Milton Keynes so that all the employees could be on one site rather than 3 separate sites currently. As we've already ascertained, spatial awareness is possibly Tony's biggest nemesis and so to arrange such a big move, with state-of-the-art equipment and layout, was never going to be his forte. However, what Tony is VERY good at is recognising when he can't do something and bringing in those that can.

Over ninety percent of Amway's unique household, cosmetics and nutrition products were developed and manufactured by them, but like all direct selling companies, the products were not available in shops and were sold, often by demonstration, direct to the home by distributors. Amway is what is known now as an MLM (Multi-Level Marketing) company. Amway created the MLM distribution method as we know it today and ninety percent of the world's direct selling companies now use an MLM structure. Independent distributors with a business of their own, earned commission on both the products they sold and on commission and bonuses on the products sold by the people they recruited.

The more recent examples of this I can give you are Forever Living and Arbonne. I'm sure you will have come across at least one friend or acquaintance involved with these companies and may understand how they work.

In 1981 however, MLM direct selling still seemed relatively new in the UK. Recruiting distributors to sell the products were not a big part of how you made money in the traditional direct selling companies like Tupperware, Avon and Kleeneze. In these traditional companies - either party plan or selling by distributing catalogues - there was no hard sell, nor were they pitched as 'get rich' business opportunities based on recruiting others to your team.

Over the next five years, during Tony's time at Amway, the company became big news for the hold it was taking in the UK. Household cleaning products and cosmetics were the main selling lines, but Amway owned its own aloe vera farms and the nutrition products were taking off too. The founders of Amway had devised their Amway version of MLM that is prevalent today, with distributors of a nutrition company called Nutrilite. Amway Corporation now owned Nutrilite.

Amway always stressed that being an independent distributor was a part time opportunity, but most of those that joined hoped it would become their full-time own business and their route to becoming wealthy - new car, new house and new lifestyle. This was the American Way - the American Dream in action.

Although he was joining the company primarily as an HR Director to build talent, reduce costs and improve productivity, the next five years for Tony would be also be a crash course in entrepreneurship and would introduce him to the workings of government, trade associations and the mainstream media. All useful for the campaigning he does today. It was this knowledge that he learned at Amway which allowed him to create organisations like the Sales Qualifications Board and the SFEDI Group and made him an in-demand consultant on entrepreneurship, direct marketing and leadership development.

As everyone had said it was pyramid selling, which

is illegal. Tony had done a lot of research on Amway before he joined - particularly the legal position. He'd met the other directors and they were all top professionals and, like Tony, had been recruited from some of the UK's largest blue-chip companies and between his research and the other directors' answers to his questions he was re-assured. He had to understand the legalities from the beginning, as a part of his Corporate Services responsibilities. Along with HR, payroll, purchasing, catering, reception, post room, facilities, grounds and maintenance, he was to be responsible for Amway UK's legal and PR functions too.

Being a man, he of course didn't listen to his wife and discounted her fears, after all they weren't going to be distributers so the 'cult' aspect wouldn't affect them. Amway was going to be a challenge for Eileen too. It was not a challenge that Tony would have many late nights and be away from home a lot of the time. Eileen was used to that at NCR and both enjoyed their own company. The challenge was that the executives' wives were expected to attend major distributor events and seminars because the leading distributors were all husband and wife teams. Tony describes Eileen as razor sharp and brighter than he is, but also says she can't help telling people what she thinks, and Eileen really disliked many of the dream makers!

Fortunately, Eileen through world-class self-control, of maximising the smile and nods, combined with her Derry accent and speed of speech which could be confusing to the listener, she was able to avoid confrontation. Eileen also had a series of ready-made excuses not to attend all the events in the UK and overseas. So, she managed not to scupper Tony's job - but it was a close-run thing. Eileen's ready-made excuses were Carl who was born in Hemel Hempstead, where they'd bought their first flat, in April 1980 and being pregnant with Alan, born in January 1984 and Sinead, born in November 1985. Eileen did enjoy the many events at Amway with the staff rather than distributors, and her favourite overseas trip was to Venice for a World Direct Selling Association Conference.

Tony had been sure that he needed to be at director level by thirty and here he was, but he was also being thrown in at the deep end. No-one in the company, apart from his fellow executives, knew what he was there to do and as they'd never had a HR manager before they had no idea what Tony could bring to the party. Tony knew it would be hard, but he was surprised by the resentment and isolation he found in his first few weeks there. There was no way he could recruit any of his former team from NCR - they'd be fish out of water.

As you know by now, Tony had experienced this resentment and suspicion before at work and in sport and he knew that he needed to act quickly and assertively. This meant three things; one - walking around the three buildings daily and chatting to all the staff so they knew who he was and what he'd be trying to do for them; two - getting a quick win to benefit the staff

- he improved the payroll function; and three - most importantly building his own team, but as much as he could from the existing Amway workforce.

This approach of Tony's to creating winning teams, at sport and at work, is he believes fundamental to successful business ownership, entrepreneurship and intrapreneurship.

Large and medium scale companies - NCR was 6,000 and Amway UK 200 employees - if they are going to be entrepreneurial, flexible, innovative and fleet of foot need to be run like a series of self-sustaining micro-businesses (0-9 employees). The business owner, in this case Tony as Corporate Services Manager, needs to lead his or her own high performing, self-reliant, small team and be enterprising in the decisions they take. Larger than micro companies can easily drown in bureaucracy, politics, meetings, measurement (of what's gone) and processes. Micro-business owners with a team clear in their direction and individual roles achieve more than corporate 'talking heads' in Tony's opinion.

If you want a successful intrapreneur in a large company, and nearly all Tony and Clare's clients have been large companies, Tony says the last thing you should do is give them a team, a budget and some required outcomes. Let them start from scratch, test the water, be innovative and be prepared to learn from setbacks and successes.

What was really helpful to Tony and what he loved about the company, in the USA and UK, and loves in most owner led businesses - like Charlie Mullins OBE's Pimlico Plumbers - is that among the employees there was total openness with no stuffiness or pandering to any status needs. Even the co-founders in the States had coffee and ate with different groups of staff in the shared cafeteria. It was so different to NCR where managers tended to bring people to their offices rather than going outside to chat.

Tony quickly realised that if he could assemble the right team, he really could make it a brilliant and productive working environment for all. He began his unorthodox recruitment programme. Tony brought in people that had the basic skills and attitude he needed even though they hadn't been in that type of role before. He needed quick, enthusiastic, trustworthy self-learners - people like micro-business owners that learn by doing.

To give some examples: his PA, Jean, was plucked from the pick pack line; Tanya had never done payroll; Peter became head buyer having been in sales and Clare, who he later founded his own business with, became Personnel Officer having temped in Customer Services. The two receptionists had been in admin roles and he got them involved in the design of the reception area, right down to the furniture, coffee and flower arrangements… and they designed their own uniforms.

So, it went on until a complete team was in place. No-one left the team until Tony left the company. He'd started in an unhappy and often vindictive environment but by the time they moved into the new HQ - the ground floor was Corporate Services, where there was also a superb cafeteria/events space - coming to work was fun.

A great example of his off the wall recruitment was Fred Kruck, another late and much missed friend, who features in Tony's poem '*Who's pulling my plonker?*' Fred was a panel beater in a local car repair company. His wife was working at Amway and asked Tony if he could find a position for her husband. As it turned out, Fred was a genius who not only could read and understand schematics, he grasped circuit diagrams and all the technical things that Tony didn't. They spent a few hours having an interview in the pub and Tony realised he'd found someone he could trust.

As time went on, it became apparent that Fred could learn anything technical very quickly. He oversaw many of the tradespeople, grounds and maintenance personnel, became facilities manager and eventually became the company's official photographer and videographer attending and managing many major events in the UK and overseas. It was Fred that produced all the visuals and memorabilia for Tony's 'This is Your Life' leaving party.

These people were made up, first and foremost from Tony's ability to trust them to support him and each other and their sheer enthusiasm and willingness to learn. He wasn't interested if they didn't have the professional qualifications for the role, and they didn't, but he wanted genuine people that he knew could get the job done and have fun doing it.

Tony had a stack of professional qualifications and institute memberships by the time he joined Amway. He attended and led some great leadership development courses at both NCR and Amway, but he still believes that though all this is good for career progression, in terms of performance, learning by doing wins hands down. The move to the new HQ and Warehouse went well, thanks to Fred, and as a result Tony and his team helped to create an environment that had a fantastic atmosphere and made walking around the office and warehouse buildings (which he continued to do twice a day) a pleasurable experience.

I think this is a good point to reflect on how Tony has grown up to nowand how he has blended all the people skills he's learned.

It takes a good manager to step into a new role and run with it; it takes an exceptional one to observe how people fit and make a cohesive team that becomes almost a family unit. They began to run charity events, not necessarily sponsored by the company, smaller events that they would use to support local causes. Christmas parties for the elderly, summer parties for children with special needs. They set up international football matches with other Amway countries like Holland and France.

It was a great low-cost weekend away for players and partners and supporters. Tony would play and it was a really good way to build the cross departmental teams as well as give something back to their local community and charities. With a couple of guys in the warehouse he entered an Amway table tennis team in a local league and in the summer, there were all sorts of crazy events including rounders, baseball and American football that all the staff, who wanted to, participated in or came along to support.

He said that he first realised how precious it was, that he was in a superb job working with people he really liked and had a lifestyle that was almost luxurious, when he first visited Amway Headquarters in Ada, Michigan after a year or so. Up to then, he'd just been working all hours to keep the job and learn all about many new things too - like understanding the Amway bonus plan, speaking on stage to thousands of people, being grilled on radio and TV and working with top firms of lawyers like Baker & McKenzie and Clifford Chance and top firms of PR Companies like Shandwick and Kingsway.

On this occasion he travelled business class, which he loved, to Amway Headquarters to attend a conference of all the HR Executives at Amway sites around the world. It was this trip that was to show him what he'd achieved and what his position actually meant. Tony had already made quite an impression with the salary and benefits policies he'd introduced at Amway UK and was to lead a session.

Fortunately, for Tony (not Amway), he couldn't make the connecting flight to Grand Rapids in Chicago because of delays, so the airline put him up free of charge in a suite in a hotel close to the airport.

He wandered down to get something to eat and found to his delight a Jazz Club with restaurant. He had a lovely meal and what is more there was a top female blues singer. Tony is a blues addict and, unfortunately for friends and family, often performs his version of 'Got My Mojo Working' after a few drinks - yes, that regularly! It was a perfect evening but was topped off by being able to see on a big screen a live world middleweight boxing fight - Tony's family were all into boxing. The next morning, he flew into Grand Rapids and saw the fleet of Amway planes and helicopters on the tarmac. He was picked up in a large Granada, he had a smaller one back in the UK, and (fortunately) was driven to the Grand Plaza Hotel which Amway owned which remains, and he's stayed in some of the finest hotels in the world, his all-time favourite and most luxurious hotel.

He checked in and there were gifts, including clothing, from Amway on his bed and then he was driven to Amway's facilities in Ada, Michigan. The Granada was his to use for the rest of the stay but he got so lost, once being 70 miles from his hotel because he couldn't get off the motorway and went through so many traffic lights, that they decided it was a good idea to drive him everywhere. Only once has he driven on the right-hand side again and his family refused to go in the car with him.

The tour of Amway Headquarters, research and manufacturing plants is breath-taking in its scale but also in its innovation. In the UK they'd started monthly weekend tours of the new facility for distributors, and these were very successful, but it seemed pitiful in comparison with the tours in Ada, Michigan - Amway was a tourist attraction. The HR Conference of about 30 practitioners from around the world was interesting too and one aspect Tony had never seen before. The room they were in had a balcony and interested staff could come in and observe proceedings. Tony was informed afterwards that he'd done well.

It was a good life, of this there is no doubt, but it took its toll. He wasn't there for the family or Eileen very much, he was making a living for them and saw that as his duty. Eileen has always been the homemaker, coming from the children's home, Tony understood that being part of a family, her own family was what drove her and what made her heart happy. He on the other hand had an ego that needed to be fed and the demands of executive life did just that.

Tony admits that when you're surrounded by wealth it changes you, not that he became nasty but perhaps less approachable and had an air about him that suggested he'd rather be with those of a similar position. Some of his friends and family, particularly in Hull and from Sunningfields Road days, would get jealous or irritated by his actions and he possibly kept himself apart from them.

Being a top exec in a 'pyramid selling' company seemed like a sell-out, although his childhood friend Bruce's sister and her husband, Pip, a milkman were loving being Amway distributors as a side hustle.

Amway was very family oriented, both in the company and in the distributor network. The monthly Direct Distributor seminars, which Tony says were an excellent two day and night business development event, would be almost exclusively husband and wife partnerships. Qualifying at the Direct Distributor level meant a distributor could order and communicate directly with the company. It was also the point at which the husband or wife may consider going full time in their own Amway business. The two days were full of practical business development sessions but also covered things like cashflow and tax. Many years later Tony was able to draw on the best practice in these seminars when trying to reform a lot of the publicly funded 'start your own business programmes'.

The Gala Dinner evening of the Direct Distributor seminar was one of those events Eileen was meant to attend, if she didn't have a good enough family excuse for not being there. It was always a fraught experience. Eileen's opinion of the company and many of its distributors never changed and she disliked the events. Once a month of social suffering wasn't a bad price to pay for a lovely house, garden and time with the children and other Mums with children too. Eileen was sensible enough to realise what they had and was able to bite her tongue or at the very least comment in a heavier brogue so that it wasn't quite caught!

There was still cricket in the summer and Eileen and the kids had a childhood from 1982 to 2000 going to cricket matches on at least one Saturday a month as

Tony was now playing for Great Houghton Cricket Club in Northamptonshire. He captained the team for twelve out of the eighteen years.

It was here that Tony met Dave Parbery. Tony is unusual in preferring not to mix business with pleasure, especially when playing and watching sport, theatre and gigs. He hates corporate hospitality boxes as he believes that if professionals are playing or performing, they deserve the respect of an attentive audience.

As a result, some of his closest friends have never really known what he does. I asked Dave what Tony was like as a friend. Dave was a postman in Northampton when Tony first met him, playing for the Cricket Club in 1982. Tony and Dave have played and watched cricket, rugby and gigs at all the best venues in the UK, including Eric Clapton 8 times at the Royal Albert Hall. I asked him what he was like as a friend 'on tour'.

"*Tony and I have known each other since 1982 and we share a love of both cricket and music. I have been very fortunate to know the man rather than the businessman and to me he's simply my friend. We don't really talk about business, any time that we have together is spent doing the things we love. We've been to so many cricket matches together, although one of the highlights would be 1999 World Cup. Tony had at least 13 different hats for the tour, he really makes me laugh. People gravitate to him as he's so good-natured and he is naturally inclusive.*

I was working in an awful warehouse job when Tony suggested that I downsize and move near to him.

My wife and I talked it over and realised it was exactly what we should do. We now have a lovely home in beautiful countryside, and I get to go out every day with my dogs. I can't thank Tony enough for suggesting the move. It may have been slightly selfish on his part as he does love the Scarborough Cricket, in fact we used to travel from Northampton every year to the Scarborough Cricket Festival, and now I'm close enough to go with him to cricket at Scarborough and Headingley every season!"

Tony also organised a number of cricket tours and in 1984, the year of the Miners' strike they were in Easingwold near York. The Miners' strike with the police violence and phone tapping of the miners' and the bravery of the miners' families, particularly the wives and mothers, has affected him to this day.

Like Schumacher, he still believes large scale enterprise is usually unjust and exploitative and that successive Governments in the UK and USA prioritise wealth creation by large scale enterprise at the expense of social welfare. One of the only escape routes available for those being exploited is to run their own small-scale enterprise or be employed by an independent business owner who puts employees and customers first.

Tony gave up his union membership when he became Industrial Relations Manager at NCR and admits that his college friends, like Jeremy Windust, who was one of the strikers at GCHQ and became a prominent trade union official, had every right to label Tony 'a champagne socialist'.

Tony and Eileen's respective roles in their partnership kept them apart, but they were both equally happy.

Tony as main bread winner and Eileen as Mum and homemaker. Eileen, like most of the employees, really liked Amway products; they were high quality but always had a little something that made them different and therefore far more expensive than the high street version.

After three years Tony was made Chief Executive. He was considering leaving the company at that time but he admits his ego made him accept the role. At that time, he was the only non-sales manager to get this role at Amway internationally. His boss and friend Stewart and the Vice President of International Sales, an Australian, both felt that his negotiating skills, PR and legal know how made him the best choice to tackle some tricky leading distributor issues. Tony is convinced that his American superiors, in allowing the appointment had forgotten about Tony's beard and unusual dress sense. He was later advised to shave off his beard but having had one since aged 17 said that was an impossibility. Tony also became Vice Chairman of the Direct Selling Association, so all in all he was well respected by his peers and loved by his staff.

Then there was the luxury travel. Part of his job with professional travel companies and the internal events team was about setting up annual distributer events and seminars in holiday resorts abroad. These were part incentive and reward and part training and pampering. A few hundred Direct Distributors, and above, would go to places like the Algarve, Majorca and Corfu and about eight Diamond Direct Distributor couples would go to places like Monaco, Nice and Montreux.

It was when checking out the possible venues for a Diamond's Seminar in Cannes that Tony managed to insult the world's leading chef and, probably the whole of France.

Roger Verge, the inventor of cuisine du soleil and co-inventor of nouvelle cuisine was the world's most famous and commended chef. He was also an international celebrity and was regularly in the news for being the chef to the rich, famous and royalty on their yachts and at small private gala dinners. Roger Verge had a small restaurant, but it had sixty chefs. The restaurant, Moulin de Mougins, in a village close to Cannes, was booked solid by the rich and famous in the south of France.

Tony went to the Moulin de Mougins with a travel rep, on a lunchtime to check it out for an upcoming Diamond Distributor evening. If Clare had accompanied him the following disaster, like many of his disasters in foreign locations, would not have occurred. The dish Tony ordered, from the menu in French, was a knuckle of veal. It had a typical cuisine nouvelle accompaniment - not much. To Tony, it looked as though the only thing on the plate was a tennis ball's worth of raw meat drizzled with a few drops of a white liquid.

He struggled with the knuckle of veal for about half an hour, but beginning to feel quite nauseous, decided he had to do the Yorkshire thing and say, "*It was delicious but I'm afraid I'm full*". This statement led to the table immediately being surrounded by six waiters and chefs trying to establish what he didn't like about it. After a while, the concerned crowd dispersed presumably re-assured by the travel rep that Tony had found the veal to be delicious. Tony and the travel rep continued to work at the table on the arrangements for the Diamonds visiting the restaurant. Half an hour later a horrified Tony spotted three chefs approaching their table with another knuckle of veal. He tried to eat the new offering with heavy perspiration and increasing nausea, but had to give up early again - adding insult to injury!

Happy staff and family, wonderful lifestyle, great friends, international travel, fulfilling work and a growing reputation - so what went wrong? I imagine you're thinking, why give it up?

It took four years for Tony to see the full picture and to realise what was going on in one of the major distributor lines of sponsorship - perhaps up to thirty percent of total sales - and for a shrewd man you might think that this was odd, did he have his head in the sand or choose to overlook what was happening? I don't think that this is the case. Hindsight is a tremendous thing and yes looking back it's obvious, but that's not often the case when you're in the thick of things.

In order to fully understand, I think it's important that you have an insight into Amway itself.

I need to stipulate here that Tony has never said anything inflammatory about the company and in fact always said good things about his boss Dick Devos. Whilst he may not now agree with the "American-Way", the people he worked with at the time were genuine and he respected them. I've done my own research, read between the lines and added this to my own experiences.

A Multi-Level Marketing (MLM) company is what you would call a Buying Club, those at the top make a great deal of money whilst those at the bottom struggle with feelings of inferiority and the fear that they'll miss out. It's commonly known as a pyramid scheme. An MLM is the worst nightmare of someone that has FOMO syndrome.

In Amway's case this is most certainly true and in fact in 2006, in the UK Lord Mandelson argued that the company was "*Selling Unachievable Dreams*". Since 2009, the company has restricted selling in the UK which has seen it all but disappear here. Not so across the rest of the world, and in the US it is an institution, one that sponsors the Olympics and Harvard entrepreneur courses and also advertises during the Super Bowl - what could be more reassuring?

The pitch is that by selling the stock and recruiting people to sell it on your behalf, you can make a full-time job, become very rich and live a luxury lifestyle.

Now, this isn't exactly a lie. Amway have what they call Diamond Distributers and they do indeed live this lifestyle. They are, however, very few in number. You can count on two hands the number of these in the UK compared to the millions of distributers worldwide.

To encourage people to join they are given a 'moneyback guarantee' that if their business does not succeed in the first year, they can request back the money they paid for their starter pack and start-up stock. They're then invited to seminars where they're given motivational speeches by their uplines (distributors that sponsored them), telling them that it's all down to the power of positive thinking. If you want it, then it's yours to grab! Picture in your head what you want, put pictures on the fridge, see yourself living that lifestyle and then most importantly Fake It Until You Make It!!

Now at no point are any distributers ever told that they have to get into debt or to buy that fancy car, bigger house, luxury holiday, but how else can you fake wealth when you don't have it? How else can you convince people that you're a success?

Then there are the 'Losers'. These are the people that are not a success, the people that tell you it's a scam, the friends that don't want to hear your spiel or buy into your lifestyle. You must disassociate from these people, regardless of whether they are your friends and family, if they're not supporting you and Amway then they're losers and you must cut them out…

Is it sounding slightly cultish yet?

Once you reach a certain level of success you can 'win' the opportunity to attend holidays and seminars and here you get to meet the Diamond Elite. They're wheeled out to give talks on how you too can gain the same success. These people have genuinely worked for it, they're super recruiters and immense sales machines, but they're also convinced by their own hype. They're mixing with the celebs and the powerful and so they think that by being in these circles that they too, deserve the lifestyle. The wealthier they get the more entitled they become. This is the American Way (Amway).

Now, I did say that they've earned and worked up the ladder, but that's not where the extreme wealth comes from, no, it comes from the addons. Once a distributer had reached a certain level, their upline sponsors (this was nothing to do with Amway the company) cut them into the programme of selling tools and tickets for events. Family re-unions, retreats, motivational courses, DVDs, books and of course major rallies. One UK distributor network was able to book Wembley Arena and fill it, when the top (Crown Ambassador) distributor speakers came over from the USA. They may or may not allow Amway UK a speaking slot.

A few of the UK Diamond (DDs) and Double Diamond Direct Distributors appeared to be making more from the sale of motivational tools and events than they were in commission and bonuses from the sale of Amway products. Their stateside leaders could literally fly back to the States from the big events with a suitcase of cash. In the USA this seemed normal and to the leading UK distributors it just seemed like entrepreneurship, after all it was their own business. Yet to Tony and others at Amway UK, it was a problem that was getting out of hand. The company was, in some instances, just being used as a front for the leading distributors' money-making schemes.

In DD speak, helping others to get close, achieve their goals and dreams and find the 'secret' so that they could be wealthy too and live the same fabulous lifestyle of a DD - was a real money maker. This sounds familiar to some of today's 'Gurus' does it not?

One of Tony's roles was to facilitate the events that the Diamond Distributers (DD) would be attending. It was an orgy of self-indulgence and petty demands; the transportation had to be 'just so' no luxury mini-bus was good enough, each couple (yes DD's were almost always a married, white couple) required their own chauffeur driven limo. They expected gifts on their pillows each night and expected to be treated the way the celebs around them were. A Rockstar party (it was Rod Stewart and Freddie Mercury in Montreux) in the hotel? Then why were they not attending?

I imagine that on the one hand, it's fantastic to be in this place, living this lifestyle and yet in the other, how fragile and fake it all sounds.

You only have to go online and listen to ex-Amway distributers or 'Losers' as they would be known, to hear how badly lives have been damaged. The mental health issues, the pressure to succeed, loss of relationships and the devastation of financial debt. Is this the true picture of the American Way?

One thing that Tony does say is that it's not enjoyable, no matter how lovely the place, or how fantastic the event is, if you're surrounded by horrible people. He liked many leading distributors, and most were kind and not exploitative in any way. However, there were some that had all the traits of many American entrepreneurs, which so many Brits seem to admire - whatever they do to make money is OK - wealth gives them respectability.

You have to realise Tony had been appointed as CEO to battle with these leading distributors and ensure the bad practices didn't ruin it for everyone. The leading distributors kept the Company at arm's length and I think in the end Tony realised it was a hopeless task to medicate the patient - it needed major surgery.

In the end, it wasn't attending these retreats and seminars or listening to the 'motivational' material that was the reason that Tony put on the brakes.

I believe that Tony's 5 years at Amway UK and the guilt he felt when he found out about the unsavoury side of the MLM sector have profoundly influenced his work since. Particularly, his work to get better support for new business owners and his investigations into what he calls 'the business opportunity industry'.

He is keen to point out the ladders to success as a start-up and #happipreneur, for example, 'bootstrap don't borrow', 'test trading and 'multiple income streams' but he is also motivated to expose the snakes that lead to debt and depression.

He has been forthright in his opinions in blogs, interviews and articles. He gets trolled for his views. Even his fictional work references the business opportunity industry. In his most recent novel 'Loose Cannon' there is an MLM senior executive that is being blackmailed by network leaders.

His fictitious satire, with real business tips, 'Freedom from Bosses Forever' exposes how easy it is to get sucked into the scams, fakery, 'get rich quick' and secretive peer pressure groups.

See this conversation between the narrator of 'Freedom from Bosses Forever', **Leonora Soculitherz**, and a representative of the Tochen Network. They are meeting at the request of Soculitherz' all action, American lover and 'walking on toenails' guru - Ant Cracie.

"But I've never heard of Tochen."

"Cool. Sorry about that. Didn't Ant tell you anything? What do you want to know?"

"Who'll be in the audience?"

"Sure. Well look, there are four branches of the Tochen Network and the majority of the meetings are on a branch by branch basis. The Madrid meeting is for the 'Entrepreneurs' Club' branch. So, members and their guests will all be successful business owners or leaders of industry and commerce - nice people - your kind of people".

"It's not a network or multi-level marketing/pyramid selling, is it? I hate all that happy-clappy, achieve your dreams, get rich quick rubbish. Anyway, it's illegal in Canada and I am a Canadian citizen."

"No, it's not that at all. I can't deny it's a network, but no one gets commissions for selling anything. Neither can you apply to join it - you have to be invited. Members pay their annual subscriptions to a charity of their choice if they feel they're getting value. Anyone can leave the network at any time."

"Not a religious sect is it?"

"No, although one of the four key values includes 'being Christian'. That only means the network goes by the values prescribed in the Bible. It's quicker than writing some out. In fact, nothing is written - no rules, regulations, agreements or paperwork. It's all about personal development. We just enjoy our networking and enjoy developing. No prayer meetings and no-one has to go to church - I promise!"

"How long have you been in it?"

"No-one says whether they're in it or not. I've just been asked to see if you'd like to speak with Ant at the Madrid event. Look, I have to dash Leonora. Why not have a chat with Ant, see if you want to do it and he'll

get hold of me to let me know?"

A good-looking guy, but a bit intense I thought.

Tony and many others believe that the language used to control minds and hearts is the most insidious aspect of both the business opportunity industry and politics today. Lies are dressed up as truths and very quickly become the truth.

Tony particularly hated the deceit in MLM. Most independent business owners were taught by their up-lines that the way to build their business is by recruitment and, even, there's no selling involved.

The way to recruit is to 'show the plan' of how money is made in the business and to get potential recruits to the regular events where they could see successful people in 'the business'.

It was a rule never to mention the name of the company - Amway, Herbalife, Nu Skin, until the very last moment in getting the recruit to sign up. Then they'll say the company's products are only the vehicle - the means by which you develop your own business by recruitment.

In other words, the exterior looks no-risk and squeaky clean but there's a peer and status pressure, grubby game on the interior.

When Tony was at Amway UK a number of books, of which he has signed copies, were published on the Amway 'phenomenon'. Re-reading these books today, Tony was struck by how the authors, none involved in

MLM, were entranced by the excitement and positivity they had encountered from leading distributorships (mainly husband and wife) they spoke to.

If they began their books as sceptics, they were convinced by the end of their tours that Amway was a force for good and enterprise. The word 'excited' crops up time and time again about their experience. It's amazing, that with over a million distributorships at that time worldwide, there was a unanimity in the language used. Even the conservative Brits had decided to follow the 'American Way' and use the language of winners, goal setting and dream making.

These authors encountered Diamond Direct Distributors speaking the same language about 'the business'. Whatever their background, but usually rags to riches, they had similar aspirations and luxury lifestyles. A Rolls Royce's was the accessory of choice.

Tony says it is not surprising these authors were convinced of the potential of the Amway business opportunity, after all, he knew how much the leading distributorships were making from Amway bonuses and never questioned how they were funding their lifestyles.

Take these two examples of two independent authors who, from their interviews and travels around the country to meet Amway independent distributors, came to similar positive conclusions. These extracts are from *'The Dream Makers'* by Derek Wilson and '*The First Eleven* (*Diamond Direct Distributors*)' by Stephen Littlejohns.

"Take your average cynic. Show him the Amway Plan and what will he say? He might start with "It's a con - it could never work. You're showing me a dream that can't possibly come true". So you get in the car and drive him to the gates of a glorious mansion somewhere with a Rolls Royce parked outside, and you say to him, "You see that? There lives an Amway distributor, and he doesn't have a job apart from the business'. what will your cynic say to that?

One of the favourite lines is "It's alright for him - he got in at the beginning and grabbed all the success there is. ...Any money I make will just go back to the people at the top of the tree - it's too late for me now."

There is one story that's guaranteed to reduce the cynics argument to shreds in no time. It's the story of the Diamonds who got into the business after all the rest, took the system by storm, and made it further than any of them - the story of Amway's own whiz kids xxxxx and xxxxx. So any distributor up against that sort of argument would do well to ensure it's their Rolls he is pointing at when he answers it." (The First Eleven - 1984*)*

and:

"IT WORKS - That was the principal opinion I had formed by the end of my tour. It was abundantly obvious to me that Amway was providing thousands of British people with not only extra income but an extra dimension to life".

"Yet there is one aspect of the business which is

vital to Amway's success and which I would love to see taken up by people in all walks of life. It is called 'positive mental attitude' and it is basically what has made grade A failures into high flying Amway successes."

"I did not believe that the Amway story belonged solely to the people who had achieved the Mercedes, the big houses, the financial independence and the holidays in Hawaii. The story I have tried to sketch is of people who are building their own dreams." (The DreamMakers - 1982).

We talk about Edward Bernays later in the book, he's the father of Public Relations. Tony firmly believes that it is the American influence on the UK and our ability to fall head over heels with the mantras they espouse that is the main problem. To most American entrepreneurs whether they be senior executives in Goldman Sachs or the White House what they are doing is normal.

Even Tony was impressed by meeting ex-President Gerald Ford, ex-Secretary of State General Alexander Haig and Bob Hope, along with countless stars of music, film, stage and sport, even royalty, who had bought into the Amway phenomenon. Steve Bannon, with Trump, and Dominic Cummings, with Johnson, are only using the same proven techniques to manipulate public opinion.

Always remember, says Tony, that Bernays persuaded the medical authorities, through a survey of GPs, to say that a 'heavy breakfast' with bacon and eggs was essential and good for you. He was working for a bacon manufacturer whose sales soared.

Through suggesting cigarettes were a better option than sweets and his 'torches for freedom' campaign, conflating the right to smoke in public with equality, Bernays persuaded tens of millions of American women to start smoking or smoke more.

Tony believes that if people can be persuaded that war is necessary for democracy, letting old people die is acceptable, smoking makes you desirable and a full fried breakfast is healthy, then persuading people that proven business opportunities are better than starting from scratch is a doddle.

The reason most people want to start a business is to control their own destiny. Yet, because many format business opportunities are oversold on income expectation and time required, the new business owner ends up exhausted, tied into the business opportunity because of their investment, in debt and it feels like they're 'working for the man'.

The fakery of the role models that have succeeded in the MLM scheme, the franchise or as laptop millionaires is a real problem. Tony believes that it is up to people like him, the late Stefan Topfer, Brad Burton and Mike Winnet to call out the fakes. We'll hear from Brad and Mike later in the book.

Mike coined the term - the Contrepreneur, the 'rich' role models with millionaire lifestyles, like Amway leaders, faking it until they make it.

Many format business opportunities treat those that

take up the opportunity as just a 'punter'. If one punter fails or gives up there'll always be another one coming along, preferably with their redundancy money, to take up the opportunity. *PubCos* appear to work on this principle.

Tony's preference is not to copy a format or programme, but to start-up a business that is uniquely yours. That's what Tony did, with his partners and is what most highly successful, fulfilled and Happipreneurs he's met have done.

He says not to believe the fake 'only 10% of start-ups survive' which justifies the business opportunity industry format offers. Tony has seen 80% of new starts surviving over 3 years if they get the right support about them and follow certain guidelines. These guidelines are all the ones we talk about throughout the book and of course, asking for help from business owners who understand their customers.

Do not believe the sales spiel of the business opportunity sellers.

Tony does believe that some franchise opportunities and direct selling opportunities are good for people that like to sell those products. He is a fan of many high-end franchises and some part-time direct selling opportunities. But the acid test is 'do the numbers stack up' and will you 'love 'doing it. If the answer is 'No' to either, then you are just swapping one lousy job for another lousy job in your own business.

Here's a list of some of the format business opportunities you'll find being sold daily through social media, mainstream media and at start-up exhibitions; taking on a franchise, e.g. *Subway*; running a *PubCo* pub; being a distributor for a household brand; driving people, parcels or products e.g. *Uber*, becoming a laptop entrepreneur with ready-made products and monthly support and building a network through multi-level marketing.

Then there is the programme or process type business opportunities such as pitching your business idea to an investor or a lender that will get involved in running the new business - no controlling your own destiny there then!

Many people are attracted to a government, university or bank start-up programme which gives you funding, advice and a mentor. Tony says you'll probably learn how to develop your scale-up and millionaire mindset, but do you really want to be advised on entrepreneurship by people in salaried jobs? There are many more and the sales process is always slick.

Throughout Tony's long life as a founder and business owner, many of his friends, clients and colleagues have marketed and sold business opportunities, self-help books, seminars and events. Most of them claim their way is the better way to go into a business of your own. As you've read already, Governments, Media, Academics and Banks play their full part in this business opportunity industry too. It looks wonderful and most of us think we're too smart to fall for a way of starting a business which promises success yet doesn't deliver it.

That's a mistake as the way business opportunities are sold is ever more sophisticated and the sellers are often the most respectable, even revered, people. Many famous people claim these ready-made business opportunities provide a safer and proven route to entrepreneurial success.

The people selling the business opportunity are totally convincing because they don't see anything wrong in what they're offering and they believe it's your fault if what they're selling doesn't work for you. The business opportunity sellers are usually salaried employees so my starting question to them is usually 'If it's such a good business opportunity why aren't you doing it?'

Even Bankers and Government approved providers of start-up support and loans have been known to over-promise and under deliver in order to meet their sales targets. Who knew?

Tony says there are more snakes out there than ladders for people wishing to start a business. Avoiding the snakes is as important a skill as being very good at what you do, winning customers, managing cash flow and making deals. Seek help from existing business owners that are succeeding in the same sector that the format business opportunity is in. He believes nine times out of ten it is less risky and you have more flexibility to cope with emergencies, pandemics, family commitments and your own health in your own business than a format business opportunity. How many happy PubCo landlords and landladies have you met?

Q&A Time

Q Do you now accept that your wife was right and you shouldn't have joined Amway?

A: Eileen was proven right in the end with her 'cult' remark, but I can't regret joining the company - most of my time at Amway UK was very happy. It was only into my second year as CEO and fourth year with Amway UK that as a result of an investigation, which I instigated, that I found out about some lines of independent distributors being pressurised into buying positions through the monthly stock and then exploiting their 'downline' distributors. Buying a high position got them a cut in the independent from Amway, rallies, seminars, books and tapes programme.

The level of debt that some people were plunged into when all they were initially looking for was to have a part-time business of their own, was totally unacceptable and wrong. But it wasn't illegal, and it definitely wasn't condoned by anyone at Amway UK.

Q. Surely you knew that it was a controversial company and a risky business to become an Amway distributor?

A: If it looks too good to be true it probably is, but Amway's total refund policies were genuine and I implemented them. No-one should ever lose any money but, of course, I was proven totally naive on distributor mind control leading to a parallel trading system. All the biggest MLM companies in the world I now see as favouring the few at the expense of the many and I should have worked out why this happens long before I did.

Q. It's pyramid selling, isn't it?

A: No and maybe. Amway ensures that it abides by the laws and regulations of every country it is in. Pyramid selling in all countries is illegal. I did in the end, find some independent distributor practices with their book and tape programmes that I'd class as pyramid selling.

Every member of staff at Amway UK, in my five years there, believed that we'd put in place all the policies and processes so that no-one should lose any money from becoming an Amway distributor.

Q. Maybe every member of staff was turning a blind eye?

A: No, I don't accept that. Remember, every one of our Executive team and Management team, including Clare, had been recruited as professionals from some of the most reputable companies in the UK. We all loved the products which Amway manufactured.

The dark practices that left people in debt and under great stress, were not easy to find and fooled us all in the UK. I can't say the same for staff in America though. This parallel trading system and bad practices were instigated by the distributor leaders in the States and the US staff should have stopped them exporting them into the UK.

Q. But weren't you aiding and abetting these practices by speaking at distributor rallies?

A: That's a fair point. I spoke at rallies and seminars to tens of thousands of people. These events were independently organised by distributor leaders, usually featuring an American upline distributor leader.

I praised these leaders in my speeches, but I didn't know at the time that what they were doing was wrong. In fact, all these American leaders were Christians. They preached family values and helping others less fortunate.

I could be forgiven for thinking they held the moral high ground, not me. They believed I didn't meet their standards. After all, I liked a drink, chain-smoked hamlet cigars, shouted blues songs, had a beard, often wore a light coloured suit and, quite often, Eileen wasn't by my side.

Q: Don't all cult leaders con people into following them?

A: We see it as a con, but they don't. It's narcissism and the more people look up to them the more they believe they're doing the right thing. These distributor leaders and nearly all of America still don't think anything they do is wrong.

That's the same with leaders in any club, with secret rules and hidden practices - Freemasons, Banks, Trade Associations, Government and Monarchy. It all looks squeaky clean on the outside, the leaders appear to be the most upstanding but there's often dodgy practices, bullying, blackmail, pay-offs, cover-ups and loyalty is gained through fear of the consequences.

To them, it is just business, but they've created seemingly legitimate entities that exploit others. The Amway distributor leaders were using the purported sale of Amway products as a front for other moneymaking activities and that's wrong.

The whole dream building, goal setting, status trappings, winners and losers nonsense fools an awful lot of people. It's like Government propaganda through the media. If you repeat the same 'facts' and 'messages' for as long as it takes to capture hearts and minds, then you create a new normal. Fake truth replaces the real truth.

Q. How do Amway, Herbalife, Nu Skin, Forever Living and the rest get away with it?

A: There'll always be a demand for low entry cost, part-time business opportunities. Amway is not only the largest direct-selling company in the world it is also one of America's greatest success stories. It is one of the most successful American companies ever in China.

My Amway boss' wife is Donald Trump's Secretary of State for Education. Trump has been the face of a number of MLM companies. Amway and MLM are here to stay.

The Direct Selling industry is massive and doing very well around the world. All trade associations, for example, financial services including banking and insurance, construction and retail, are self-regulating. They have an Ombudsman and complaints procedures to protect the consumer.

So does the direct selling industry with the Direct Selling Association. It took me years to realise that these Trade Associations are actually there to protect their members and lobby government. They keep Government and its investigatory bodies at arm's length. Protecting the public is low down on their priority list.

After saying that I personally detest Herbal Life. One of the greatest motivational speakers and authors, Jim Rohn, who Tony Robbins worked for and whose material he still uses, was often the face of Herbal Life, but if I'd had my way they wouldn't have been allowed into the UK.

Q: So, were you too hasty in resigning?

A: No, I was right to resign over one particular issue and to set up my own business, with Clare. Not much later after I left, most of the Executive team and Management team left to go onto highly reputable Director and Chief Executive jobs - including Harrods! I had a great team and Amway is a good employer and I feel lucky to have four good years out of five.

Q. Did it put you off the Direct Selling Industry?

A: It put me off some of the world's biggest MLM companies, but not of direct selling as a part-time, independent business opportunity. It's still a good side hustle and extra income stream if the products are good. For the first ten years of our business, some of our best clients were direct selling companies or household names wanting to set up direct selling companies.

Image Set B:

1. 94 (right as you look at it) and 96 Sunningfields Road Hendon - Tony lived in about 7 different bedsits in these 2 houses
2. First of many crazy ideas at NCR Limited
3. Eileen and Tony in the Chequers pub, Hendon 1976
4. All of these friends travelled from around the UK - quite a wedding party
5. Wedding photo - Tony, Chris, Dave, Colin, Digby and Eileen
6. Wedding Day Eileen and Tony on January 21st 1978
7. Amway Convention 1984 - looks like a Trump Rally
8. Tony as CEO of Amway writing on Amway Convention 1984
9. Tony, Eileen and Dick DeVos at a World DSA Conference in Venice 1984
10. Clare and Tony handing out the cake at one of the many Amway Christmas parties for care homes in Milton Keynes
11. Not your usual CEO! An Amway staff party 1985
12. Tony riding into John O'Groats - the other two cycled from Brighton on penny farthing and upright - Clare is on far right
13. Help the Aged Silver Jubilee fundraising Brighton to John O'Groats summer 1986
14. Tony with ex-President Gerald Ford and Stewart McArthur
15. Early Business Advisory Bureau Limited publicity shot for our book and seminar Murder at Mill How to prevent managers strangling the business
16. Clare and Charles
17. Eileen, Sinead, Alan and Carl on holiday 1995
18. Tony with Dave Parbery at the 1999 World Cup

BRIGHT IDE
BRIGHT IDEAS
PLEASE TAKE
A PROPOSAL

Special Souvenir Pull-Out Section
Amway National Convention 1984
NATIONAL EXHIBITION CENTRE BIRMINGHAM, MAY 19th, 1984
Together we mean business

Special Souvenir Pull-Out Section

Amway National Convention 1984

MESSAGE FROM TONY ROBINSON GENERAL MANAGER, AMWAY (UK) LTD

It was quite a Convention wasn't it? There were moments when you couldn't hear yourself think, when thousands of excited and enthusiastic distributors applauded and greeted our guest speakers. And there were times when you could hear a pin drop as 15,000 Amway distributors listened intently to the business news and advice coming from the stage.

The packed programme included some very positive and professional speeches by recognised Amway leaders from the U.K. distributor organisation, presentations by Parliamentary Consultant to the DSA Jim Lester, M.P., and Amway (U.K.) corporate executives, and some exciting new audio-visuals made especially for Convention.

The whole programme built up to a marvellous climax with our very special guests – the DeVos family. First we saw Dan and his wife Pam. Then newly appointed Amway Vice President International Dick DeVos with his wife Betsy. And finally, the highlight of our 1984 Convention, with his wife Helen, Amway President and Co-founder, Rich DeVos.

Words cannot express the reception that greeted Rich, so I must let these pictures tell the story of Convention. A tape of Rich DeVos's speech to Convention will be available on August 1st (see page 17 for details – Editor).

I was excited to be part of such a positive group of committed business entrepreneurs – the largest number ever to attend an Amway U.K. National Convention. Let us now work hard and work together to translated that enthusiasm and commitment into renewed vigour, sponsoring and selling Amway products.

Never in the U.K. have we had a more businesslike group of leaders: I and the Amway staff team look forward to working closely with them and you in the months ahead to ensure the success your business.

Tony Robinson

General Manager
Amway (UK) Limited

john o'groats
KNITWEAR

Help the Aged

World Cup
asics

I made many friends in the Direct Selling industry and especially loved party plan, like Ann Summers and Undercoverwear. It's not politically correct to say so, but I really loved being on the catwalk with models in lingerie. I loved working with the educational book companies like Encyclopaedia Britannica, Dorling Kindersley and Grolier too.

"How could we even begin to
disarm greed and envy?
Perhaps, by being less greedy
and envious ourselves,
perhaps by resisting the
temptation of letting our
luxuries become needs."

EF Schumacher

VI
Integrity First

This was a time of plenty for Tony. His salary was large, his car was better than he'd ever owned (or would again) and he was mixing with the cream of society. He was valued in his role and challenged which kept him from getting bored.

However, there were several aspects to Tony's job that I imagine, looking back, he feels uncomfortable with.

Firstly, Amway had a large legal budget, which Tony managed, and a top law firm happy to spend it. The company was quite aggressive in protecting their intellectual property and reputation and ensured that any competition 'passing off' their products or denigrating the company were 'put down'.

As the largest MLM company in the world, they had to have good relations with the government and part of this came from being a member of the Direct Selling Association which interestingly, for his last 3 years, Tony was Vice Chairman of and Chairman of the DSA of Ireland. Tony remembers trying to prevent several, now massive, MLM companies becoming members of the Direct Selling Association - Herbalife was one.

Like all trade associations, think Financial Services,

the Government stays one step removed from the companies in the sector by allowing the trade association to self-regulate. If a company isn't a member of the trade association it is likely to be regarded as disreputable and is vulnerable to not being able to trade or engage in legal recourse. If this seems like a conflict of interests to you, then I'd probably agree. The organisation set up to police the actions of MLMs being chaired by the Chief Executive of the world's largest.

Being part of Amway and the DSA meant that Tony was travelling globally, but more importantly meeting people that in later years would come to be of assistance in his own companies and with his own campaigns on behalf of micro-business owners. It was here that he found himself attending meetings of many other self-regulating trade bodies, such as retail and financial services, policy forums in 'posh buildings' and committees in the Houses of Parliament. He learned how lobbying is done by wealthy corporations and how policy is made. Over the years Tony has been fortunate enough to be in the places he needed to be to see how business s was really done, how the big decisions were made and to see first-hand that in business, at the top, it really is a case of who, not what you know.

Whilst working for Amway, this would be in his favour, no matter how distasteful he might find some of it, but as time would prove, government and parliament would become a battleground. Amway and such companies needed to have an MP on their side, one that would help with any legislations or sticky political matters and of course they needed the banks to be saying good things about them too.

That last bit is quite surprising when you realise that almost every year Amway is practically bankrupt, the company isn't there to make money. No, the people make money. They also have all of that 'refund' money to consider, you know, from the unhappy distributers that could claim a refund. Therefore, they weren't a lucrative business on paper.

That is in the UK, of course. Tony has explained to me that Amway's global sales when he joined in 1981 were 1.4 billion dollars and will be ten times that now and every year will be very profitable. Like most large US companies that pay little or no corporation tax in the UK, because they have not made much or any profit, they sell their products and sell service charges to their UK subsidiaries.

Out of interest how many distributers ever claimed back their money do you think? I doubt it was ever many, such was the feeling of failure instilled in those that left.

It was also Tony's responsibility to spin positive stories about the company, despite the press hounding and negative news.

They had a top, successful London PR firm which enabled the positive to outweigh the negatives, although at the time of a Canadian Customs legal case against Amway Corporation, they were sacked by their first PR company.

It was by watching how these firms in league with

the establishment worked that he learned the 'dark arts' of public relations and government affairs.

What Tony was doing, along with the PR company, is something that every Insta wanabee knows all about, creating the Ladder of Trust. We'd call it influencers today, but it's the same thing. You bring in celebs, politicians and important people to talk about your product and company, to endorse the events you're holding and genuinely tell people what a great company this is and how much it's doing to give back.

That's not to say that they didn't.

A few months before Tony left Amway, he recalls a charity event he organised in aid of Help the Aged, the year of their Silver Jubilee. Amway UK arranged for a bike ride from Brighton to John O'Groats with a difference. It was ridden by two men in their late seventies on a Penny Farthing and a Victorian Upright bone shaker, dressed in period clothing. At various points throughout the country Amway distributers and usually the Mayor and Mayoress of the town, would hold small events, arrange press opportunities and raise money for Help the Aged along the way.

Tony himself rode part of the journey on a tricycle from Wick to John O'Groats. He travelled with his secretary and Clare in a tiny plane from Inverness to Wick. He was given an old tricycle which was a nightmare to ride, it was easy to ride on flat ground but pulled horrendously when on an uneven surface. It was funny to see these two old chaps sailing away ahead as Tony battled to control his three-wheeler! He was never so happy to arrive at John O'Groats! They raised an incredible amount of money and garnered a massive amount of positive press on the back of it.

Amway UK sponsored golf tournaments, such as the Bob Hope Classic, where he met both Bob Hope and ex-President Ford, both Amway influencers, held classical concerts and even entertained royalty. How could this company endorsed by so many, be so bad?

However, it was the actions of a particular group of Amway leading distributors that finally brought things to a halt for Tony. He'd tried to enforce many of the Amway rules, which were designed to ensure Amway was neither a buying club nor that people got into debt, (he's now paranoiac about debt) by buying positions through filling their garages with stock. One example was the ten-customer rule, which meant no distributor could receive monthly bonuses unless they could prove, by customer receipts, that they had ten customers. I'm sure the canny ones would have forged them. There were still some disturbing reports about distributor scams, which, often anonymously, were brought to his attention. In 1985 he got his national, regional and area sales managers to investigate.

He realised that there were deals going ahead that he could not condone and that the people in those positions needed to go now. He knew getting rid of independent distributors with large businesses of their own was not easy legally, but he felt there was no option. What was going on was wrong and he and Amway UK should not be associated with it. He brought his findings to Dick Devos and explained what needed to happen. He was told that whilst they understood his reservations and that they appreciated what he was bringing to them, the company could not let these distributors go now and would resolve the issues a different way.

Tony at this point resigned explaining that he wanted to start his own business which Dick was naturally, as an entrepreneur, very understanding of. Dick and Tony agreed that it would really help retain the confidence of the staff and the overall business if Tony had a twelve-month notice period in which he could recruit and induct his successor.

It was the end of an era and an end of the time of plenty. Never again would Tony earn this much money, live this lifestyle or have this power/position. Did he feel sad about it? I imagine at the time that there was a loss of ego, position and maybe credibility, but none of those things in the long-term were what Tony thrived on. He loves a challenge, he loves freedom and most of all, he loves doing the 'right' thing.

Q&A Time

Q. What do you miss the most about Amway and the lifestyle you had while you were there?

A: I really miss our house in Milton Keynes, on the edge of Great Linford village green. The difficult part of becoming a #Happipreneur is that you have to keep costs as low as you can and sometimes that means downsizing. I've downsized twice, but leaving 55 Granes End was the toughest.

Eileen and I and our three children loved that house. We'd a flat in Hemel Hempstead for three years so to move to a large, nearly new detached house at the end of a row of four houses with only one neighbour was a fabulous feeling.

After selling our flat, until we found our house in Milton Keynes, I stayed in an Amway flat while Eileen and Carl stayed with my Mum in Hessle. We lived in Great Linford for nearly twelve years including seven years after I left Amway.

We even built a granny flat there for my Mum and when my Mum moved into sheltered housing and care, Eileen and I had three years in the granny flat too. Sheer luxury. I think the garden was the thing Eileen will have missed more than anything. Occasionally, my Uncle Ron came from Hull and enjoyed helping Eileen with the garden. It was big at the front of the house and very big at the back.

We planted some amazing trees and bushes and built a

small pool for the kids to splash and swim a few strokes in. We had a sandpit, lots of furry animals and Eileen turned out to be an awesome gardener. The Nags Head pub in the village was five minutes' walk away and surprisingly I was quite a frequent visitor. I still miss that house but I'm so lucky to have had so many years there.

Q. Anything else - the big company car and expenses allowance?

A: Well you've met Clare, so you'll know that there was never any chance of all that corporate status stuff continuing. We were lucky to start our business with an overdraft from the bank and so we leased a small, used second-hand car so we were paying monthly.

There are very few people in the world brave enough to ask Clare to pay expenses other than the cheapest travel and accommodation. In fact, if she were controlling MPs' expenses, the money the Government would have saved could have built four new NHS hospitals a year.

Only with the benefit of hindsight, I missed having enough money to really look after my Mum. If I'd still been working in a well-paid job at Amway we'd never have moved from Milton Keynes to Northampton and the social and medical care my Mother received would have continued to be great.

The move to Northampton turned out to be a nightmare for my Mum and I'll always regret I didn't have enough money to get her into a home where she would have had better care and more fun.

Q. I know you don't miss the business opportunity and positive thinking scene - why are you so anti the dream builders?

A: Most of us think we're too smart to fall for a way of starting a business which promises success yet doesn't deliver it. That's a mistake as the way business opportunities are sold is ever more sophisticated and the sellers are often the most respectable, even revered, people.

Many famous people claim these ready-made business opportunities provide a safer, proven, route to entrepreneurial success. If you don't succeed, then it'll be because you didn't dream big or you associated with losers or you've got a negative attitude. Anything but the business opportunity is overhyped rubbish.

Because it's overhyped rubbish is why very few make any money out of them. It's why so few succeed through buying self-help books and attending Tony Robbins' seminars.

The people selling the business opportunity, self-help books, DVDs and seminars are totally convincing because they don't see anything wrong in what they're offering and they believe it's your fault if what they're selling doesn't work for you.

These business opportunity sellers are usually salaried employees or just earning money out of being speakers, so my starting question to them is usually *"If it's such a good business opportunity why aren't you doing it?"*

Q. I saw you do a show where you said avoiding snakes is really important - explain?

A: There are more snakes out there than ladders for people wishing to start a business. If you want to be a #Happipreneur then avoiding the snakes is as important a skill as being very good at what you do, winning customers, managing cash flow and making deals.

The 'follow my way to success, wealth and happiness' business opportunity, positive thinking and self-help industry preys on the most vulnerable in our society.

Everyone needing to make money as quickly as possible, in order to make ends meet is vulnerable. Everyone who believes successful people have 'secrets' to their success, which can be copied, is vulnerable. Everyone who wants a much better lifestyle with all the status trappings - better house, a better car, better holidays - and who doesn't? - is vulnerable.

If you're interested in finding out how the 'dream big' sellers and all the speakers and writers promoting positive thinking and the law of attraction, all of which looks great, can actually cause real harm then google *'American Dream Turned Nightmare'* or read *'Smile or Die - How positive thinking fooled America and the World'* by the famous American journalist, *Barbara Ehrenreich* or *'The Antidote'* (to positive thinking) by the acclaimed British journalist, *Oliver Burkeman* or *'Happy'* by *Derren Brown.*

Donald Trump would call Ehrenreich, Burkeman and Brown 'losers' and they haven't written the type of self-help books Oprah Winfrey endorses and promotes on her show - so I promote Ehrenreich, Burkeman and

Brown instead!

There are much better ways of earning a living out of your own business, but they all look so much more like hard work. Every successful entrepreneur I know has worked very hard for their success. It's easier to work really hard and build your own business if you're doing something you love and something you're good at.

Q. So, you recommend doing as you and I did - setting up your own business in your own way rather than to someone else's formula?

A: Absolutely. My contention is there is more chance of a successful own business career which you'll enjoy if you start a business from scratch rather than buying into a business opportunity. I've met a lot more miserable franchisees, PubCos landlords and landladies and new business owners with investor money or angel money and even, Government Start-Up Loans, than I have people who have started their own business from scratch and grown organically.

It's always better to do something you enjoy and are really good at. A problem with the business opportunity industry is that they're selling formats and formulas which have worked for some people in the past but that doesn't mean they'll work for you right now and in the future.

You need ultimate flexibility to survive and thrive. You need to always remain in control of your own destiny. You always need to be building new income streams and test trading new products and services. Formats and programmes are restricting, they stop you being fast on your feet, flexible and grasping opportunities as they appear.

This makes formats and formulas just not as much **fun** as starting from scratch and learning by doing. These are all the advantages that business owner led enterprises can have over large companies.

Q. You say the more staff you and Clare had, the more the financial headaches occurred?

A: Yes, we had awesome staff such as Paul Crook, who I see most years, he lives and works in Africa, but we didn't get the balance right on cost against fee earning. On lengthy contracts, such as with my friend, Peter Huntington, at the Meat Training Council, I should have negotiated deals so that we shared the employment costs. I would advise people starting out to use freelancers, rather than employing staff, if this option is possible.

"Work and leisure are complementary parts of the same living process and cannot be separated without destroying the joy of work and the bliss of leisure"

EF Schumacher

VII
Leaving the 'Man' Behind

As I mentioned Tony was not alone in starting his venture. At the point whereby he handed in his notice he'd already spoken to Clare about going into business. It had been agreed and she was all set to go when Tony dropped the bombshell that he'd be working at Amway for an additional twelve months. I think this sets the stage of how things were to be for the remainder of their business partnership - 32 years. Tony with great ideas and Clare holding the ball.

Tony had met Clare in 1981, recently married she'd been looking for work having just moved to the area and had been temping at Amway. A position came up in the personnel department and having the relevant skills she duly applied.

Clare tells me that she was "*singularly unimpressed*" by the young man who interviewed her, dressed in a "*ghastly black Mac and crimplene trousers*", he gave her cause to seriously consider whether she should take the role, however, the company seemed interesting and so she accepted the job.

They were a very young team and gradually she got to know him and revised her impression. Although he would always appear to be chaotically disorganised, when it came to meetings, he'd always manage to have thought of the one thing that no one else had considered. Clare also recognised that Tony had high moral values.

Clare said that Tony was unhappy with the actions of some of the managers and their extracurricular activities. He'd noted that at the 'family' get togethers wives would often be hurt to find out what was happening and it also created a difficult working environment for the staff who knew who was doing what with colleagues. Whilst it didn't make him popular, Tony worked his way through the company, changing behaviour and making it a practice that was unacceptable. It was this side to Tony that made Clare realise that there was more to him.

At the point when Tony was promoted to General Manager (CEO), he took his team with him. Clare notes how unusual it was for a man with a beard to be offered such a high position. Amway had a very clean-cut image and beards were considered scruffy. I smile to think of him refusing to bow to convention even then.

The move up had created a lot of pressure for Tony and Clare recalls some of the difficult issues he had to deal with; she also notes that he never shied away from doing this and always tackled them head on, albeit as sympathetically as he could. Whilst never holier than thou, he would not let something slide, even at personal cost to himself. His humour may well have got him through this.

Clare also fondly notes that whilst he was very much a sportsman, in those days his fondness for the Amway 'food bars' of which he had boxes of, and the rich living I presume, had made him a little tubby!

This makes me laugh, as when you see him today running marathons and eating healthily (when he's not on the choco wine diet) it's difficult to imagine him with a food bar addiction and smoking Hamlets.

One of the favourite sporting events of senior management and leading distributors was golf and Tony, as with all sports was happy to join in, however, as previously mentioned, Tony has dyspraxia and a golf club in his hand become a lethal weapon! He's terrible at golf and so not his best sport. Table tennis is another matter; not being that sporty, I struggle to see how you can be good at hitting one small ball but not another, however Tony is full of such oddities and table tennis is one of his best sports!

Over time Clare and Tony would have to work closely together on policies, processes and events. Whilst seemingly very different, they both came from similar backgrounds, with parents that instilled a good business ethic and eventually realised that neither wanted to be employed for the long term. Their business partnership made sense, whilst Tony is all about the ideas, for Clare it's the details and you need both for a business to succeed.

Tony was always good at oration, but the written word following his speech pattern and sentences could go on for ten or more lines, punctuation also not being a strong point. Clare realised that she could help with this as she could write and so they decided to take the plunge.

Having asked Clare about Tony leaving her in the lurch a little when it came to him staying at Amway, she notes that, as Tony himself has said, he has an intrinsic need to be loved/liked and always wants to be seen to have done 'the right thing'.

Perhaps this dates back to his father never having thought much about him or given him his approval, but for whatever reason, the decision to stay was just another way that Tony did this. There may also have been an element of ego, that they needed him to stay on and of course, leaving behind that salary with three young children was not an easy decision to make.

Clare was a little taken aback, particularly as her husband had also just made the decision to become self-employed. This meant that things took a lot of adjusting, however it is a testament to their friendship that they overcame it and continued with the business.

Looking back Clare says that they were very naïve. Having both come from large corporate backgrounds, they thought that they knew what businesses needed, however, the reality was that they didn't have a clue!

The initial idea was to offer affordable personnel management consultancy to small businesses, something that they thought would be in high demand. In reality, it was not something that their demographic felt that they wanted to pay for, their budgets were all marketing driven.

This is a good time for me to talk about start-ups, something that Tony is totally passionate about.

What Tony and Clare did right was to start their business based on something that they knew and enjoyed. Yet, like many new business start-ups they didn't initially factor in test trading to see what the market wanted. It would be a brilliant lesson and one that Tony would make one of his top five things for businesses to consider first.

We think of starting and running your own business a game of snakes and ladders. It should be great fun, but there are always ups and downs. Starting and running your own business is hard work but it is not complex. Your sales revenue needs to exceed your costs and your cashflow determines whether you survive and thrive.

Where you go to get the know how to succeed is as important from one sector to another. That you don't need funding, coaches or a twenty-page business plan to start-up is as true today as it was in Schumacher's day.

There are many people who try to complicate enterprise in order to sell their expertise to you but as Schumacher said:

"*Any intelligent fool can make things bigger, more complex and more violent. It takes a touch of genius - and a lot of courage - to move in the opposite direction*".

Surviving and thriving in your own business is like a game of snakes and ladders. You need guidance to help you find the ladders to climb and the snakes to avoid, luckily for Tony, he had Clare and some very good contacts.

At the beginning Clare held on to the finances (quite tightly) whilst Tony came up with big, bold ideas on how they could market, this led to "*quite heated arguments*" as Tony can be quite infuriating!

He broods and doesn't speak about things as he doesn't feel it's right to speak about them, when people around him can see that they need to come out. Tony admits to being quite manipulative when it comes to getting his own way and, in some ways, controlling - not in any kind of abusive way, just that his behaviour makes people throw up their hands and give in! Normally not something that you'd recognise since Tony will with a genuine heart do anything he can to help people, but once his mind is set… Well that's another matter.

Clare worked at getting a few short-term personnel contracts in the early days to keep the business going and Tony supported her as much as he could whilst still working.

After twelve months they started working together on the business.

In the early years of the business they were required to take on Civil Service skills training work, using video cameras and some of these contracts led to skills that they still have today. Clare notes that one of Tony's worst skills was listening. You'd think that he was, but actually, he was planning what he was going to say next or thinking about something else entirely!

However, taking on new contracts meant that Tony had to retrain himself and 'listen' to what he was being taught. This has meant that it's now one of his best skills, although Clare is still one of the only people he'll actually listen to when told "*no*"!

They're still poles apart as Clare is very cautious and Tony is 'nothing ventured nothing gained'!

Clare was always mistaken as Tony's secretary rather than his business partner, something that was often enforced by Clare's need to make notes, knowing that anything Tony wrote would either be illegible or have missed great chunks! Being detail orientated Clare always made sure that they had the right information to do the job being asked of them.

Having started business in 1986 it wasn't common to have a male and female business partner; the expectation would be that the business owner would take his secretary. At times this could be advantageous as it would mean that Clare was overlooked or underestimated and so she would have time to formulate plans and strategies that would benefit them.

Clare would make the decision not to put them right knowing that they would speak more freely around her, however I know that it did often gall her. It's important to recognise that Clare is a successful businesswoman on her own as well as being involved with Tony in his ventures. It would seem that even today, where this misconception still arises, that we're not as forward thinking in accepting that a woman could be the business owner.

Within the business there were definitely two sides, Tony doesn't like to tell someone they've done a bad job and Clare likes things done well, this would mean that Tony would be in charge of staff whilst Clare looked after the 'nitty gritty' and the money, making sure that everything was written well and was professionally done.

"Mr Motivator" as Clare called Tony would never tell anyone that they'd let him down and this would infuriate Clare. He still does it today, if he is let down, he simply lets it go. Clare reflects that Tony's first impression of people isn't as sharp as it might be and in business this can lead to costly mistakes. He will assume that people are nice until he is proven otherwise, whereas Clare is quite the opposite. He'll never call anyone out on a lie, even if he knows.

No matter what his financial situation, Tony would/will always be the first to put his hand in his pocket to buy gifts or drinks, to spend money even when it's tight. This is another of his Father's traits, one that Tony admits he does, again for that desire to be liked and thought well of. This surprises me as he's so well liked anyway and being a Yorkshire man could get away with not putting his hand in his pocket!

By now Eileen had the children Carl, Alan and Sinead. In his penultimate year at Amway, Tony built his mother a Granny flat on the house in Milton Keynes so that his Mum could be close to the family too. This again has caused tension in the business. Tony has often wanted to spend and to give away money where it wasn't necessary. Both Clare and Tony had father's in business, both of whom were gregarious and the first in the pub to buy drinks, so it is interesting that it is only Tony that has continued this habit and not Clare too.

As a business owner myself, I understand sometimes the need to give the right impression or be seen as successful, but to spend where money isn't available takes me back to the 'fake it' attitude of the Amway distributers.

Maybe it's the feminine 'homemaker' (I can hear the politically correct screams of outrage as I write) that allows both Clare and me to see through the showmanship and understand the need for restraint, whilst Tony retains the peacock aspect of being seen and admired.

It is one aspect that profoundly irritates Clare, as she feels that if you're always the one giving, you don't allow others the chance to 'gift' you. Tony is not good at receiving gifts, he likes to be the giver and often has something ready to handover should he be presented with something. I can imagine this to be tremendously irritating, how do you treat someone who only ever wants to give? Also, the money could often be better spent elsewhere.

Over the years Tony has become a more caring person and is better at understanding people, he's a far better listener and has taught himself to write. Something I'm delighted about! He's a lot more self-disciplined, he's gone from simply being driven to being focused - he knows what he wants and how he's going to get there.

All that aside, he's not a saint to work with. Tony has a capacity to get very, very angry, although he battens it up. He may grit his teeth, but not often does he lose it. They would have absolutely terrible, vicious shouting matches but Clare feels that she's probably one of very few people who have ever seen him lose his temper.

She says that it's a testament to him that he keeps it controlled; she understands that when it does go, it's a total fury but it's the exploding bottle scenario, if everyone only ever sees the happy, personable and pleasant person and you never allow the smaller niggles to get loose, at some point there is going to be a powder keg release. There's also an icy cold side, where he refuses to speak. Clare however, prefers to poke him into anger rather than suffer the silent brooding!

Throughout this book there are many examples of what Tony and Clare have learned about running a micro-business from their own experience and from their larger sized clients. They have spent thirty years working with and learning from entrepreneurs and many of them are famous. It is important to recognise that the first ten years of the Business Advisory Bureau Limited were very different from the last twenty years.

Ask Tony which years of running his own business

he's proudest of and he'd say the first decade, but ask him which years he would say where his most 'Be Useful' (to quote the title of a book by Jos Burton) years and he would say from 2000 to 2020.

The difference came from their experiences in founding the Small Firms Enterprise Development Initiative (SFEDI). If their fathers and Amway had fuelled their interest in entrepreneurship then SFEDI, which was only ever a part of their business, fuelled their interest in making life better for micro-business owners in the UK.

Q&A Time

Q: Did you and Clare leave Amway with any skills that helped you survive the early years?

A: We were lucky that we'd received a lot of training - Clare at Metal Box and then Amway and me at NCR and then Amway. Clare's skills and know-how initially proved the most useful as Clare got some really good interim Personnel Management contracts and turned my knowledge of things like salary surveys for local companies into actual products.

We published two books on which we ran business seminars around, this was all down to Clare turning my ideas and poor writing, into work that was readable and saleable. I've kept many of the newsletters we produced for local companies. Mailing out quirky but informative newsletters with invitations to free seminars was our main means of marketing.

We wouldn't have survived without Clare's professional and practical skills. Later on, as we picked up more national clients, particularly in London, then my professional speaking, direct marketing and training skills in influencing, selling and negotiating gained us some big contracts.

Q: What about knowing how to start and run your own business skills?

A: No, we didn't have any of those. At Amway, we ran that kind of programme for our Direct Distributors but I now realise that a lot of generic business start-up training, coaching and mentoring is of quite limited value. It's better if it's in context of the business and is best delivered by another business owner who understands your prospective customers.

Certainly, there are a lot of other things a generic business adviser can help you with, such as what not to buy, pricing and how to deal with tax and regulations; but the important help you need is about how to win customers. So, someone who has a high street clothing shop is best to help someone who wants to start a clothing business.

There was none of that good kind of training around - it was a bit like business studies courses - hopeless. In retrospect, we know now that it's mainly about learning by doing which is why test trading before you give up your job is so important.

It was my fault that we cocked up the first eighteen months, as I'd expected a large contract to come in and it didn't. Stupid but we learned.

We did follow our own 'Ask a business owner for help' start-up advice. We made a good deal before we started in asking Brian, a Business Owner of a Recruitment Agency to help us in our first year. He introduced to us to do a number of our first local clients, including a Conservative MP, Bill Benyon, who gave some of his secretarial allowances to us to do half a day a week local press releases for him. He thought we made a great contribution to his winning re-election a couple of years later. He bought Clare and me a lovely meal at the House of Commons.

Q: You did work for a Conservative MP? - as a staunch Labour supporter, shouldn't you be ashamed of yourself?

A: Maybe we shouldn't print that! He was a brilliant constituency MP and I really liked him. Like most Conservative MPs he was a millionaire, but I never felt he was anything else but a caring man trying to do the very best job he could. I'd starve if I only worked with people who supported Labour - in fact, I can't think of a boss, partner or a client that didn't vote Conservative.

Q: You and Clare had to do a lot of things you'd never expected to do in order to make ends meet. How did you find that?

A: It's a good job we get on so well and have complementary skills, because for the first ten years of our business we were continually out of our comfort zone, and like most business owners, we were working ridiculously long hours too. I tip my fedora to those who work totally alone. I don't know how they do it and I certainly don't recommend it. Even if it's just some help from friends and family you can never have all the skills yourself.

Being outside our comfort zone, which I now realise is not unusual, started early on, when to get some money in, I did a year of part-time lecturing at the local college for the Institute of Administrative Management Diploma students. There were too many diagrams for a dyspraxic to learn for a start. Teaching stock control was a particular nightmare. But they all passed their exams and I was offered a full-time job there. I couldn't go back to being employed and, also, it was taking me two days of unpaid preparation for each evening session I was paid for.

After, that I did many years of training, starting with a lot of five-day residential courses in influencing skills for the Department of Education and Employment, at their Ranmoor Hall Management Training Centre, in Sheffield. That nearly killed me.

Q. This doesn't sound much like Happipreneurship - why was it killing you?

A: In the first few years of the five-day courses at Ranmoor Hall and in hotels all over England and Wales, I was running courses which we hadn't designed. They had to be delivered to a very high standard and in a set way. I'm not great at rules and formulas. As an external trainer, there's huge pressure to get great marks on the evaluation sheets at the end of the course. Two average weeks and you were out.

'Conscientious' is my middle name, one of the many unusual middle names my parents gave me, so I really went the extra mile. The sleep deprivation, four packs of Hamlet a day and barrels worth of booze are what nearly killed me. I partied with the delegates each evening and then when they got to bed, in the early hours, I'd do my prep for the next day.

If I was doing the course with Colin Hussey, now a friend, we'd also do traditional rugby drinking games like bar diving. With my co-ordination, me diving off the bar top into the outstretched arms of drunken delegates is life-threatening.

Q: Did it get better then because it certainly didn't kill you?

A: The first five or six-week-long courses were terrifying, but eventually I loved working with the civil service tutors, some of whom became friends, and some started their own businesses and then worked as associates for our company.

After three years our company was asked to design courses in leadership development, marketing, negotiating and selling. This of course, is a lot easier to deliver. It also meant much bigger fees, as we gained a reputation for writing the best skills exercises and case studies for delegates, which replicated their day to day jobs. Great learning is all about context, isn't it?

Training and vocational education work became about half of our fee income each year. Clare and I hadn't expected to be doing any of that type of work when we put together the client offer for the Business Advisory Bureau Limited. It's why micro-business owners can succeed where larger companies can't - we can change our businesses to match what clients and customers will buy.

In fact, looking back over our thirty years in business together, Clare and I became acknowledged as developers of excellent learning media - courses, seminars, videos, guides, books, manuals and e-learning.

Q. Is success in your own business, mainly about trial and error, then?

A: I do believe it is about learning by doing, which is why too much time in a classroom or reading and planning, is often time wasted. Our research doesn't prove the 'fail to plan means plan to fail'. Test trading and learning from it is the key to survival. Furthermore, most business advice and planning guidance is boiled down big company stuff and not appropriate for start-ups.

The late Professor Allan Gibb OBE, who inspired many of us to investigate the real world of new business owners, had a mind-boggling map of all the know-how the 'experts' said you needed to successfully start a business. We never met anyone that had a tenth of this know-how. He was great at explaining to Government and other academics that, starting your own business is not that complex and it's nothing like being a manager in a company.

I believe in what Dr Ernesto Sirolli calls 'enterprise facilitation' and what my colleagues and I call 'joining business owners and entrepreneurs in their world'.

Sirolli says much of the advice on offer from the experts is 'paternalistic' and 'patronising' and we both think much of it stifles rather than encourages enterprise.

The first rule in Sirolli's enterprise facilitation, which he adapted from Schumacher's 'Small is Beautiful', is you should only help someone that has invited you to help them - in their community - in their world.

By great questioning and even better, listening, you find out what the business owner is truly good at and are passionate about spending their time on. You need to be good at three things: making the product or service, marketing and selling the product or service and managing the money.

We've never met any business owner that is good at all three; the role of the enterprise facilitator is to help make connections and partnerships with people, so all three are covered and being implemented 'beautifully'.

After about eighteen months to two years, Clare and I had learned how to do all three, but if we'd had some good start-up help like Charles Cracknell and his team provide to young people in Hull, and Jenn Crowther and team provide to the Scarborough business community, we wouldn't have got off to such a bad start.

Q: Is there better support now for start-ups in the UK?

A: There is but it's patchy. It's exceptionally good with Hull Youth Enterprise, Yorkshire in Business, Portobello Business Centre and many enterprise agencies but is still poor in many towns and cities. It's brilliant in the Highlands and Islands of Scotland, which is as good as many enterprise-friendly countries in the world. England is poor in comparison.

Start-up support in England isn't as good as it was in 2004, when Government policy changed away from micro-enterprise.

When I did the Loch Ness Marathon in 2019, I checked to see whether there was still a high street presence for free start-up support in Inverness. There was.

With 1 in 6 of the adult workforce starting and running their own business, I've always felt that high-quality support at the very beginning of the journey should be a right. In most countries that have an ecosystem of support to micro-enterprise, Government helps with funding free support to ALL #Startups who ask for it, it's not necessary for most countries, but I keep campaigning for it in the UK because it's vital to people, being able to make ends meet.

Q: You've been scathing about the wrong people providing advice, coaching and mentoring on Government-funded start-up programmes - why do you feel so strongly about this?

A: You have to remember that, partly through research contracts, I've interviewed thousands of micro-business owners over the last twenty years. Most of the people that have got into real trouble with a new business have received bad or no advice.

The most common mistakes are that they borrow instead of bootstrapping, don't reduce their personal and business expenditure to the minimum, don't test trade while they've still got income coming in and aren't in contact with people that can help to get their first customers.

Existing business owners know all about these mistakes and have probably made them and many more. But, unfortunately, many of the people providing start-up advice, coaching and mentoring have only worked in management in large organisations. They've never successfully started a business. It's outrageous, patronising and arrogant.

Q: So, it was a better standard of start-up support in England years ago?

A: One of the reasons I resigned from the Board of the national skills body for enterprise and entrepreneurship, SFEDI, was because it was a government-funded programme. They were training up redundant bank managers, corporate executives and trainers to be start-up mentors. These mentors would help with work on such as the Government's Start-up loan scheme.

Every f***ing scheme the Government inflicts on indie business owners involves loans, investors and is aimed at businesses that will have over ten employees. They're always looking for the unicorns. It's purely lip service to the 95% of businesses that are micro including 99% of #Startups.

Q: You seem fuelled by anger whenever you talk about Government schemes to support start-ups and micro-business owners. Can you give me a recent example?

A: You've even seen that in the coronavirus pandemic. On April 20th, 2020 during the peak of the pandemic in the UK, the papers hailed a new £1.3 billion Coronavirus Government scheme to help start-ups. The organisations campaigning for this scheme included the Centre for Entrepreneurs, Crowdcube, Capital Enterprise, Coadec, Draper Esprit, The EIS Association, The Entrepreneurs Network, Founders Forum, Huckletree, Seedrs, Tech London Advocates, The UK Business Angels Association and VCTA.

At the same time, I was campaigning with some of the small business membership organisations, for at least 2.5 million self-employed people, including self-employed start-ups, to get some income support as they'd been left out of all the Government schemes. The start-up investor sector campaign won and I lost.

£1.3 billion is massive, isn't it? On the same day, they announced the same amount of support to all Local Councils in England. The catch was that the start-up business had to have raised over £250,000 from private investors, within the last five years.

So, that's £1.3 billion to a few thousand investment-led larger businesses, leaving 5.6 MILLION micro-business owners, including 1.2 million start-ups in the lurch. That's why I'll never stop campaigning.

Q: Is it ignorance or attitude?

A: It's a patronising attitude based on anecdotal rather than real evidence, that prevents everyone having an equal chance of success. It's lobbying power too, as they listen to the wealthiest donors, banks, the financial sector and big business. They give us lip service and spin to gain votes every few years.

It's the same attitude that says we won't protect the UK, by closing borders to prevent importing coronavirus. Other island nations such as Australia, New-Zealand and Malta were successful in containing the virus by doing just this. The UK and USA always think they know better than the rest of the world.

Our government seemed to work on the theory that they didn't need to stop importing the virus because only the old and vulnerable would die.

The rest of the population will become immune or able to get back to work in the biggest companies, faster than the rest of the world. They let the infection spread through borders and institutions like hospitals and care homes.

They believe our economies will flourish, at the expense of others. South Korea told everyone how to save lives and countries like Germany that went straight to it succeeded and then they turned their attention to the economy. We always put the economy first and people second. That's why Schumacher called 'Small is Beautiful' - economics as if people mattered. The UK and the USA like no other countries in the world believe in 'Big is best' and 'Pick winners ditch the losers'.

It is why I'm still campaigning on behalf of others that are bullied into submission and poverty. That's why the Government believe that voluntary business mentors can help the 99% of new business owners, that they couldn't give a damn about, to succeed. It wrecks enterprising lives. Happipreneurship is the way to go - don't have anything to do with Government until I win some campaigns!!!

Q: Surely, volunteer mentors can help start-ups?

A: They can, and I was one of the 'experts' that explained to the future Conservative Government that mentors had a big role to play in start-up success rates. There's nothing wrong with pastoral support and these voluntary business mentors are well-meaning, but if they're not teamed up with a professional business adviser, they can be downright dangerous to the health and wealth of a new business owner. It can be the blind leading the blind.

For many start-ups with a government loan, the only help they receive is from one of these mentors that had no long-term experience of starting and running their own business. So wrong. No wonder 40% of start-up loans have defaulted and many more commit the new business owner to years of debt and despair.

Q: But these mentors meet the SFEDI standards which you created. SFEDI got over one million pounds to do the training. It's your fault, isn't it?

A: For a few years in the early noughties every Government-funded business adviser, coach or mentor had to be accredited against the SFEDI Business Support standards. Assessing the competence of the adviser, coach or mentor by observation with start-ups and business owners was important.

Equally important was that they could not be accredited unless they had three years of practical experience of running their own business. As a tennis player would you want an adviser, mentor or coach that didn't know how to play tennis? Would you like an accountant that couldn't do their own self-assessment?

These voluntary business mentors were being given by SFEDI a one-day course and a little test to see if they'd remembered what they learned on the day. I went on a one-day course to see for myself and I've got my IOEE certificate.

It's what the Government wanted SFEDI to do but it's not good enough. These ex-bank managers are practising their mentoring on vulnerable new start-up business owners, who already have a slowly tightening noose around their neck from the start-up loan. They shouldn't even be allowed a start-up loan unless they've test traded or already have customers.

Q: What's the best piece of business advice you've been given?

A: Never have to cross the street to avoid someone.

The best advice I received as a new start-up was from a micro-business owner who ran a successful recruitment and temp agency in *Milton Keynes*. This was in the mid-eighties - that's the 1980s for those who question which century I was born in. The business owner, Brian, said: "*I live, work and play in this community and I'll never do anything which would mean I have to cross the street to avoid someone*".

Brian lived and worked in Milton Keynes and being respected by the whole community was the most powerful marketing tool for his business. It also made for a very happy life at work and at play. Positive word of mouth was more influential and lower cost than advertising, direct marketing, PR and employing salespeople.

Q: Over the years you've interviewed a lot of business people, what's one of your pet peeves?

A: When I'm interviewing entrepreneurs I often ask "*Give me a tip that you think will be useful for a start-up?*". I'm always disappointed if they just repeat one of the motivational quotes we see every day on social media.

At least they should give these guru quotes their own twist. When I'm asked for my tip I often say, "*Surround yourself with people who make you giggle*". When my parents were running their business, they seemed to be always surrounded by close friends and were always in fits of giggles. The laughter Clare and I have shared in our business is the greatest treasure.

We know that the happiest, longest living people are in countries where they live very simple lives, haven't got wealth and haven't even heard of goal setting. As Bob Dylan said,

"A man is a success if he gets up in the morning and gets to bed at night, and in between he does what he wants to do."

Q: You get a lot of stick on social media, how do you feel about it

A: The trolls go with the territory and I understand why so many businessmen, for it is predominantly men, can't understand why I try to level the playing field to give the smallest of businesses, including all the self-employed, the best possible chance of making ends meet. 'You can't be a socialist and an entrepreneur', they say. I'm not an entrepreneur, but I am a very proud independent business owner and I am a socialist.

The critics' argument goes that I'm supporting 'losers' and unambitious people lacking a positive or 'scale up' mindset. To these businessmen winning is everything and by winning, they mean getting rich. If you're not wealthy it is your own fault.

I understand why my wanting every new business owner to have the very best opportunity of surviving their first three years doesn't chime with 'dream bigger', 'survival of the fittest' and 'fail fast, fail better' mantras.

***Q: Why are you not in favour of government funding scale-up support to existing business owners*?**

A: They always get it wrong. I haven't the time or energy to explain all the mistakes they make, but I must have seen at least 20 government-funded business growth schemes that haven't delivered. Most Government schemes are patronising, to say the least. Most of them believe that big companies, universities and banks can show existing micro-business owners what they're doing wrong and how they can grow their own business. There are an amazing number of people that, without ever having started and run their own business, feel that they can advise micro-business owners how to scale up.

Private sector support is always better quality than these government schemes. My feeling is that the government should only get involved in helping new business owners and much evidence presented to them supports this. Microbusiness owners that have been running their own business for a couple of years are totally capable of deciding what help they need to grow. They can pay for it. Free start-up support should be available as a right.

The Government should get involved in doing things

within their control rather than playing God with our livelihoods. So, they can help all micro-business owners reduce costs. It is way too expensive to run a business in the UK in comparison with most other countries. The Government can reduce costs that are killing micro-business owners in such areas as utilities, rates, the cost of regulatory compliance, fast broadband and #PayIn30Days.

"Rational beliefs get us closer to getting good results in the real world"

Albert Ellis

VIII
What do you do?

You must remember that Tony and Clare, who to this stage had only worked for giant multinationals had received the very best formal business training that their employers could buy. They'd just finished working for a company that was founded by two of America's most iconic entrepreneurs which promoted and trained people to start a business of their own.

So when they say that when they started their business in 1986 the start-up advice was terrible, I believe them. They say there wasn't a book or a programme or any advice from publicly funded bodies, including their local enterprise agency which Amway had sponsored, that was much use to them.

In fact, most of it was wrong - come up with a business idea, write a business plan, use the business plan to get funding. Sound familiar? They say the only thing that matters to most businesses at the beginning is getting customers and learning from them.

Furthermore, the formal training they'd received, particularly Tony's post graduate diplomas, were of no use either. If they'd started the business a year earlier, then they would both have had some contracts to keep them going until they found enough customers to make ends meet. As it was, once they'd realised that their initial plan of offering services people didn't think they wanted to pay for, they knew the first year at least, would be about test trading.

Their original aim was to concentrate on providing HR Management and Development Services themselves and to use contractors to provide related business services such as Health and Safety, Taxation and Pensions.

A supplier of theirs at Amway, Brian, ran a local recruitment agency which had the type of small and medium sized businesses which may need their services. This chap had a cashflow problem because of late payment but couldn't get a further overdraft. Tony persuaded his mother to lend him £20,000 from the sale of her house in Hull, to give to Brian and to be repaid monthly and in full in one year. Tony would become a Director of Brian's business and Brian would become a Director of Tony and Clare's until the loan was paid off then they'd rescind their directorships.

What was the big idea? Well, obviously Brian needed cash but in return he could give Tony and Clare leads and some stationery for a business - the Business Advisory Bureau - which was in its formative stages. Tony and Clare didn't even choose their own name for their business - hopeless!!

There was method to this madness though. Tony and Clare then wrote a business plan purely for the bank and because of Brian's clients and involvement and their positions previously at Amway and in the local business community, the bank gave them an unsecured overdraft of £10,000.

This is a great example of why business plans really have very little use. You can make them say whatever you need them to in order to fit the bank narrative, but in reality, they're usually obsolete within a week or so or writing them - unless you're constantly updating them. From my own experience, working with several different business coaches, I can tell you that once I've gone through the motions, I've never looked at it again, never used it and quite frankly I'm too busy running my business to update another unnecessary excel spreadsheet!

You can understand why Tony believes that winning customers and making deals, not developing products and services and planning, are the most important skills for a start-up. The first year was test trading and it was hard. It would take three years before they'd really worked out which of the professional services they offered clients would buy at a fee level and often enough for them to make ends meet.

They both had to take interim contracts to make ends meet - Clare as a locum personnel manager to companies such as Scania, and Tony part time lecturing in Administrative Management (well he had got the diploma even though he was lousy at it) at a local college. Having multiple income streams is another 'must have' for start-ups in Tony's opinion.

This is another thing that both Tony I agree on is so

important when starting up a business, multiple income streams. Because micro-business owners are earning less than ten years ago and there are two million more micro-business owners competing for the same share of the economy, it takes a long time - eighteen months to four years - to make ends meet out of your main business. This is why more start-up entrepreneurs today have other side hustles and part time jobs to stay in business for the vulnerable first 18 months. Tony was aware of this good way to keep the business afloat even back then.

Eventually they found that locally they could provide HR, they even ran salary surveys and Press Release writing services to small companies and individuals, including a Conservative MP (Tony - how could you?). They are proud that the CEOs of their first clients at Sonatest PLC and Duo-Fast are still friends today. Tony believes, controversially, that those who criticise him for always trying to do more for a client than he is paid for don't really understand professional services marketing. It's not just that the cost of getting a new client from cold is very expensive and difficult whereas a referred prospective client from a happy, satisfied current client is no cost and easier. It is also about the nuggets of gold you learn from a happy, satisfied, current client.

Take Mike Reilly who was the CEO of Sonatest PLC in Milton Keynes. He's an accountant and a serial entrepreneur in electronics manufacturing. Sonatest was a management buyout in the flaw testing equipment market - all a bit techy for Tony. He and Clare helped Mike out in many HR aspects - they had about 50 employees and they always gave him more hours than they charged for.

He hasn't been a client for at least 25 years, but Tony remains in touch, primarily now by LinkedIn, and is always interested in each new company he founds. Why? Well he's a great Bruce Springsteen concert goer so they have gigs in common, but he also has a business life that is so different to Tony's that learning things from Mike helps Tony in working with his other clients, contacts and government.

Mike went onto become the Chair of the Milton Keynes Business Link, so they even had business support in common. You may not have heard of Mike but he's really one of the UK's finest entrepreneur manufacturers because 90% of everything he makes is exported. He knows more about trading in all the other countries of the world, most of which he's visited on business, than the Government.

Mike learns from Tony and Tony learns from Mike. This shows that the real value of a deeper client relationship is what you learn from each other - priceless!

But it was nationally, providing Direct Marketing, Selling and Negotiating Consultancy and Training to large organisations where they'd make their money.

So, started Tony's thirty years of commuting into London and big-name clients such as Dorling Kindersley, Encyclopaedia Britannica, Grolier, Ford, Steelcase, Clerical and Medical, Abbey National,

Bose, Amstrad,

Prince Johnson Controls, BT, Sage, Nuance and party plan and catalogue companies such as Betterware, Kleeneze, Oriflame and Undercoverwear (like Ann Summers).

Bose was particularly interesting as they wanted to sell their acoustic wave music system by demonstration in the home. They flew Tony out to Framingham; Massachusetts and he was picked up from the airport in a wonderful white stretch limo with full bar at the back. 24 hours later and after refusing to become the CEO of the new company they were setting up in the UK, he was packed off back to the airport in a taxi. I asked him why he turned the job down and he said:

"It was remarkably easy to turn it down even though I was in their HQ in the States. I'd had a few offers of great and amazingly well-paid jobs before. Clare and I had committed to each other to run our own business and that was that. I've never regretted starting and running our own business with Clare. It's the best thing I've ever done. I hadn't expected to be offered a job and didn't think I had misled them. The money was mind-boggling but I didn't want to work for the man again. They became a client and we recruited their UK CEO for them so all's well that ends well."

Bose were one of his favourite clients and Tony and Clare helped set up their, short lived, direct sales operation.

Clare and Charles found BAB's dream office premises in the village of Clifton Reynes outside Olney in

Buckinghamshire. They'd previously been in an office above an excellent Turkish restaurant in Newport Pagnell. Our new office was an outbuilding of a farm. Naturally, the farmer and his wife became their friends. Their location and the way Clare made it, became BAB Limited's biggest selling point. Clients would travel to us from around the country. There was an awesome pub with awesome food close by. It was so different from corporate-dumb. Most big corporate executives and senior civil servants love getting out of the office on expenses and they realised that their Clifton Reynes office was enticing. They saved a great deal of time and money in travelling but most of all it made them accessible 24/7.

The most employees they ever had was seven, so they were truly a micro-business. They worked with about twenty freelancers to help on contracts, particularly on executive training contracts. Tony and Clare became well known for writing bespoke training courses with real life case studies and practical exercises that meant any skills learned on their courses were immediately transferable to the workplace.

It was their training know how, combined with their direct marketing expertise which brought the Business Advisory Bureau Limited to the attention of national government departments, primarily the Department for Education and Skills and the Department of Trade and Industry and their successors. This would ultimately lead to a contract which would have a profound effect on their business - good and bad - but because the contract was about helping small and micro-business owners to survive and thrive it would define their future.

We're in the mid-nineties, almost ten years into Tony and Clare running their own business. They were doing well with blue chip clients and a great reputation, but the hours were long, Tony was still travelling a lot and they were beginning to resent the fact that they had five employees to find a wage for each month. Five years earlier, Tony had a bit of a health scare, where he crawled into a police station at a services area off the M6 and they got him into intensive care in a hospital in Nuneaton. He'd gone on a bit of a fitness kick after this scare; that is doing more than just captaining Great Houghton Cricket Club, which now seemed to be more about pre-match and post-match pints than scoring runs.

He wasn't prepared to do as much training away from home as previously. Clare, likewise, wanted to spend more time on her active pursuits with Charles, her husband - particularly walking, cycling and skiing.

They'd never really solved the fee-time puzzle of clients always wanting Tony and Clare to be upfront on the projects, so the rest of the team were more of a cost than value adding. As a result, in this riches to rags story, Tony downsized for the first time, to reduce his mortgage and moved to Northampton with Eileen, Carl, Alan and Sinead. Tony's Mum had moved out of the granny annexe into sheltered accommodation and eventually followed them to Northampton.

One of their early clients and then a customer for many years had been the Meat Training Council, the CEO then is still a cricket watching friend of Tony's today. One of the many projects they'd undertaken for the Meat Training council was developing and direct marketing national vocational qualifications (NVQs). This led to the Director of the DSA, who had been asked by Government to develop NVQs in sales to ask Tony and Clare to help him.

Eventually they founded the Sales Qualifications Board and Tony and Clare ran the secretariat for this from their offices and Tony spoke at the major events like at the CBI. Senior civil servants were now looking at Clare and Tony as the answer to their problems in trying to get high take up of national vocational qualifications. It was the perfect combination for their HR Development and Direct Marketing expertise. They got involved in several sectors and occupations - including forklift truck driving - good job Tony didn't try to drive one of those.

One day, a request came in to see if they could do anything with the Small Firms Lead Body which had been set up to develop NVQs and SVQs (the Scottish equivalent) for Owner-Managers (Small Business Owners) and Business Counsellors (later to be called Business Advisers). Tony and Clare were knackered and not really interested but Bill and Christine in their office put together a proposal and presented it to the government officer, who they liked a lot, and the secretary of the Small Firms Lead Body.

They won the contract so Tony and Clare had to go meet the Small Firms Lead Body (SFLB) which was made up of all the small business membership organisations in the UK - FSB, FPB, British Banking Association, CBI, British Chambers of Commerce, ACCA, IAB, Prince's Trust and the rest of the alphabet soup. These are all the same organisations Tony works with today to back #MicroBizMatters Day and #PayIn30Days campaign. Although back then they weren't so friendly and were threatening to quit developing these NVQs and Government were threatening to pull the funding.

BAB managed to keep them all together and reprised the creating a brand and a secretariat to do the marketing tactics just like they'd done with the Sales Qualifications Board. Government were please and gave them more funding.

Tony and Clare still weren't overly interested in the small firms sector until a series of events made Tony angry about the patronising and paternalistic treatment small and micro-business owners were getting. A banker and government official even used the terms 'the great unwashed' and 'life-stylers' to describe micro-business owners. The qualifications Tony and Clare had been given to market were terrible and looked like something written from a business studies college course - no practical use at all.

Business advisers in Britain, he felt, were just as likely to give the wrong - business killing - advice as the right advice. By this time, his friend Bill was running the SFLB secretariat from his office and Tony was doing the marketing and public speaking on these dreadful qualifications.

When the Government said they wanted to create a network of National Training Organisations, with substantial Government funding, Tony saw his opportunity to improve the quality of start-up support and training in the UK. Why? He'd read the research that showed the failure rate in the first three years was appalling, but more importantly it was avoidable if the prospective business owner had the right skills and advice.

He was lucky to have worked with several senior civil servants for a number of years on a number of successful projects and believes Clare and he were thoroughly trusted by Government to give maximum value for money.

Learning from their many mistakes in starting their own business, led to Tony and Clare, helped by Tony Bedford and Alan McDonagh, to write 'The Essential Guide to Earning a Living as an Independent Consultant'. This updateable and loose-leaf guide was one of their greatest successes. Tony learned how to market it from a successful employment law guide he'd seen. It was sold by direct mail and outplacement agencies would buy the innards of this BAB guide in quantity and put their own covers on it. It became a good extra income stream.

They won an award with it and ran free Saturday morning start-up seminars funded by the local Training and Enterprise Council. Today it would be a brilliant product for all freelancers. Tony and Clare had realised how important context-specific start-up support is to a new business owner. They knew this from all the mistakes they had made. Helping start-ups to learn how to survive and thrive became a driving force in their business when they founded SFEDI.

He founded, formed a company, a board, an advisory council (many of the same organisations as on the SFLB) and launched the Small Firms Enterprise Development Initiative Limited (SFEDI). SFEDI partnered with the Management Charter Initiative, to form the Management and Enterprise National Training Organisation with Gordon Roddick, Anita's husband, as Chair and with offices in Russell Square in London.

SFEDI is pronounced "Sfeddie" and there's a story behind why instead of the initials S.F.E.D.I. In the early days of SFEDI their meetings were held at the British Bankers Association and the previous secretary of the SFLB and the first SFEDI chairman both had banking connections. This led to Tony and SFEDI holding major events at the Bank of England - a wonderful venue with a hi-tech conference facility. The Governor of the Bank of England was Sir Edward George who had been nicknamed by the press as 'Steady Eddie'. When he first addressed the SFEDI audience he said, "*I was in my office minding my own business and one of my staff burst through the door saying 'Right, Steady Eddie, let's get ready, it's time for SFEDI'*".

Although Tony's time was still paid for as a contract to the BAB, Tony assumed the role of Chief Executive, recruited a team and worked most days from the Russell Square offices. I'm not going to take you through the history of SFEDI and all it achieved in the UK for small and micro-business owners. However, on a personal basis it made Tony the 'in-demand' expert on the learning and support needs of start-ups and business owners in the UK.

He had the research, the backing of all the major small business bodies and the leading academics, such as Professor Allan Gibb OBE who established the first European university-based Small Business Centre at Durham University Business School in 1971, which developed over the next 30 years into a substantial organisation. It delivered the first national UK programmes in schools and college enterprise education, the first UK programmes for new venture management, business survival and growth and the first programmes for the national development of the official UK small firms counselling service and enterprise agency development, the latter in partnership with Business in the Community. Many of these programme models have been disseminated around the world often in partnership with international organisations.

If you've understood how important he believes deal-making is, you won't be surprised that two new deals he made took SFEDI and Tony into the 'really influential with the establishment' bracket:

Firstly, one of the SFEDI Advisory Board members, David Irwin became the first Chief Executive of the Small Business Service, reporting directly into the Prime Minister, Tony Blair. The deal made, was that every publicly funded business adviser, including from the emerging Business Link network and all Enterprise Agencies would have to be assessed and accredited to SFEDI standards.

Secondly, he persuaded Government of the importance of treating small firms separately from Medium and Large Firms when it came to forming policy on learning and support needs. He started campaigning in every meeting with Government that using the term 'SME' was wrong and that positive cashflow, which Government could do something about with #PayIn30Days, was essential to surviving and thriving.

He was succeeding to persuade many in Government that business owners were not the same as employed managers and that increasing the success rate of start-ups and new micro-businesses would create more economic growth than 'picking winners' from existing small, medium and large businesses.

SFEDI became the sector skills body for small firms which strived to achieve all of the above. SFEDI gained funding to leave Russell Square and move to lower cost offices in Sheffield where they recruited a team of twelve in the office, including a research director - now great friend - Nigel Hudson - and eight business owners that were also brilliant business advisers to conduct assessments and train assessors. A full time employed Chief Executive, Christine Tolson replaced Tony and Tony replaced the first SFEDI Chairman, Stuart White.

Nigel was not only incredibly well qualified as a professional researcher, he was a Director of research for a Government department. He has also been an independent business owner since 2003. Nigel went on to become one of Clare and Tony's great collaborators. Today he coaches and mentors' start-ups, mainly from disadvantaged backgrounds, day to day.

Most of their research has shown that the pursuit of happiness and fulfilment is more important today for people starting their own enterprise than the pursuit of wealth. This leads on to where Tony is today and his goal to increase the number of "H*appipreneurs*". Entrepreneurs work long hours and rarely can 'switch off' but because eight out of ten are happy they combine their business with the lifestyle they want. They earn on average 20% less than they would do in an equivalent job. It's hard work too, but it is not as stressful as 'working for the man'.

When Tony started campaigning for a supportive environment for those starting their own micro-business, Government officials and major influencers from the financial sector would tell him disparagingly "*But they're all 'lifestyles not serious businesses' - they're of no economic or social benefit*".

These critics were wrong; lifestyle is important to new entrepreneurs. It's almost impossible to stay happy running your own business unless you integrate your lifestyle within it.

Not only did SFEDI achieve a great deal in raising the quality of business support and learning in the UK, but Tony was at the heart of helping create enterprise friendly government policies for all independent business owners and every start-up had access to quality advice, free of charge, if they wanted it.

This all stopped in 2004, when Government policy changed to preferring to support high growth start-ups and scale ups and the focus was on businesses with 10 or more employees. In other words, the 95% of all businesses in the UK that are micro, or start-ups were no longer a priority. They withdrew all funding for SFEDI.

Government, Banks and Investors 'programmes' sell a process, or programme, of support. Often, this process is just as likely to build a business dream in Never Neverland as an MLM opportunity. They try to find a winner out of several start-ups and aren't worried about the collateral damage with those that don't succeed and get into debt.

At the top end of programmes in tech, at Silicon Valley equivalents, they're looking to fatten the next unicorn (valued at a $billion dollars). The unicorn doesn't even need to make a profit and is sold within 5 years to make investors and founders mega rich. They are one in a million but in the process of finding one, investors' burn hundreds of thousands of companies, lives and livelihoods each year throughout the world - this is not fulfilling business ownership as we know it.

At the lower end of 'picking winners' through programmes, Tony has seen too many rubbish loan + mentor/adviser/incubator/growth/accelerator schemes.

When the Government began, years ago now, its Start-Up loans scheme, Tony begged them to only grant a loan after the new business had enough customers to show the business was viable or shown it through 6 months test trading.

The business plan is what Start-up Loans assess but this is worthless until you've found out why and how many customers will buy the product or service. Naturally, they ignored Tony, and Government's Start-up Loan providers were targeted on getting the loans out. As a result, they've seen a 40% default rate on the loans and loads more business owners struggling forevermore with a personal loan of average £12,000. A financial noose around your neck at start-up is not a good look.

The Banks and Government never lose money - the banker always wins - but the new business owner is not in control of their own destiny. A bad credit rating makes life very difficult in the future. The business owner feels out of control as they're just working to pay back the loan or investment. How dare they give these new business owners a mentor who has never started a business of their own!

By this time Tony had done his second downsizing and the family had moved to his dream location, Scarborough (he'd attended over forty annual Scarborough cricket festivals). Tony had one member of staff, an ex-pop star who was a digital whiz (his unusual recruitment policy yet again) and Clare was sharing someone else's office in their original location.

Although their BAB, business years and SFEDI years had highs and lows since 2000 when Tony moved to Scarborough, their personal lives were about getting the maximum happiness and spending as many hours as they could with friends and family. They were Happipreneurs now.

Both were working much less hours - Clare was trying to be part time and often when times were hard with SFEDI, didn't take any salary at all. Tony had all the pleasures of living at the seaside, albeit still commuting to London a few times a month and had far more time to play.

One of the non-financial reasons they'd moved back to Yorkshire, after his mother's death in 1998, was to be closer to Uncle Ron, his mother's brother who had lived at Tony's house before his Dad kicked him out. There's a poem about that too. Tony particularly has enjoyed since 2000 spending twice as much time with his family, re-uniting with all his Yorkshire friends and watching twice as much sport and live gigs.

Tony and Clare made all the SFEDI staff redundant, with maximum redundancy pay and in-lieu notice and were to be found sat on a floor in Sheffield at 4am in the morning getting everything ready for a shredder lorry to take away all the contents of the office at 9am.

The career high of receiving an OBE at Buckingham Palace seemed a long time ago. It was only three years earlier and he'd received it for services to small firms and training. Following the investiture by Prince Charles, Tony's family, minus his Mum who'd died in 1998, were taken to a top restaurant hosted and paid for by Clare and Charles, where 30 of their BAB/SFEDI friends, including Tony's oldest friends, Jude, Nick and postman Dave celebrated the gong - he still doesn't know who nominated him.

Other huge highs he reflected on had been the number of visits to St George's House and Library in Windsor Castle to help formulate Government policy. The Dean of St George's Chapel gave the fifteen or so guests, theoretically, of the Duke of Edinburgh an after-dinner tour of St George's Chapel and Tony always went on it. He loves history and the whole history of Britain is at St George's Chapel. It's where the Queen's knights have their crests, most of our monarchs are buried and of course, more recently it's where Prince Harry and Meghan were married.

Tony was Vice President of the National Federation of Enterprise Agencies, Vice President of ISBE (small business academics), Investors in People Small Business Champion and had contributed to many Government committees, the best being the Council for Excellence in Management and Leadership and The Review into the Costs of Regulatory Compliance - all to benefit small and micro-business owners.

Tony decided to keep going with all his voluntary positions, only the Investors in People Small Business

Champion role was a fee paid to BAB, in order to re-start SFEDI. One of the board directors of SFEDI and a previous SFEDI Award winner, Ruth Lowbridge MBE, agreed to help and a small number of files were moved to a small rented office near Darlington and near where Ruth lived. Clare who had resumed the role of Company Secretary and looking after the SFEDI accounts eventually handed over both these roles to Ruth and her team in the North East.

Tony isn't a fan of '*the fail fast, fail better'* mantra in your own business. But he does believe learning from the '*downs'* as much as the '*ups'* is essential.

Between them, Clare and Tony founded several (still successful) businesses over a thirty-year period. They also had massive failures too. As an example, they invested a lot of money in a cosmetics business called *Sudden Change*, but it was Sudden Death for them as their partners lost the license to sell the products in the UK.

When faced with the lowest points in business, Tony's fall back is a high-profile launch or re-launch. He believes it's the fastest way of getting happy existing customers to positively influence prospective customers. After all, they'd started their business with the launch of a book they'd written - '*How to prevent managers strangling the business*' and every few years since they'd found an excuse for a party. However, the next two parties they put on were the boldest yet.

Firstly, they held an '*18 years and up for it'* celebration of BAB‘s 18th anniversary and entering adulthood at the Café Royal in London and then a year or so later, held a new SFEDI Awards event on HMS Belfast. Previous SFEDI Awards events had been at the Bank of England but then they had big sponsors, now they had big nothing. They nearly sank HMS Belfast because Tony forgot who he'd invited and didn't expect more than 50 to turn up - they had nearly 200 and you can see on the video the buzz you get from a sit-down luncheon that has many people standing.

By the way, at the Café Royal event each guest received a 116-page book 'Buzzing with the Entrepreneurs' written by Ms Leonora Soculitherz who was later to write ***'Freedom from Bosses Forever'*** and 'Soculitherz on TV' with Tony. Don't ask - she doesn't exist, except in Tony's satirical mind, and in my mind as the creator of the Incredible Choco-Wine Diet.

Q&A Time

Q: In 2001 you were awarded an OBE and since then you've received two Lifetime Achievement Awards for Enterprise and are currently the National Enterprise Network's Business Support Champion of the year. Do you deserve these awards?

A: Probably not in that free support to start-ups is not as good as it was in 2004 and I must be the most unsuccessful campaigner ever with #PayIn30days - 24 years and counting!

Q: What did you and Clare achieve that led to an OBE - weren't you just doing client work?

A: Initially it was just client work but the beauty of having your own business is that you can follow your instincts and Clare and I have put zillions of hours, unpaid, into things we think are important. We've always accepted every award that the Business Advisory Bureau Limited that Clare or I have received.

We're very proud that we went into business together and I've only got more awards than Clare because Clare isn't and doesn't want to be the 'talking head'.

The OBE is a bit different because I don't know who recommended me for it and since I received it from Prince Charles I've tried as hard as I can to be worthy of it. It was for services to small firms and training and I hope that there are many thousands of micro-business owners that might say I deserved an OBE, even if I didn't at the time.

It was another great opportunity for me to get dressed up in a morning suit and as a family, we had an awesome two days in London. My daughter, Sinead and I pretended to be celebs and my favourite photo of the day is Sinead and I standing in front of a massive posh white limousine - I don't know makes of car - pretending it was ours.

Q: Why did you get an OBE?

A: I can only guess that a senior civil servant or Minister felt that I'd gone the extra mile in working with the government to improve the quality and accessibility of enterprise support and training in the UK. I must admit that by 2001 we thought we had made a lot of progress.

I was voluntarily and unpaid on every one of the most influential policies proposing organisations and forums in the UK. SFEDI standards were underpinning both policy and practice.

When you consider that in 1996 I'd been ashamed of how hopeless the 'owner-manager' standards that we inherited were, then to have revised them and made them useful to underpin all help to start-ups and indie business owners in the UK was a bit of an achievement.

It's still 'Other Buggers' Efforts' though. Clare, Julie, Stephan and especially, the late John Copsey and his team of assessors, plus the senior civil servants like the late and great Linda Ammon CBE, Derek Carr and Verni Tannam were the heroes. I just did the standing up and sitting down work - all the showing off.

Q: You were in the Establishment then weren't you?

A: I hope not. I was used to being at posh places like the Grosvenor House Hotel and House of Commons from my time at Amway. Clare had ironed out my table manners. But I always thought of myself as being the token micro-business owner that had the research to back their opinions. Most of the people I met at that time were male, private school educated, wealthy and, for some reason, thought that I wasn't a 'life-styler' but a serious thinker. How wrong they were!

Q: Yet you're critical of many entrepreneurs and small business membership organisations that lick the boots of the Government?

A: I understand how it happens and, hey, I'm a Happipreneur so it doesn't bother me much that so many people get sucked into the bubble. The Establishment bubble has fine food, fine wines and the most wonderful places and entertainment to enjoy. It's no different to Amway leading distributors going to luxury hotels in Cannes and Montreux - once you've tasted the prestige and luxury you want more.

For example, Chief Executives of small business membership organisations will enjoy being in the bubble but also can't afford to not be liked by Government and Banks - same thing. Their membership won't be very happy if their CEO is not involved in all the important talks. So, they have to 'welcome' whatever policy announcement comes out even though they know that they're not what they lobbied for.

Similarly, leading entrepreneurs will be asked to Chair

Committees for the Government and these entrepreneurs will love how well they're looked after - locations, VIPs, secretariat and comfort. Although these leading entrepreneurs can afford their own luxury they are now mixing with the really powerful.

Remember all our current cabinet of ministers are multi-millionaires but more powerful than any entrepreneur. It's like a drug they don't want to come off. That's why they lend their name to reports and policy recommendations they haven't written. They go native.

I'm no angel. I hate posh clubs, but I still go to Lords to watch cricket, when invited by my friend, a Lords member, and take my champagne through the Grace Gates and meet the dress code of the Warner stand. But I can only do it occasionally. I love being outside the bubble.

Q: But you miss think tanks at Windsor Castle?

A: I was only there for a small number of days on a handful of visits, but they're etched in the memory. A lot of policy forums are under Chatham House Rules. You're very well looked after in terms of environment and food but of course, you don't get paid. Rituals are very important to the Establishment and I would never breach confidentiality - it's the most important aspect of being trusted. But I really was at my best then.

It was an opportunity for me to contribute at the highest level to small firms policy from the research I've been involved in. There's joy in finding creative solutions to problems. Just a lot of bright people in a room trying to be useful and some of it eventually finds its way into

Government policy to benefit the lives of business owners.

It was also a nightmare staying in the Queen and Prince Philip‘s home. Prince Philip had given St George‘s House and Library to the pursuit of thought and public endeavour and those lucky enough to be invited there were very well looked after - including an honesty bar. My problem is that it was a home not a hotel so the rooms in St George’s House didn’t have locks on them and as a dyspraxic, after using the honesty bar, I was tiptoeing up the stairs and gingerly opening many doors before I found my bedroom.

Q: Not long before you received the OBE you’d downsized again and moved from Northampton to Scarborough, where you still live - was the Business Advisory Bureau Limited in trouble?

A: It wasn’t in trouble, Clare always cut the costs, including her own salary in order that we survived but we were at a crossroads business-wise and personally.

I’d made the same mistake that I made before my first downsizing of putting all my eggs in one basket. In 1994 it was setting up a UK company for a Chinese Company manufacturing home alarms and personal attack alarms which were set off for no apparent reason.

Then, in 2000 it was SFEDI. We’d again put in loads more hours than we were paid for and lost other clients and opportunities during that period. As we’d now appointed a CEO and recruited a team I was able to go back to promoting our company’s services and one main product ‘The Essential Guide to Earning a Living from Independent Consultancy’ but we knew it would take a while to build our client base again and I couldn't expect much in terms of salary.

You can see why I'm so assertive about the need for a business owner to build multiple income streams. In time fee businesses, like ours, it's also important to have a mix of retainers and some products too so that money keeps on coming in when the unexpected happens.

Q: You are known for doing more than is expected of you. Where does this come from?

A: When Clare and I were at our most successful with BAB we were charging from £450 right up to £1200 a day for my time. That sounds and is very good but both Clare and I were so desperate to give value for money that we always did many more hours and days than we charged for. One of my obsessions, from being ripped off by solicitors and accountants, was to detail pages and pages of information as to exactly what we'd done for the client in every hour we charged for.

We even detailed the extra hours we weren't charging for. The accounts departments in the large companies that were our clients weren't at all interested in this detail, but there was some good psychology behind what we were doing. The first recipient of the invoice is the executive in the company that we worked with and nearly always these invoices require a second signature of their boss before it goes to accounts. We gave such detailed information that the executive would look great in the organisation as to the value for money that he'd achieved from contracting with the BAB.

Clare made it her business to know who in the company was signing off our invoice and who in the accounts department would be processing it. We rarely had a problem in being paid promptly - certainly #PayIn30Days. Very few people are brave enough to lie to Clare. Eventually, on many contracts we asked for a third up front, a third on delivery and a third within 14 days. As these clients knew we always delivered more than they asked for we became able to dictate our payment terms rather than theirs.

Q: What were the personal crossroads?

A: My mother died in 1998 and for a number of years before it had been a full-time job for Eileen and a weekend job for me in keeping her going. After the funeral, we went to Scarborough for a few days. I'd been going to Scarborough for the cricket festival with my friend Dave, every year.

I've loved Scarborough and the cricket ground all my life and as Schumacher says 'quality of life' is the most important thing. Scarborough was the place I most wanted to live and Eileen and I would be closer to my Mum's brother, Uncle Ron in Hull.

Added to this Clare and Charles wanted to have more time travelling and enjoying life and less time working. I wanted to do much more fiction writing. As a family, we saw in the Millennium in Trafalgar Square and it just seemed the right time for all of us to have a new adventure in Scarborough. It wasn't a sensible business decision as any work I would get would still be in London, but the 3-hour train journey was worth it to be by the sea and eating cinder toffee ice-cream.

I love it so much that I convinced one of my best friends Dave to retire up here with his wife and I know that he is as happy as I am with a quieter life.

Q: Were you looking to slow down and retire in Scarborough?

A: No, I haven't met many micro-business owners who look to retire. I had the view that 57 would be about my life expectancy, the age my father died, so I certainly wasn't looking to slow up. I wanted to achieve more and faster, but not in a wealth-producing way. I certainly wanted to do a lot more creatively, especially with fictional writing.

It's ironic that I've lost so many friends that were 57 or under and here I am still. I'm so lucky and live every day to the full as happily as I can. While I have my marbles, that's debatable I know, I'll always have to earn money as Carl doesn't work or claim any benefits and Alan earns very little from online trading. Eileen has now retired from the Hull University library after 18 years in a job she loved and was loved by the students.

So, it's up to me. There may even be a last downsizing around the corner if we move to Ireland where Eileen would like to live. I'm so lucky if it ends tomorrow, I've had a wonderful time and I learned how to enjoy every day.

Q: You loved your offices in Buckinghamshire, did you have to work from home in Scarborough?

A: No, I've only worked from home in the last few years after we closed the Business Advisory Bureau

Limited. I rented three offices in three different buildings owned by the Enterprise Agency I now co-chair. I started in Scarborough with high hopes of creating Entrepreneurs UK as a brand of our company and as a publisher of advice, learning, books and guides.

I was lucky to recruit Ocean Reid, a multi-talented techie and ex-pop star to help me and I had a few good client contracts in London, like being Small Business Champion for Investors in People, to keep the wolves from the door, while we built our new brand.

Q: I've not heard of it so why did it fail - you seem to have had a lot of failures?

A: *'He who dares...'*, *'Nothing ventured, nothing gained'*, *'The world is my lobster'* - to paraphrase Del Boy in Only Fools and Horses. I don't think of them as failures.

Ocean, Stuart as he was then, and I produced some good stuff leading up to our re-launch at the Cafe Royal in 2004. It's just that SFEDI reared its head again in 2004 when the Government didn't renew its funding and I had to make all the staff redundant. I've still got the EntrepreneursUK domain, the Rat Race Escape kit and many of the guides we produced are freely accessible on my current website.

The next six years were a fight for SFEDI's survival. Maybe I should have just let it go, but Clare was helping me, unpaid, fulfil the few contracts in Europe that SFEDI still had. Clare also took over the Company Secretarial duties and bookkeeping and we used our accountant, John, and our fabulous designer friend,

Alan, who we'd worked with since 1987. Ruth was really into creating new income streams through being an Awarding Body. Nigel was helping out too.

I recruited a new board, chaired by Elsa Caleb. I was surrounded by so much goodwill from friends and voluntary effort that I really believed we could save it and that Government would then start supporting learning and advice for all start-ups and micro-business owners.

Q: Tim Campbell MBE obviously has huge respect for you, and recognises, as you say that people need to learn from doing, how do you see this working?

A: My whole motivation since founding SFEDI has been to help new business owners as they're the ones vulnerable to the snakes and the snakes stop them finding the rock-solid ladders.

As business owners with the 'been there, still there and got the T-shirt', we can help them find the ladders AND show them how to avoid the snakes, (including charlatans, scams, stuff they don't need and many government schemes and loans).

The difference is only 30% succeeding to trade over 3 years and 80% succeeding to trade over 3 years.

I know where Tim is coming from because we both believe it is learning by doing business. It is not learned by formal teaching, planning, strategy and deep thinking. We can, as Schumacher suggested, make starting and running your own business a simple and good thing, not a complex and dangerous thing. He didn't say it like that but that's what 'Small is Beautiful' and Happipreneurship is all about.

I knew nothing about what worked in practice and didn't work in practice until I met the late Professor Allan Gibb OBE and Terry Owens. Terry Owens was the Founder of Inbiz who had helped 10,000 start-ups, from mainly deprived backgrounds with his Inbiz centres.

Allan helped me to iron out my thinking as to all UK start-ups could get the right help to see the ladders and avoid the snakes. He also helped me get the research to demonstrate to the Government that there was another way of practically helping new business owners in the UK. He was really interested in all I knew about the charlatans and fakes.

That work we did is still in evidence in many countries - in Scotland it's great and in England it's patchy.

On the enterprise education side, it's a shame that so much of his work - particularly the 30 years between 1971 and 2001 when he founded and ran the Small Business Centre at the University of Durham, and a little of my work, which improved enterprise in schools, colleges and universities have largely been forgotten.

That's not the fault of enterprise educators, many of whom were taught by Allan Gibb - it's the fact that Government and the Banks (same thing) like formal teaching (schemes, programmes, accelerators etc). They also like business planning and pitching to investors for funding or pitching to banks for loans and NOT test trading, learning from that and being helped by business owners in the context of your unique personality and your unique business.

Tim Campbell is an awesome business and young people's mentor and I know would agree with this. He's just saying, as I say, that there's absolutely no substitute for the learning by doing and taking a few knocks along the way in the context of your business. After all, it's so sophisticated, any one of us can fall foul to the charms of the charlatans.

Q: Your partnerships with most people seem to have worked very well but you've had some that have ended up badly. What advice would you give other business owners about making successful partnerships?

A: *One: Complementary skills, passions and resources* will be what you need to grow your business not 'another you'.

In 2003, Antony Chesworth founded what is now the UK's most popular online shops service - EKM. He works very hard, has a state of the art, £3million HQ housing 85 employees and has the lifestyle of a successful entrepreneur, even piloting his own plane.

Antony is the only successful entrepreneur who I haven't established who the partner, with complementary skills, was that helped him move his business forward. It may be that partnership is with his wife, Alison, who works in the business too. They're a great team.

That's how important partnerships are. For example, I know that Antony spent 2 years hardly getting any customers for the platform he'd built until he learned telephone selling.

That's a very brave and excellent way Antony solved

the problem of a great, distinctive product and service but not enough customers. Another way of doing it in Antony's early days would have been to find another freelancer or new micro indie business owner that understood online shops, maybe one of his early customers, and was brilliant at telephone selling. Offer them a great cut of the value they bring in - make it more of a business partnership - help get them clients.

Two: A partnership is not the same as buying a solution. Most start-ups given lots of money will blow it on developing the product, service, shop, restaurant or whatever it is that they're passionate about. If they haven't done enough test trading or practical research, they won't know what they need when it comes to marketing and if they don't know what they need they'll waste even more money on marketing staff or contractors.

It's not good enough to get an average supplier either - your business needs to be 'beautifully' distinctive - excelling in product/service, selling/marketing and financial management - particularly cash flow. Supplier partners are likely to be people you can't afford to pay what they're worth, but the loyalty and enjoyment you both get from committing to each other are enough.

It's why family and friends are often the sources of great partnerships in the early days. Remember, with a partnership 2+2 must = 5 not 4. Chris Percival, one of Britain's most successful entrepreneurs and still under 30, credits the skills and resources that his Mum and Dad brought to his fledgling, paramedic and ambulance business. Chris has fully resourced fleets of ambulances and thousands of employees in many countries today and his Mum and Dad are smiling too as they have a share in the business.

Three: Trust, shared passions and values are important. One of Sirolli's wonderful true stories is of five Australian fishermen working together to sell their fish at a higher profit. As individuals, they were struggling and all they knew was how to catch fish. Through Sirolli's enterprise facilitation they found out the solution was to learn how to prepare tuna to be superior grade sashimi and supply it to Japanese restaurants at ten times the price they'd been getting before.

It took many 'partnerships' to make this a successful business venture - each partnership was a win-win, primarily because of shared values. The two partnerships which went badly wrong in my businesses were both due to our partners not valuing the work we were passionate and proud of doing.

These partners would do anything to make money. It was a disaster. Since then, we've always stuck to people that our friends or family can truly recommend, and we've tested the water before making a deal with any new 'partner'.

Like Tina Boden and the more famous *Warren Buffet*, I now only work with people I like, trust and admire. In a 1998 address to University of Florida MBA students, Buffett reiterated this golden principle, saying *"I only work with people I like. If I could make $100 million with a guy who causes my stomach to churn, I would say no."*

Image Set C:

1. Prince Charles presenting Tony his OBE 2001
2. Family photo at OBE 2001
3. Family & Friends at the 2001 après OBE meal and party
4. Tony and Saint Jude at the OBE after meal and party
5. "Friends in memory of" for Tony's runs
6. Tony's IAB Lifetime Achievement Award for Enterprise
7. Clare-&-Nigel with their SFEDI awards at Kensington Roof Gardens
8. SFEDI House of Lords
9. SFEDI Awards at the Bank of England 2003 Christine Tolson and the late great John Copsey is next to her
10. Ethnic Minority Business Task Force with Lord Mandelson, James Caan CBE and Tom Riordan OBE
11. Tony in Malta for a year
12. Launching Enterprise Rockers on Scarborough Beach
13. The moment Sway met Tony - first #MicroBizMatters Day
14. Tony & Tim Campbell
15. Tony, Tina, Charlie Mullins & Kanya King
16. Tony alone in a onesie in a studio
17. MBMD Cupcakes
18. BBC Breakfast Weston Super Mare 2018
19. The man in the Red Hat
20. A Yorkshire business board of directors
21. A selection of books I've written to date

22. #PayIn30Days on back of jacket
23. Trip of a lifetime 2003 Cricket World Cup South Africa
24. Tony's Proudest possession - East Yorkshire Schools Cricket Cap
25. Carl & Tony at a very wet Rhythm Festival
26. Tiger, Eileen & Shaggy
27. Marathon Man - Loch Ness 2019

ELIZABETH
great north run
I'M RUNNING FOR
IN MEMORY OF:
MACMILLAN CANCER SUPPORT
DIGBY
JUDE
CHARLES
MANDY
ELIZABETH
GREATRUN.ORG
WE ARE

IAB

Enterprise Rockers
.CO.UK
ENTERPRISE ROCKERS

MicroBiz
recognition

MicroBizMattersDay
recognition • action • learning
Friday 13 January 2017 • www.microbizmattersday.rocks
ScanSnap
PIMLICO PLUMBERS
sage
123 Reg

I believe
MicroBiz Matters

BBC
BREAKFAST

ARE YOU
LOOKING
AT ME?
WHY NOT?

@MicroBizMatters
Buzzing
ENTREPRENEURS
How to be a Brilliant
Community Based
Business Adviser
STRIPPING
for Freedom
Earning a
Living
from
Good
Practice
Guide
LOOSE
BBC
MAKE OR
BREAK
A Perfect Little Gift
Tony Robinson OBE
#PayIn30Days

E.R.S.C.A
ENGLAND

Baxters
LOCH NESS
MARATHON
and Festival of Running
567
LOCH NESS
Anthony Robinson
Baxters Loch Ness Marathon
TIME
5:32:39
MARATHON PHOTOS

"There are three musts that hold us back: I must do well, you must treat me well and the world must be easy."

Albert Ellis

IX
Bye, Bye SFEDI I'm Malta bound!

Ensuring SFEDI survived was the work priority from 2004 to 2009 for Tony and Clare. They'd put so much voluntary time into it and it now had their values stamped on it, that they just couldn't let it go - or, more accurately, Tony couldn't let it go.

Ruth put her business into SFEDI, and Tony and Ruth split Tony's shares 50/50 and then when Ruth's son, Nathan Hardwick joined them it moved to them owning a third of SFEDI each and that is the position today. Tony's friend from when she was Chair of the London Group of the Institute of Business Advisers, Elsa Caleb, became Chair of the Board and Leigh Sear, who is now Chief Executive of SFEDI Solutions, became Chair of the Advisory Board with Clare as Company Secretary.

There were many battles with Government and those who 'offered' to take over SFEDI; but today the SFEDI Group, including the Institute of Enterprise and Entrepreneurs, which Tony co-founded with Nat and Ruth is more successful than any time in its history, even more than in 2004 when the government funding rug was pulled from under it. This success in recent years is none of Tony's doing. Sarah Trouten, Ruth's daughter, is now Chief Executive and they have a loyal, long serving team in their offices in Darlington. SFEDI remains recognised by the Government as the sector skills body for enterprise and business support.

Tony decided in January 2012 to have nothing more to do with SFEDI in an executive capacity. He still attends SFEDI Advisory Board meetings and their award ceremonies at the House of Lords. What went wrong?

Tony regards it as a matter of what went right rather than what went wrong, although not being involved in SFEDI was another big step down in his financial situation - the riches to rags story is now gathering pace.

In downsizing again and moving to Scarborough from Northampton in 2000, Tony had decided he wanted to spend the remaining years of his life primarily as a writer and in earning a living as a Happipreneur; a term he more recently coined to describe someone who pursues earning a living from their own business as a means of happiness creation rather than wealth creation. It includes doing things like Tina Boden's 'Don't work with Tossers' which is not necessarily good for earning money but is great for gaining happiness.

Tony believes that 'doing what you love', family, friends and happiness are much more important than money. Making money is not the main reason people start their own businesses. The main reason is to control their own destiny.

It is his belief that happiness, doing what you love,

is a prerequisite for successful and worthwhile entrepreneurship and intrapreneurship. All of his talks, keynotes and interviews are now about what he's termed, *'Happipreneurship'*.

Goal setting, data and process driven, strategy, planning and management led enterprises will never achieve as much as the Happipreneur - entrepreneur or intrapreneur.

John Lennon, a rock-star entrepreneur with a famous micro-business, put it perfectly:

"*When I was 5 years old, my mother always told me that happiness was the key to life. When I went to school, they asked me what I wanted to be when I grew up. I wrote down "happy". They told me I didn't understand the assignment and I told them they didn't understand life"*.

Tony feels he's achieving all of what he thinks are important for happiness in 'bucket loads'. After all he only had 5 years of the status trappings of success and that was so back in the day that he wasn't missing anything by giving his happiness meter a boost at the expense of his piggy bank.

There were also some significant and unexpected events leading up to his resigning as a Director of SFEDI and Chief Executive of the Institute of Enterprise and Entrepreneurs (IOEE).

First, you must understand why he was determined to 'do what you love' in being a writer and Happipreneur. His father had died at 57 and Tony had certainly beaten up his lungs, like his father, through asthma and inhaling small cigars. In 2000 when the Robinson family downsized again to move to Tony's paradise in Scarborough; he was 48, given up smoking and like one of his heroes, Charles Dickens, loved walking long distances and had re-discovered an appetite for reading and writing fiction. He started writing poetry again and more importantly, started improving his writing, naturally with Clare's help. Practice, practice and practice - remember. He regarded every year up to the age of fifty-seven as a happy bonus and has regarded every day since passing the age of his father's death as a happy bonus too.

In September 2002, Clare and Charles bought Tony the holiday of a lifetime for his 50th birthday. This was a three weeks tour of South Africa, in Spring 2003, to watch the Cricket World Cup. He had a marvellous time but more significantly for the future, had written a 150-page travelogue as a thank you present for Clare and Charles. It re-enforced his resolve to make the most of every hour.

Encouraged by the reaction to the book 'Buzzing with the Entrepreneurs' given to BAB clients at the Café Royal Tony then wrote 'Stripping for Freedom' by Leonora Soculitherz. He'd written it in the style of a writer called Miles Kington, with a little bit of PG Wodehouse too, and it got some wonderful reviews and also, some readers didn't get it all.

They really thought it was just a self-help book for prospective entrepreneurs not a satire - the last chapter is quite dark satire. Most people didn't realise that all the characters in the book and the author of the book was fictional. That's where me and my partner came in as Tony wanted to rewrite 'Stripping for Freedom' as 'Freedom from Bosses Forever' to make the Soculitherz joke clearer to readers.

Tony loves writing satire and when 'Freedom from Bosses Forever' came out it gained excellent reviews and he knew his decision to be a writer was the right one. The late millionaire entrepreneur, Stefan Topfer, who loved Tony's campaigning on behalf of small business owners and against big company and government bullying gave Leonora Soculitherz a weekly column on his Small Business Blog. This reached many thousands of readers as Win-Web, Stefan's cloud software company had tens of thousands of customers world-wide and the blog was open to everyone. It was another confidence booster for Tony as a satirical writer.

Writing and performing have been the main sources of income for the business Clare and Tony started and ran. In most service businesses and 70% of all businesses are services, writing and speaking, will form a part of the business even if it is just to attract clients and customers.

At every turning point in their thirty-two-year business story was a new book and a new seminar about the book to attract new clients.

They originally launched their business with two short books. One they sold to a publisher on *'Job Hunting'* and the other they self- published called *'Murder at t'Mill - How to Prevent Managers Strangling the Business'.* They wrote and self-published loose leaf manuals and software as a non-time-fee income stream. The most successful was the *'Essential Guide to Independent Consultancy'.*

Because they could write good copy and were fast learners, they developed new income streams writing press releases, case studies, websites, video scripts and direct marketing media. Whenever there was a prospective downturn in income, they would launch a new niche service with a niche publication and niche seminar.

Business humour and satire in their newsletters and publications became part of their brand and difference. So it was no surprise that *Freedom from Bosses Forever* would be such a hit. Being entertained by the quirkiness seen in their writing became a reason for their corporate clients from London wanting to visit them in their amazing, non-corporate, offices in a village outside *Olney* in Bedfordshire. After the formal work was done, their clients enjoyed an informal chat and snack in the local pub. They hardly ever tendered for business - even with Government. That shows the power of writing.

For their business 18th Anniversary party at the *Café Royal* in London they launched *'Buzzing with the Entrepreneurs'.* This book introduced 200 clients to the mythical fashionista, Leonora Soculitherz (pronounced So-cool-it-hurts).

Writing is still Tony's passion and is now his

profession. He feels that as he's coming toward the end of his life, he's now writing more fiction than business and is enjoying doing so. He'd have preferred to only write fiction for the whole of his life, but then he wouldn't have had the life he's had and of course, as I know only too well, there is no magic wand when it comes to publishing. A study, conducted by the *University of London*, showed just one in ten authors can afford to earn a living from writing alone, a drop from 40 per cent just a decade ago. A typical professional writer, it found, earned just £11,000 annually, less than the minimum wage. So, if you are a budding author, bear this in mind!

So back to Tony…

At about 9am on the 7th July 2005, Tony approached Kings Cross Underground station to see crowds running towards him. At the time he did not know that a bomb had been detonated between stations at 8.49am and although it had occurred 8 minutes after leaving Kings Cross there was panic and shocked and injured survivors trying to escape from all tube stations to Aldgate. Tony walked to Russell Square tube station to try to get a tube to Oxford Circus from there, he had a 9.30am meeting at Investors in People on Chandos Street.

The scene at Russel l Square tube station was even worse there and people in total shock were walking and running covered in soot and there was blood too, some people just sat on the pavement looking totally lost. The noise of the sirens and helicopters overhead increased minute by minute, it was deafening. There was no noise at all from the thousands of people now being cordoned off and trapped in the area of the incidents. Tony later found out that the whole area between Aldgate, Edgware Road and Kings Cross was cordoned off and all three bombs had been detonated at 8.49 on trains leaving Kings Cross on different lines. Tony nor anyone in the cordoned off area knew that bombs had been detonated.

He wandered to one of his favourite cafes, Night n' Day on Southampton Row to get a coffee and ring Investors in People to say he'd be late for the meeting. The television screen and BBC News was repeating reports of a power surge affecting certain tube stations. Tony thought this news sounded a bit odd and not inline with the mayhem he could see outside the café. Later he would be as angry with this deliberate misreporting as he was with Orgreave and other incidents during the Miners' strike, some twenty years earlier.

The noise outside was frightening and the amount of police vehicles, fire engines and ambulances arriving made everyone in the café disbelieve the news story on the TV screen. After Tony had been in the café about 40 minutes, he was on his second cup and croissant, there was a loud explosion behind him in Tavistock Square. A double decker bus had the top deck blown off it by the fourth bomb - although, again Tony did not know this at the time.

It took many hours before Tony was allowed to leave the area and, naturally there was no public transport. At about 5pm Tony and Mike Chitty, who was then Chief Executive of the Business Link University, were having a pint of London Pride in the Civil Service Club, which Tony was a member of, and both realised how lucky they'd been. All other pubs were shut as were all office buildings in the cordoned off area. The silence in London was eerie. It was like a ghost town and the memories of that day, night and the next morning will never leave them.

Arriving eight minutes earlier into Kings Cross would have likely put him on one of those tubes. Their and everyone else's thoughts in London that night were for all those that died and about the kindness of the whole London community, including the emergency services, coming together and supporting each other in this tragedy. It took Tony a couple of days to get back on the tube, but understanding the fleeting nature of life and the need to make the most of it is with him forever.

Having been caught up on the Docklands bombing in 1996, I know exactly how he feels. London is a vibrant, loud and bolshy place; and yet the day after the bombing I walked through Docklands to my offices and there was not a sound, it was as though the area was surrounded by a muffler, no birds sang, no traffic noise and people spoke in hushed voices. It's the weirdest thing I've experienced in London and it still haunts me.

I had driven past Canary Wharf ten minutes before it blew up, like Tony, minutes away from a vile act that would change so many people's lives forever.

Tony admits that any success they had with the BAB Limited was down to Clare and him working together and the joy of it was the laughs they had together, even when working hard. He credits Clare with keeping him on track as he's always looking to create something new rather than finishing the client work in hand. If you speak to Clare, she will tell you that this is true! He can be a bit of a butterfly, attracted by the excitement of the new challenge.

As a Chartered Marketer, he loves the marketing but not the doing and it's only the doing that makes the money. Working 200 miles away from Clare meant he easily got distracted, not that he was in any way unhappy, him and Stuart Reid were having a fabulous time when in Scarborough and Tony was still commuting to London on SFEDI business. Tony also recognised how much he missed working creatively with their designer and digital printer, Almac, owned by Alan McDonagh.

As well as producing all the marketing media Tony and Clare wrote, he was ostensibly their partner in publishing books and guides, up to and including '*Stripping for Freedom'*. Tony believes winning partnerships are a massive part of own business success.

Ruth and the day to day SFEDI operations, as an Awarding Body of qualifications, were of little interest to Tony. Although he enjoyed launching Entrepreneurs UK as a new brand for the BAB, he admits he wasn't that keen on doing consultancy or training again to make ends meet. Even though consultancy and training paid the bills, Tony had spent so long on his SFEDI obsession that he'd lost confidence that he had anything to offer private sector clients. The world of marketing, particularly digital, moves very quickly.

Tony and Clare had always been at the top of the consultancy game but now they were nowhere. Again, this is something I can relate to. I hate to hear people in marketing call themselves 'experts', the industry changes almost daily with Google and the large online platforms changing their algorithms, so unless you're reading and checking in on updates (or writing the algorithms) you're never really going to be an expert. I teach it at university level and I still wouldn't class myself as an expert. It's about knowing what works and there are still tried and tested methods that are successful, but word of warning, watch out for any marketing company who cannot show you their own success or that of their customers.

The few times a year Tony and Clare got together and by now were on SFEDI's European projects, at the SFEDI Awards events they organised at BAFTA, the Magic Circle and Kensington Roof Gardens and, of course, SFEDI Board and Advisory Board meetings. Oh, and the ballet, theatre or walks with Charles, but that was pure pleasure.

Tony had lost the earning money plot without Clare's practical input but was very happy.

He and Clare particularly enjoyed writing start-up

learning media for the European projects and writing the programmes, in true satirical style, for the Awards events. They also enjoyed creating events that were totally different from anything businesspeople had experienced before. Tony and Nat, as the 'voice from above', would MC SFEDI Awards events and the entertainment on offer would be second to none.

Tony fondly remembers that the magicians, on stage and at tables, at the Magic Circle were truly spellbinding. The SFEDI Awards Event at the Magic Circle also had three of his all-time heroes attending, Kanya King CBE, Founder of the MOBOS, Tim Campbell MBE, the first 'The Apprentice' winner and Victoria Lennox who went on to found Start Up Canada. These people are true heroes to Tony and he'll tell you why in a heartbeat.

Kanya is a perfect example of what Tony believes is a true entrepreneur. Creating the globally televised MOBO Awards to showcase new urban music talent sounds 'beautiful' and is amazingly creative, difference-making and 'disruptive'. But the reality is simpler. Through her upbringing and a short career as a television researcher for talent booking, Kanya gained the large dose of common sense she would need in the music sector.

Kanya matched this sector-specific common sense with her enterprising attitude, hard work, influential contacts and a belief that she had the skills to seize a TV opportunity. In a time frame which most said was impossible, Kanya was able to remortgage her house and use the money to run the first MOBO Awards event, persuading stars, like Lionel Richie to cross the Atlantic.

From this one successful televised event in 1996, Kanya King has developed a movement which has changed the face of Urban music and exported tremendous new talent from Britain. The MOBO organisation is unique and it can't be copied because the founder's values are integrated into the brand.

SFEDI's Annual Awards ceremonies in the House of Lords in the last ten years are nothing like those up to 2010. But again, Tony acknowledges that Ruth's way is better for making money and gaining sponsors - Tony was viewed as rather anti-establishment and a bit crazy. Maybe he still is, but he's certainly a lot of fun and knows from his days at Amway what makes a successful event, maybe not the political money maker but one that recognises the real success in people.

Tony and Clare also enjoyed being in various European countries and Clare's fabulous language skills made it tremendously easy for them to enjoy their SFEDI working trips abroad. It was in Budapest that this true story happened;

The talk was on 'What improves the success rate of start-ups?'. Tony's talk was simultaneously translated. His jokes went down well, in fact Tony claims he got the best response to any of his talks. He said to the translator afterwards - 'thanks so much - they even enjoyed the jokes'. His translator said 'No problem. I just said to them 'he thinks he's being funny - LAUGH'!

Ouch, but I'm sure they would have found some of it funny at least…

By the summer of 2010, SFEDI was relatively safe but it wasn't doing the kind of work Tony was interested in, involved in or why he founded SFEDI in the first place. Tony had also lost faith in the Government toproperly support start-ups and micro-business owners. In fact, he thinks that since 2004 they haven't been that bothered. Successive Small Business Ministers have concentrated on 'growing SMEs' and anything they've said about start-ups and 5.8 million micro-business owners has been purely spin.

For the last two years of the Labour Government Tony was on Lord Mandelson's Ethnic Minority Business Task Force, co-chaired by the entrepreneur, James Caan and Tom Riordan, now the Chief Executive of Leeds City Council. He loved the work they did and all the people on the committee, especially the entrepreneurs, all giving their time voluntarily.

However, the final report contained hardly any of their recommendations to better support ethnic minority businesses, including adopting community-based business advisers, which Tony had shown was successful as he'd worked on one such programme for five years in Islington. All the recommendations were on access to finance, which is what the banks wanted. Tony was ashamed that the Government and Banks had deliberately, for their own policy reasons, wasted the time of the ethnic minority entrepreneurs on the committee. Tony had also been involved in consultations with David Cameron's new Conservative Government.

Tony was fine with them dismantling Business Link but not fine with the fact that there was nothing of any quality to replace it for pre-starts, start-ups and micro-business owners that needed help. It seemed that voluntary business mentors were to replace highly trained and qualified business advisers, coaches, facilitators and mentors. Over £400 million had been spent developing a website to provide facts, guidance and information to help start-ups and new business owners but there were no plans to keep it going.

Furthermore, personal start-up loans would be given to people against a business plan, repeating the mistakes of twenty years earlier. Tony had suggested that no loan should be given without evidence of customers, either through test trading or from 6 months 'bootstrap don't borrow' trading.

Tony has been proven right there's a 40% default rate of these start-up loans - it's like putting a noose of personal debt around the neck of the new business owner for the rest of their life - just like student loans.

You only have to look now at Tony's most re-tweeted message, to understand where he's coming from with this.

Thinking of starting a business?

1. *Bootstrap don't borrow*

2. *Test trade first (preferably while in a job)*
3. *Ask for help from a business owner (particularly one that understands your customers)*
4. *Build multiple income streams*
5. *Enjoy!*

Many who sell to micro-business owners don't like this 'bootstrap don't borrow' tweet, particularly the banks and financial services companies. Small and micro-business policy has been dominated by the financial sector throughout my lifetime.

Tony had spent the previous 12 months doing what he could to help Eileen through her cancer treatment. Eileen was now back at work in the library of Hull University campus in Scarborough, a job she'd loved since 2001.

Tony was 57, the age his father had died, and approaching 58 - all bonus months to Tony. In December 2009, his best man Digby, regarding as the "*best district judge we ever had*" and the only solicitor in Hull to receive a full court eulogy had died - age 57. In August 2010, 'One Saint Jude' Tony's closest friend from his teenage days, and his life mentor, died suddenly. You've guessed it - aged 57.

Tony desperately wanted to fulfil his ambition of writing a psychological thriller. With the agreement of Eileen and Clare and probably, the relief of SFEDI, he was to take a year's sabbatical in Malta and write to his heart's content.

He rented a flat in Sliema, only ten minutes' walk and ferry from the gorgeous capital of Valletta and had the finest year of his life. Apart from two weeks when Eileen and his daughter Sinead visited and a week when his next-door neighbour Bob, a self-employed plasterer, visited he could do exactly as he liked - even cook himself a midnight feast of fish fingers, beans and smash accompanied by a carton of Maltese red wine.

Now to a lot of people this might seem strange, could he really spend an entire year away from his wife and family with only sporadic contact? The answer is most definitely yes! Eileen and Tony have a marriage that is based on mutual trust and understanding. They both have their passions and the things that drive them, for Tony, the opportunity to go away and write was something that Eileen recognised and wholly supported.

I think this is strange, that they lead such independent lives but Tony believes it is the reason why they're still best friends after fifty years of knowing each other. Eileen as an orphan had no choice but to be independent and Tony chose after the death of his father and leaving the family business behind that independence gave him the best chance to excel at whatever he chose to do.

He's proud of the fact that there are never enough hours in the day for either of them; and there's still so much that they individually still want to achieve.

Not that they never come together, after all, they've had three children. When the children were growing up there were two fun-filled holidays each year. One, some years two, holiday would be abroad such as the Canaries, Greek islands and the Algarve. Even today, Tony and Eileen make a weekend of it in different cities during the summer for his marathons and half marathons for Macmillan Cancer Support. When either of them is ill, the other does everything they can to help the recovery of the other.

Tony says they both love a new project and because the project is individual to them, they just get on with it in their own way. Tony believes that Eileen having religion and him not, has meant there is a difference to what they each spend time on with family and friends. They very rarely argue and love life and being creative as much as when they first met. It's just that, even when they're at home together they're nearly always doing different things.

Tony considers that only best friends that are very independent and proud of their differences could have remained together through the ups and downs of their jobs, health, family and Tony's business ventures. They just let each other get on with it and manage the fallout. Sinead, their daughter, shares this independence and exceeds it.

Sinead has travelled the world on her own and worked for charities in tough conditions in many African countries, even returning from Madagascar completely blind. She left school without A levels yet later completed an OU degree and recently an MA in International Development. Yet Tony and Eileen say they often don't know which country she is in. Tony regards Eileen, Clare, Sinead and the late, Jude, as the best of all his friends and regards himself as exceptionally lucky to have so much fun in their company.

Against the picture of non-stop hedonism in Malta there was a tragedy panning out with Clare and Charles. Tony was in weekly, sometimes daily contact with Clare and it was the saddest, toughest time for his best friend. Charles had surgery on a brain tumour not many weeks after Tony arrived in Malta. It was not to be the saviour that they had hoped and in fact the last weeks until his death were mainly horrible for them both. Charles died a few days just after Tony's return to Scarborough and two days after Tony's birthday. Charles was only - you've guessed - 57.

Tony believes the most courageous and finest speech he's ever heard was delivered by Clare about her wonderful, happy, super fit, guitar playing, cyclist, charity fund raising and so caring husband, at a packed Woburn Church at the thanksgiving service.

Clare had arranged the whole celebration of Charles' life to be joyful. Wearing black was not allowed. There was laughter, tears and applause. Clare's speech, remember this is someone who would never speak in public, gave the audience most of the laughter - and the tears. The service finished with Morecambe and Wise singing '*Bring Me Sunshine*', Charles loved them and everyone in the packed congregation knew that the song typified Charles purpose in life - he loved making people happy and never had a mood, unlike me.

It's why he did so much volunteering and raising money for the charities which he actually got involved in.

His concerts with the band he founded (at the prestigious Stables theatre in Milton Keynes) were joyous affairs and all for charity. He made the whole of the hundred-strong Milton Keynes chorale happy every Tuesday, his village happy, his cycling colleagues happy and his motor racing colleagues happy.

Charles went out of his way to help people several times a day and on top of this he had a day a week being front of house, unpaid at Milton Keynes hospital, directing people to where they needed to go. We all know just how frightening hospitals are, whether you're a patient or a visitor and Tony could think of none better than Charles and his smiling, friendly demeanour to help them.

Charles brought sunshine to many thousands of people's lives. He is remembered dearly.

Sadly, around this time, Clare's father died too.

That was the end of the BAB and Clare's involvement in SFEDI. It was the end of their business partnership, but they remain the closest of friends to this day, enjoying theatre, opera, ballet, tennis and walks together. Charles and her father had run the multimillion commercial property business that her father founded, and now Clare would have to run it for the family.

Meanwhile, Tony who was in weekly contact with Nat whilst in Malta knew that SFEDI were accepting contracts which were taking the organisation in the opposite direction to where he'd wanted and had originally created it for. None of his ideas on focusing on recognition and support for start-ups and micro-business owners were acceptable to his co-owners either. The final straw was in accepting massive contracts from Government and Banks to train up business mentors to help start-ups and small business owners, particularly if they'd received a loan from the government or banks.

Tony was all in favour of business mentors being trained but it was not acceptable to him that the only business support a start-up or business owner might get, was from a redundant banker or ex-corporate executive that has never started or run a small business.

In the early years of SFEDI every publicly funded business adviser as well as being assessed as competent needed at least three years small business experience, before they were let loose on vulnerable start-ups and new business owners.

Sadly though, these were the contracts SFEDI was winning and delivering. It seemed to Tony that SFEDI was going backwards in terms of what he'd aspired to achieve with it.

Tony knew that his co-owners were taking the right decisions for SFEDI to be very successful financially and everyone involved to receive good salaries, but there was nothing that interested him in the work it was going to do. On his return from Malta he tried a couple of months of working with Ruth and Nat, as Chief Executive of the IOEE, and then resigned, retaining his co-ownership and shares.

When Tony is unhappy with a situation, he becomes unwell as he internalises the problems and they bring him down, he can also become difficult to work with. He has to work things through in his own mind and also shuts off from those around him. This makes it very hard, especially when you have a close business relationship. Once he has made a decision, there's no going back. To Tony it's a '*fait accompli*', he's worked it through and that's what he's going to do. It's frustrating for those around him but often these decisions are supported on trust. It does create problems when his decisions affect cashflow, I'm sure that anyone in business with a partner can relate to this.

Fortunately, Tony and Clare are very similar in outlook, especially when it comes to morals and how business should be run, this is why they have worked so well for as long as they have. That's not to say that she didn't get worried or annoyed with many of Tony's decisions to walk away coming as a surprise leaving a deficit on work and money for the business. Being practical, Clare would want to have longer to find replacements and ensure staff were protected. Tony lacks pragmatism and perhaps forethought in this situation, because it puts a strain on the family finances and that of those working with him.

Having seen what was happening herself, Clare

supported Tony in his decision to step away, she could understand that how it was being run wasn't how they had envisioned it and could see why Tony would not want his name associated with it anymore in an executive capacity.

In early January 2012 Tina Boden and Tony launched the Enterprise Rockers CIC to make life better for micro-business owners. While Tony had been in Malta, they had been testing how to create a free, informal and virtual community, a network of networks to help business owners to help each other.

They weren't interested in what Government or Banks might or might not do - in the future they envisaged that the best help would be provided by micro-business owners backing and supporting other micro-business owners. Simple as.

Tina and Tony were laughing and shivering on the beach in Scarborough, along with about 30 business owner friends, holding a giant stick of rock. Enterprise Rockers and the #MicroBizMatters movement was born. The world was their lobster.

Q&A Time

Q: 'Put family and friends first', 'Avoid Debt' and 'Cut your Costs' are three of the ten principles behind your 'Happipreneurship' philosophy. Wasn't going to Malta for a year and then saying bye to bye SFEDI costly and risky to your family finances? Some would say it was selfish - wouldn't they?

A: 'Do what you love' is also a principle behind being a Happipreneur. I figured that there would be no other time that I could be so selfish in my life. We could afford that year as I spent very little in Malta. The wine was 1 euro a carton!

Eileen had gotten through her gruelling cancer treatment and was back enjoying work at the university library but we both knew cancer may return and it did but not until I'd returned from Malta.

Ruth, Nat and Sarah didn't really need me at SFEDI anymore and thought my ideas daft really. It was also just like 2004.

I needed to get my mojo back and crazy as it seems I felt so lucky to be alive still I wanted to celebrate that by writing something really good.

Q: Why couldn't you have written at home and used the money for the family?

A: I think that as a writer, business owner and Happipreneur you'll understand. It's the importance of saying 'No' in order to do what you love. I was quite well known in the UK for supporting small and micro-businesses and as the Co-Founder of SFEDI. I also had a lot of unpaid, non-executive positions on boards.

When people asked me to come to support or speak at their small business events, unpaid, I always said Yes, even though it cost me a lot in London.

I used the IBIS at Wembley Stadium for accommodation and used the Institute of Directors as my office for over 30 years. IOD membership is not cheap and neither are their refreshments. IBIS Wembley is the lowest cost, happiest place, I use but would average about £120 for two nights.

I was lucky to have some fab meals at posh places like the East India Club, RAC Club and so forth but I paid my share of buying lunches and dinners too. It was easy to say 'No, I'm in Malta' without causing offence and the money I spent in London each month went to pay for my year in Malta.

I'd been to Malta for 3 or 4-week breaks for a number of years previously so I knew that I could both write and work from Malta. They have free WIFI in all parks and public places. They really care about micro-business owners.

Q: So, looking back what did you get out of a year in Malta - were your expectations met?

A: It exceeded all my expectations. I feel guilty for saying it was the most 'be useful' and happiest year of my life. I'm so lucky and grateful to Eileen and Clare for supporting me.

Q: Why do you feel guilty?

A: Well, I was in weekly, sometimes daily contact with Clare and she was having the worst and most tragic year of her life, while I was soaking up the sun and doing exactly as I pleased. I was also in weekly, sometimes daily contact with Ruth and Nat and I knew that everything I'd wanted to achieve with SFEDI was slipping out of my grasp.

We didn't agree on the future direction or the principles and I knew that by the time I returned the money I hoped I'd get from SFEDI for the rest of my life, I'd put in jeopardy. My family couldn't afford to be without that money so, naturally, I felt guilty. I could see how the dice were loaded.

Eileen came over a couple of times, once at the same time as Sinead and my next-door neighbour, Bob, came over too so I was re-assured that they were managing great without me at home so that was all good.

Q: You were on your own for 48 weeks out of 52 and you'd only lived on your own for 12 weeks in all of the previous 58 years, did you ever feel lonely?

A: Not once. Of course, I thought about family and friends all the time, but I love time on my own to be creative. There were never enough hours in the day but it was a sheer joy.

I really knew how to enjoy myself by the time I went to Malta. Not everyone does bother to learn how they can be the happiest. I learned a lot from Bob Murray.

Q: Who is Bob Murray?

A: When I had my holiday of a lifetime in South Africa, to watch world cup cricket, paid for by Clare and Charles, I met Bob Murray, an ex-university chemistry lecturer. After his wife died, he decided to retire, sell his large house in Nottingham and sell or give to charity most of his possessions.

He got a small flat in Nottingham and ensured his children were OK financially. I still meet Bob and so, he's had nearly 20 years having the time of his life. He's become a great Salsa dancer, feasted on cricket, football, literature, dance, theatre and music and has travelled the world - mainly dancing and walking.

We went on another holiday together, corresponded and he came to Scarborough for the Jazz Festival with Jude from Ipswich and Chris and Verni from Sheffield. He is always happy and always curious.

He's never said it, but I believe the reason he gets so much joy out of every day is not because of positive thinking but because he's always looking for the next 'Wow!' moment.

By the time I went to Malta I was great at finding 'Wow!' moments. It can be the sunshine on the water, watching an old lady catch fish for the cats surrounding her, chocolate ice cream with a glass of wine, chapters of a book, a great workout in the gym, music, a film on video, looking at a Caravaggio painting, street entertainment, choosing fresh, warm bread at 7am and treating yourself to breakfast in your own flat at 7.15am I gorged on 'Wow!' moments in Malta.

Q: What about the business side and especially, trying to improve things for indie business owners in the UK? Had you stopped caring about that?

A: Not at all. As soon as I realised that Ruth, Nat and Sarah weren't on the same page as I was, then Tina, I and Lorraine Allman - author of Enterprising Child - started using social media to start building followers around what we felt were important for micro-business owners, to help each other and be recognised by both the larger business community and the Government.

I didn't stop campaigning while I was in Malta and used social media and Skype for about 4 hours every day. It was a year of test trading whether we could build an informal movement, through social media, to make life better for micro-business owners.

After I got back from Malta it was easy and exciting to see what Tina and I needed to do to found the Enterprise Rockers and the #MicroBizMatters movement. Lorraine supported us greatly through the first few years too.

Q: Your businesses and life seem to have revolved around partnerships with women and never men. Why is that?

A: I think it's called testosterone, Taryn. It's why in the coronavirus pandemic the women leaders won hands down in saving lives, over the male leaders in the world. It's why the financial crash wouldn't have happened if there had been more women leaders in the banks, stock markets and governments. It's why I'd never have been able to survive in my own businesses for thirty years without women partners.

Q: But you're passionate about equality and diversity and now you're suggesting women make better leaders?

A: I wasn't a fan of Margaret Thatcher, Theresa May or Christine Legarde but when it comes to hard work, really knowing the facts, practical application, responsible compassionate leadership and 'economics as if people mattered' decision making then I just find more women I've observed have fit the bill.

A favourite book I haven't mentioned is called 'Power and Greed' by the late Philippe Gigantes. I've even had friends that have been so motivated by the never-ending pursuit of great wealth and trappings of power - status symbols, sex, travel, events and so forth - that they've turned into really erratic and bullying leaders.

Behind the false smiles and motivational mantras is someone who will almost kill to retain power and wealth. They're no longer good on detail but get a macho thrill out of taking unnecessary risks, hiring and firing and justifying their decisions by spurious means

- ‘strategy’, ‘survival of the fittest’, ‘winners and losers’ and ‘it’s only business’.

Q: So, who would you recommend as role model women leaders?

A: All leadership is in context of what you do and who you are leading. It’s often not transferable. Amazingly good woman political leaders like Angela Merkel and Jacinda Ardern are not comparable with great independent business leaders and entrepreneurs like Kanya King CBE.

I’d go for Clare Francis, Jenn Crowther, Taryn Lee Johnston and Tina Boden in the important category of ‘micro-business and family and friends’. Tina and I actually got to meet Sir Alex Ferguson at a posh do at the Royal Festival Hall, when I wrote a LinkedIn article explaining why Tina was a role model leader; shortlisted to a LinkedIn final.

In the public domain in sport, then Serena Williams would be my role model. I think she’s following in the giant footsteps of Billie Jean King and Martina Navratilova - achieving far more than just being a supreme tennis champion.

Q: Why?

A: Firstly, she doesn’t know it yet but she’s a ‘Happipreneur‘. Serena Williams said, *“If you feel good about yourself and what you can do, it changes your whole outlook”*. I think great leaders have to feel great about what they can do.

Serena Williams is, arguably, the greatest woman athlete of all time. She is approaching 40. She plays tennis in an era where most female tennis players peak or suffer burn out by their mid-twenties. Serena Williams has 23 Grand Slam singles title and she has 14 Grand Slam doubles titles, with her sister, Venus.

Serena is already the record-breaking holder of most Grand Slams in the Open Era and has been number one ranked in more years, with more gaps, than any other player. She has earned over $25 million and would continue to be one of the highest-paid athletes in the world even if she was not playing competitively.

Serena has lost 4 Grand Slam finals since returning to tennis after the birth of her daughter, Olympia. She went into January 2020 Australian Open expecting to do well as she had managed to win a tournament just before this Grand Slam had started - her first tournament win for nearly 3 years.

Unfortunately, she was knocked out in the fourth round of the Australian Open by an unseeded player in a performance Serena described as ‘unprofessional’ because of over fifty unforced errors in the match. Yet she didn’t retire from playing competitive tennis.

Why does she continue to play tennis at the highest level? How does she come back from getting beaten by players that weren’t born when she won her first Slam?

Answer: Serena Williams loves playing and winning games of tennis. Yet by her own admission, it was only after the tragedy of the eldest sister - shot dead, serious injuries, a period of depression and a dismal year of performance in 2005, that she felt *she chose tennis* rather than tennis having chosen her.

The greatest leaders absolutely love being great at what they do and constantly pursue excellence. Choosing carefully what you want to devote your focus and skills towards and then choosing carefully the people around you are essential leadership tasks.

In Serena's case family are first in her team, before coaches, fitness trainers and hitting partners. All the people in the team are essential for loving what you do. They're essential for anyone to become a leader who can make a difference.

Q: You had quite the social life when you were younger, have you calmed down now or are you still the same?

A: I do own up to loving nightlife into the early hours, drinking and gambling. I love playing pool and snooker for money or beers. The all-night festivals, love of blues bands and drinking after performing plays and gigs got me into the night-time haunts. Fortunately, my girlfriends liked these places too. I got used to midnight cabarets in clubs at a very early age as it was the only place you could see one of my favourite groups, the Peddlers. Casinos, especially those in major cities with entertainment, are my idea of a great late-night into morning place.

However, as I have a fairly obsessive personality it's not a good idea for me to go into casinos too often and I certainly don't do any online betting. I tried online many years ago but quickly scrambled all my passwords and accounts so I couldn't use them. I'm transfixed by roulette wheels and have never understood why numbers 17 and 32 don't come up every other spin.

I've made it a rule to only go into a casino now when Sinead is with me. Sinead collects any 5s, 10s and ponies and tells us when we have to leave. As Sinead lives in London or is abroad most of the time this limits my casino trips to two or three a year. That is a great relief for my family. All the gambles Clare and I have taken in business I claim total responsibility for, but like from the casino visits, I'm sure I've broken even - gamblers always say that don't they?

Q: For a man with severe dyspraxia, which I know about firsthand, you play some sports to a high level, is there any you just can't do?

A: My dyspraxia has got me banned from some of the best golf courses in the world. This includes Penina Golf course in the Algarve, during an Amway distributor event, Moor Park during a DSA event and Stewart MacArthur's golf club in Northampton. Stewart only lasted three holes before telling me to stop playing. I have this unfortunate habit of hitting the ball sideways which is quite scary for those playing with me and those on other fairways.

"....because from bigness comes impersonality, insensitivity and a lust to concentrate abstract power"

EF Schumacher

X
Showing the world "Why #MicroBizMatters"?

Tony and Tina make a great partnership. Tina has bundles of energy, enthusiasm and is a successful, practical business owner of thirty years standing. Tony is full of crazy ideas, lots of influential contacts and is an impractical business owner of thirty years standing. They share the same values about enterprise, family and life. They are both used to performing in public but most of all, they both want to make a difference.

Tony met Tina in 2009 at an International Enterprise Promotion Conference, at the Harrogate Conference Centre. Tina told Tony why the Conference was rubbish and he informed her that he was the founder and co-director of the very same event!

They hit it off immediately despite the massive age and style difference and rarely seeing each other, even though they both live in Scarborough. They decided that they would do 'something' to make lives better for micro-business owners.

Since they hatched their cunning plans when Tony was on his Sabbatical in Malta, they have never looked back.

Around the time of Start-Up Britain, Tina told Tony that they needed to do something that was more about 'keep going' than start-ups. Tina created the social media pages for Enterprise Rockers and off they went.

They launched their adventures with 4 campaigns: #NotAnSME, #Indie25ER, #PayIn30Days and #MicroBizMatters.

I asked Tina why this is so important to her and she reflected that, having been in business and around business for all of her life, she felt that business owners needed a voice and she wanted to make that happen.

Tina also realised that whilst Tony had already started to make waves and was starting to be recognised, the foundation of their efforts needed more grass roots, someone that was still working in a micro-business and that's where she came in.

Their initial intention was to create a kind of networking group that would have little pockets of people coming together in towns across the country, however, it didn't work out that way.

Tina laughs that it's been a standing joke between them, that whilst she has all the micro-business experience, Tony has the OBE (Old Bugger of Enterprise) and so it's his voice that gets heard, in fact she is often, like Clare, mistaken for his wife or PA!

After creating their virtual, annual #MicroBizMatters Days they dropped the Enterprise Rockers brand in favour of #MicroBizMatters as their brand.

The early years of the free, informal #MicroBizMatters movement were all about generating loads of publicity and getting the support of all the UK networks of micro-business owners. Many of the national, small business membership organisations like FSB, FPB, Enterprise Nation, IAB and IPSE, Tony knew would support them but there are literally thousands of local, regional, sector specific and occupational networks which they had to contact through Twitter, Facebook and LinkedIn.

Tina did some awesome publicity stunts such as her Indie High Street Challenge and Tony worked his famous entrepreneur and press contacts like crazy. He was also lucky enough to pick up two high profile Lifetime Achievement Awards for Enterprise in their first year - from the International Association of Bookkeepers and Start Your Business Magazine.

It's interesting to note that when they started out micro-business was not in anyone's terminology and was one of the reasons that they created the hashtag:

#NotAnSME.

Tony was also recognised on many top influencers on entrepreneurship rankings, such as Smith and Williamson and was well known in the Enterprise Agency movement and has been a Director of Yorkshire in Business since 2005. Though he'd left SFEDI he was still getting invited to the big enterprise events and some people hated what he and Tina were trying to do - to many it was 'not serious' but others loved it. Once they'd got the networks and press support it was easy to reach hundreds of thousands of micro-business owners through social media and the hashtags #MicroBizMatters and #PayIn30Days stood out as their top two campaigns. Both Tina and Tony realised that everything that they were doing was to raise awareness and support of micro-businesses and so they decided that it needed to have just the one heart.

They needed an annual focal point for their campaigning and recognition of micro-business owners, and they needed to show the world that micro-business owners will and do help each other. The idea may have come off the back of the UK Small Business Saturday launch on 6th December 2014, Tina was an ambassador for them.

In November 2014 Tony did a 'secret' video, which he put out on YouTube to say they were going to run a virtual #MicroBizMatters Day to start 2015. The aim was for indie business owners giving a small amount of time to help each other and it would feature entrepreneur guests online. It was test trading in action. They weren't sure it would come off at all and Tina rightly wasn't going to cancel her family skiing holiday.

This is where a wonderful man called Paul Lancaster came into the #MicroBizMatters story. He was working at Sage at the time, he knew both Tina and Tony and he made the first #MicroBizMatters Day (always on the second Friday of the year) happen.

The original concept was no speeches just interviews with real, authentic business owners, some of them famous, but having to answer Tony's questions so that they gave real help to other business owners in similar sectors to the people being interviewed. After all, it's a day about helping each other.

Because they made #MicroBizMatters Day fairly zany and definitely fun there was no place for big egos and so the advice they always give is amazingly useful.

There was no sponsorship, as in money, Tony and Tina have pretty much co-funded #MicroBizMatters from the beginning, but Paul arranged for Sage's friends at Google for Work to give them some space at their London HQ and Paul would take his laptop and sort out connecting with the world on Google hangouts.

All Tony and Tina needed to do was to get enough interesting guests from around the world to chat to online and some of them to come to the 'studio' at Google for Work. Remember the idea of the day was to encourage hundreds of thousands of business owners to give a little time to help each other.

It happened and it was a massive success, Tina joined in from her ski resort in France (she tells me that she arrived the day before not even knowing if her chalet had WIFI, you can see the prelude videos the night before have her on the balcony bundled up in her coat whilst she tries to ensure she can get connected), Tony and Paul made the studio guests welcome and happy - Charlie Mullins OBE, Founder of Pimlico Plumbers and the Mercury and MOBO award winning rapper, Sway, were the definite stars. An online audience of millions was reached.

Tina recalls that Charlie Mullins had never met Tony up to this point and Tina watching from France recalls the completely shocked look on his face as he walked into a small room to see Tony and a laptop.

Speaking to Paul, he says that running the live streaming for that day will always stay with him. Watching Tony in Google glasses with a hand puppet whilst interviewing Sway, is not a memory easily forgotten! Sway had no idea what he was getting into but went with it, Paul had told him beforehand not to worry and just to go with the flow. I think that's one of the gifts that Tony has, the ability to make you feel totally at ease whilst doing something that takes you out of your comfort zone. There is an amazing video online that you can watch of a bemused Sway interview by a crazed looking man whose voice was on the way out.

Tina laughs and says that their business model was terrible, that whilst they had location support, they had nothing else, Tony even had to send out for croissants on the day just so people could eat. There was no fancy lunch - not even in Google HQ (maybe all the money went on the ball pit??!).

It was Tony's sheer determination that saw the likes of Charlie Mullins and Tim Campbell get involved.

Every January since there has been a #MicroBizMatters Day and Charlie Mullins OBE became their #MicroBizMatters Tsar and Kanya King CBE became their #MicroBizMatters inspiration. Many famous entrepreneurs, featured in the Hall of Fame at the back of the book, have attended the main event which is livestreamed to the massive online audience on Facebook and YouTube.

The venues have been:-

2015 - Google at work, London;

2016 - Portobello Business Centre, (in a broom cupboard!) London; Tina recalls this one being a challenge as it was roasting hot and they were all practically sitting on each other's laps so that they could fit in the MacBook screen.

2017 - Pimlico Plumbers, London; - This year it snowed and many of their guests couldn't make it.

2018 - XYZ Building Manchester;

2019 - Guild Hall, Hull; I went to this one and it was full on from start to finish. Tony always ends the day on humour and this year if I recall there was something to do with singing vegetables.

2020 - EKM, Preston; This year was very different and not the usual structure but was a brilliant day.

2021- Will be Yorkshire in Business, Scarborough.

The reason the annual #MicroBizMatters Day, always the second Friday of the New Year, started on January 9th January is because that's Tina's birthday. She told me that she thinks it's a "*crap*" day for a birthday as no one wants to celebrate and so at least this way she gets a little bit of a party and can spend it surrounded by lovely people.

The events are now sponsored although only the

bare minimum. This has been a theme throughout, it goes against their ethos to get banks involved for funding, any money that have received has been ploughed straight back into the event, often seeing them pay the last of the days costs out of their own pocket.

From day one it's been quirky, fun and made as simple as possible. I think the idea being that business owners can dip in and out and also see just what you can achieve when you have very little. It's a shame really that because the event has such little funding, they have never been able to get all of their footage edited and put together, I imagine that there are some absolute gems of humour and incredible pearls of wisdom, sitting in a file somewhere.

Tina and Tony have always paid for their time, attending Houses of Commons for instance to make sure micro-business owners have their voices heard, this has come out of their pockets. Any sponsorship they had meant greater costs, for instance screens to advertise the names of the sponsors so it always meant sacrifices elsewhere.

Over the years they have reached millions of business owners. Tina says that the mix between real people and business owners coming together is what makes it so important. Whilst Tina readily admits that there are more and more people trying to pick up the baton of micro-business support, they're not all doing it from the grass roots level which is key to making it better understood. It's real people helping real people.

It's hard to imagine that Tony has only known Tina,

for about ten years but in that time, they have such a strong relationship. In that time, Tina has set up and run four businesses or new income streams to fit in with lifestyle she wants for herself, family, friends and the many charities she supports. Like Tony, some of her businesses have had employees but she now prefers the flexibility of using freelancers to help her.

Two years ago, she turned her hospitality skills and knowledge into a 'B&B Keeper' service. Her service allows the owner of a small hotel or Bed & Breakfast to take a break. Tina will do everything from breakfasts to reception to marketing. It is a business based on referral, brilliant service and trust. Would you let your house and business be occupied and run by a stranger?

Tina is usually booked up for the 'B&B Keeper' for at least twelve months in advance. However, the Coronavirus brought that to a halt. This is where the years of experience make a difference. Despite having a successful business, Tina has kept on with other income streams such as her speaking engagements, coaching and family businesses. Now more than ever Tina, is determined to make a difference to micro-business owners and is pulling out all of the stops to make a platform for business owners to get help.

Up until three months ago, Tina had a superb and happy business life. Now, like with so many other business owners, she's had to pick herself back up and figure out what to do next. Not only has she done this, but she's put others first and made it her mission to get heard. What an achievement? Many experts, governments, banks, academics and others wouldn't give this 'lifestyle' business a hope in hell of succeeding.

Like Tony, Tina has been starting and running her own businesses for thirty years. That's a lot of ups and downs. To repeat Schumacher again "*an ounce of practice is worth a ton of theory*". If you want to know how to start and run a business and be happy running it then ask another business owner who understands your customers.

It's been very draining for them both, but the chances of them stopping, I feel right now, are pretty slim. One of Tina's frustrations is that it doesn't matter how much she knows or how long she's been in business, people in power still don't want to listen and she feels that could be the case no matter how loud she shouts or how high she raises her head above the parapet.

Tony is very proud of his association with Charles Cracknell, Mike, Graham and all the team in youth enterprise at Hull City Council because he's very proud of his home city. He attends their Global Entrepreneurship Week each year and is Patron of the John Cracknell Youth Enterprise Bank. For a few years he toured with his Micro is Magic one-hour show and he was delighted that he was asked to do it in Hull and I enjoyed it too. There is a sense of being right at the heart of it at these events. You can see Tony's passion and his absolute joy at seeing new entrepreneurs shed their fears and pitch their ideas. Having watched these new faces shine at the event I can understand why Tony is proud to be associated with the event.

The success of Yorkshire in Business in Scarborough, which he is Co-Chair of and is the venue of the 2021 #MicroBizMatters Day, is his proudest achievement. He seriously believes that if the Government was interested in finding out how to improve start-up survival and growth rates that they only have to come and see Jenn Crowther, the CEO of Yorkshire in Business and Charles Cracknell who heads up Hull City Council's Youth Enterprise and Micro-business support and founded the John Cracknell Youth Enterprise Bank.

Both Jenn and Charles are multiple national award winners so it's not just Tony saying this.

They have totally succeeded in getting micro-business owners deserved recognition and helped level the playing field too.

I spoke to Jenn and asked her what it was like working with Tony and why she felt that Yorkshire in Business was so successful, she told me

"I have worked for the Enterprise Agency as long as Tony has been a director. I initially didn't know what he did but in 2015 I approached him and told him that the agency was dying a death, that if we didn't do something to change it, we weren't going to last. At the time I didn't lead the organisation, in fact I'd just come back off maternity leave, but I'd worked there for ten years and I knew that Tony "got it" and wanted us to be there.

To be honest I thought he'd tell me 'on your bike, you're talking rubbish' but he asked me to tell him more. I thought that it was amazing how approachable he was, he was so open to having a discussion with someone he'd really only seen in passing in the office. I actually thought it was above my station to be saying anything! Tony opened up to me, what he thought the future of enterprise support should be and the fact that being reliant on government funding just meant the projects achieve a little bit until the funding runs out, whereas really it's about providing a sustainable service and being invested in the local community. I was over the moon to see that we had the same passions for it.

He worked with me and after a time the other directors to launch Yorkshire in Business. Over the last five years Tony has been my mentor in turning what a traditional enterprise agency was into what we feel is what microbusinesses actually need. It's about providing a full wraparound support, we provide peer-peer support using people who have experience of running a business working with others to help them build their business and to create more of a community.

We do still deliver on government funding but our reason for this is that we can still control and oversee what support is given and make sure that it's done properly.

The advice that people are given needs to be practical, you can only give that advice when you've lived it yourself.

We also realised that each area nationally has different issues, so the advice for businesses may differ. If you're locally based, community based then you're in the heart of it and know what the struggles are for your region.

We're proud to have created a model that can be utilised in other areas across the country, one that can meet the needs of that region specifically, rather than just be a national umbrella organisation.

We want to create an enterprise that will help make business owners stronger in their areas.

Tony is fantastic at holding me to account and making sure that I move forward.

Tony has so many ideas and knows what businesses need. He's always ten years ahead of everything else, he knows what needs to be there for the future and is passionate about creating an organisation that is sustainable for after he's no longer available to do what he's doing.

All he does is give his time for others and is such a pillar of support. He has such confidence in our abilities which makes us feel we can succeed. I know that he's doing everything he can now to make sure that we're secure in the legacy he has created."

It's really clear that Tony has left his mark on Yorkshire and that with all the hard work that is going into both Yorkshire in Business and Youth Enterprise, microbusiness owners in this region have support that they can trust.

Q&A Time

Q: Let's talk about campaigning for start-ups and micro-business owners. You've managed to nationally campaign continuously despite moving to Scarborough in September 2000. Why have you carried on despite the cost, time and failures?

A: If Labour had won either the 2017 or 2019 General Elections I would have stopped because all my campaigns and most of my recommendations were in their manifestos or were being put forward by the then, Shadow Small Business Minister, Bill Esterson.

For the first ten years, what I was campaigning for was part of the reason I founded SFEDI and for this last ten years was part of the reason I co-founded #MicroBizMatters with Tina.

Q: Clare said some of the setbacks put you in darker moods?

A: That was a lot of years ago. Some of the setbacks and the costs I've incurred did get me down, particularly the recommendations on reducing the cost of regulatory compliance not being accepted.

Sarah Anderson CBE, who is brilliant, led that review. A few years earlier just about every recommendation we'd made to Government on the Council for Excellence in Management and Leadership, Small Firms Group, which Sarah had chaired, had been accepted. I had high hopes but none were implemented. It would have made so much difference to new business owners to not get bogged down in bureaucracy and encouraged them to take on that first employee.

The Ethnic Minority Business Task Force didn't get me down it just made me angry and ashamed. It was good as it spurred me on to leave SFEDI and form the #MicroBizMatters movement with Tina.

Q: Did you hope to achieve with Enterprise Rockers CIC and #MicroBizMatters what Ruth and Nat didn't want you to do at SFEDI?

A: Partly, in that, I wanted to do something really useful to help micro-business owners survive and thrive. I also knew that my contact network of all the small business membership organisations, trade associations, enterprise agencies, accountancy bodies and so forth would be essential to achieving anything on a UK wide basis.

But the difference was that the SFEDI I founded was a standards-setting, skills and accreditation body and I wanted through the membership bodies and trade associations to create a nationally recognised certificate and a logo that would show all their customers, suppliers and, even banks, insurers and government that they met the highest standards of good business practice.

The assessment against the standards would be online and they could apply for the certification after 3 years of trading. They wouldn't need to attend any new training or go through loads of hoops, they'd just need to answer some questions online and have a one-hour skype interview.

I'd learned about the power of recognition against national standards, not just through SFEDI but from the Sales Qualifications Board we founded and then working with the guilds in the meat industry and, lastly, being Investors in People. Small Business Champion.

I get fed up with small and micro-business owners being patronised in the UK - many are providing higher levels of quality, people management, fair pay, outstanding customer service and so forth, than the large companies and big brands which get all the Government support. All the small business membership organisations and trade associations would be proud to promote to the public the benefit of working with, working for and buying from these accredited small and micro-businesses.

Q: What was different about what you were going to do with Tina?

A: Enterprise Rockers and the #MicroBizMatters movement was also going to be about recognition but it was going to be informal, free and about helping each other to survive and thrive.

Tina and I were also willing to put our heads above the parapet and campaign on behalf of micro-business owners - SFEDI would never do that as it would mean the loss of government contracts as well as big companies and bank sponsorship. Small business membership organisations are in the same boat as SFEDI - they need to be nice to the big boys.

They'll be a 'critical friend' and they'll lobby gently on behalf of their members, but they can't afford to be thrown overboard. Tina and I were willing to say what micro-business owners and their membership organisations couldn't say.

Q: What was first on your list of things to do?

A: Put 'micro' - 0 to 9 employees - on the map and stop them being confused with SMEs. (10 to 249 employees). 95% of business are micro and operate in a totally different way from businesses with employed managers in them. They get a really bad deal from Government, the media, lenders, insurers and are invariably bullied by Big Business and Institutions. The first step in levelling the playing field was to get 'micro-business' understood.

I'll leave you to judge but take a look today at the number of times you see 'micro-business' in the media, social media and talked about in local, regional and national government.

There were hardly any mentions of micro in 2010 when Tina and I started plotting. It was all 'SMEs' which the media, conveniently for the Government turned into 'small businesses'.

#NotAnSME #MicroBizMatters, #PayIn30Days and

#Indie25ER are all reasonably well known now. Not bad for two people with no money battling the mega-rich powers that be.

Q: So how do you go about this David and Goliath thing?

A: The first rule that I learned in the SFEDI years is to let the people with the money and the power claim it was their idea. There's no point in expecting anyone to do anything out of the goodness of their heart or because they want to support Tina or me.

Remember those St George‘s Library, Windsor Castle and Council for Excellence in Management Leadership days when I was at the top of my form. It seemed that every month there'd be a Government announcement giving funding for one of my ideas but there'd be no mention of me and very rarely would my businesses see any of the funding.

No Government Minister, Professional Body or Membership Organisation will ever say 'Tony Robinson had a great idea to increase take-up of apprentices by small businesses'. They'll claim it was their idea, their campaign and that's fine. The important thing is that the business owner benefits.

Q: You spent all March, April and May 2020 campaigning to get better support from the Government to micro-business owners in the coronavirus crisis. How do you go about it?

A: The first thing is to free up the time to campaign. It takes loads of time to relentlessly chip away at my contact network, So I told everyone asking me to do anything - podcasts, webinars, Skype and Zoom calls, even interviews that until there was a better deal for micro-business owners, I'd be unavailable.

I'd met with the Small Business Commissioner in Birmingham in early March, so I had a fairly clear idea which of my contacts were most likely to influence Government on support for indie business owners.

You have to remember Treasury rules small business

support policy in the UK so even if you influence the Small Business Commissioner who reports to the Small Business Minister you still have to influence senior civil servants and special advisers that have the ear of the Chancellor.

Before the Government put together a package of support I put my ideas to a lot of influencers and I put these ideas on social media too. I use all the platforms but concentrate mostly on my 20,000 followers on twitter and 3,400 contacts on LinkedIn.

The day before the Government announcement of support, the Commons committee recommendation looked pretty much as I expected. I hadn't been able to get any traction on free broadband and slashing utility costs but the income support package looked OK.

Q. But you felt it all went wrong - did it?

A: Yes. The Chancellor's announcements which, stupidly, were welcomed by the small business membership organisations and all the pundits, were a let-down. I realised there was an almighty battle ahead to get support for about two and a half million business owners that were forgotten - deliberately.

June was also too late for income support to come through.

The government know that the majority of the 5 million self-employed are only ever a month away from serious problems with debt. That the income support was backdated is no consolation, they have to borrow or more likely max their credit cards again.

Then it's a matter of me influencing individuals in organisations the Government might listen to. Anything they do gives us a chance - petitions, letters, blogs, press articles, tweets, retweet my tweets - absolutely anything. We're also fighting the banks, investors and lenders of all descriptions.

High growth start-ups got an extra £1.3 billion in support which sounds good news and the press reported it as help for struggling start-ups but it is appropriate for very few. I supported that campaign as I support everything for start-ups but it shouldn't have been a priority. To get the matched with investment support a company must have raised at least £250,000 in private investment - not your usual micro-business.

Q. What about petitions?

A: I signed at least 7 petitions that I thought stood a chance of getting enough signatures and I promoted these. I even did videos in support of petitions.

Any time the Small Business Minister or Small Business Commissioner was doing a virtual forum I tried to get to someone that would be on it with a question or a point.

I do as much amplifying as proposing and just hope that my contacts at the Small Business Membership organisations and Accountancy Bodies realise, they're letting down their members if they don't campaign too. I have some good national media contacts that pick up on my posts and articles.

Most of what I do is unseen and as I'm past my sell-by

date with Government and I'm not representing a reputable body then I rarely get asked by Government to input directly.

One person's input won't achieve anything - the object of my campaigning is to get the same message from a number of influential bodies and media, including using petitions, to Government.

I'm quite good at campaigning now and have a quiet celebration when I hear someone using my words. Often nowadays they use Tina and my hashtags which is a compliment too.

Q: You're trying to build a Small is Beautiful Roll of Honour so that more companies, including large ones, are seen to be publicly backing Schumacher's values. How's that going?

A: It's going well. There are many charters and codes, like the prompt payment code, but they're not really independent as they're created by the financial sector or Government - same thing. I know they're not enterprise friendly when they allow 60 days payment terms - outrageous. Schumacher would certainly have supported all six of the values in the Small is Beautiful Roll of Honour:

1. #PayIn30Days ALL suppliers ALL the time
2. Promoting equality and diversity
3. A fair day's pay for a fair day's work
4. Protecting our environment and communities
5. Unlimited growth is pathological

6. Small can make a difference and should be supported.

Some people are surprised about 4 and 5. "*What's the environment got to do with entrepreneurship and small-scale enterprise?*" "*What's wrong with the pursuit of unlimited growth to satisfy shareholders and hedge funds?*" Schumacher was ahead of his time. '*Small is Beautiful*' is as much about how large-scale enterprise destroys our planet and communities, as much as it is about why small is beautiful.

Nearly 50 years after Schumacher linked 4 and 5 above, some countries - not the USA and UK - and even some cities have now linked the pursuit of unlimited growth with the climate emergency. For example, Barcelona in January 2020 has stated: Barcelona has declared a climate emergency that gets straight to the point: "*The current economic model is based on endless growth, consumption and a permanent race for profit. This economic system threatens the ecological balance of our planet and has multiplied inequalities*."

Q: You and Tina say that #MicroBizMatters is not political and I know you have different views so why do you both put your heads above the parapet and criticise Government so often?

A: We do it because most micro-business owners can't stand up to the bullies - it's commercial suicide. So, we do it because they can't. We know we're doing the right thing because they thank us.

One entrepreneur who urged me to put my head above the parapet and reveal the truths about being your own boss was Stefan Topfer. Sadly, Stefan is no longer with us. Stefan was a German Anglophile who while a student in London set up an internet service provider business which he sold for many millions.

He was the only successful .com multi-millionaire that I got to know well. He was a serial entrepreneur and founded other companies, including WinWeb and he gave me a monthly column on his Small Business Blog which was read by many thousands of business owners. He loved my mythical character, Leonora Soculitherz, who starred in my satirical blogs and books. He was living proof that the pursuit of wealth is not as important as the pursuit of happiness and loyalty to family and friends.

Stefan gave me the courage to try and cut through the myths and spin on entrepreneurship and continue to back micro-business owners while the rest of the UK focused on 'high growth', 'scale-ups' and 'SMEs'. He was a massive confidence boost for Tina and I. Sadly, at the first #MicroBizMatters Day he thought Sage and Google were sponsoring us and thought I'd sold out. I couldn't keep going if it wasn't for the support of high profile successful entrepreneurs like Stefan.

Q: You always say that what it takes to succeed in business hasn't changed much over the centuries, only the environment and the technology. Is that the same for all sizes of business?

A: Yes, it is. Big business has complicated it - it's why micro-business is more likely to survive a pandemic without any bailouts. As Schumacher said "*Any intelligent fool can make things bigger, more complex and more violent. It takes a touch of genius - and a bit of* *courage - to move in the opposite direction.*"

Before we started in business the 3 million bestselling and most influential business book was '*In Search of Excellence*' by Peters and Waterman (published 1982). It's an all-time fave of mine and I've even got the videos. I still use most of the learning today and I've had the occasional tweet from Tom Peters.

Not all the 'excellent' big businesses featured are still around. In my opinion. critics that say many of the 60 or so businesses featured in the book were not 'excellent' miss the point. Through their research Peters and Waterman found several factors that would greatly increase the chances of these large organisations continuing to succeed. Being customer-centric; sticking to what you know well and are really good at and 'simple form, lean staff' are all concepts entrepreneurs believe in today. The point is these weren't commonly held views before 'In Search of Excellence'.

Drucker and other gurus of management and leadership development seemed to relish the top-down, command and control structures which often do not nurture enterprising people.

'In Search of Excellence' found by its own research of best practice that autonomy and entrepreneurship could be achieved by breaking the corporation down into small companies and encouraging them to think independently and competitively. In other words, 'Small is Beautiful'.

Q: You and Tina have never looked for Government or Bank funding, support or sponsorship for #MicroBizMatters - why is that?

A: There's a BBC documentary called Hyper-normalisation which tells you all about the way Government and Banks create their own reality to control the population, including small and micro-business owners. Tina and I need to be independent of them. It's like the Business Opportunity Industry the majority of the population don't realise how their minds are controlled by these powerful Establishment forces. I blame Edward Bernays. In the USA and the UK, the Government and the banks are there to make the rich richer and if that means, as it always does, that the poor get poorer so be it.

Q: Who is Edward Bernays?

A: Edward Bernays is the father of Public Relations. He established it as a key marketing discipline for governments, presidential candidates, large corporations, institutions and trade bodies. He first came to prominence in the mid-1920s by persuading American citizens to join the military and enter World War 1. This was not a popular idea in America as most had recently left Europe.

Bernays's 'Make the world safe for democracy' campaign has been used by every American president, since President Woodrow Wilson adopted it, to justify war having a higher purpose.

His famous book of 1928 'Propaganda' makes the case for 'psychological warfare' or 'the engineering of consent'. He later renamed 'psychological warfare' to the more palatable, 'public relations' and stated, 'the conscious and intelligent manipulation of the organised habits and opinions of the masses is an important element in a democratic society.'

He predates Orwell and many others in saying *"Our minds are moulded largely by men we have never heard of"*. Who is pulling Dominic Cummings and Boris Johnson's strings?

"It is a case of the bland leading the blind"

EF Schumacher

XI
The Business Opportunity Industry

"If it looks too good to be true, it probably is"

Tony coined the term 'the business opportunity industry' thirty years ago. It doesn't exist as a recognised business sector and there are many powerful, self-regulating trade associations in the UK which object to lumping them all together. What all the organisations, high profile speakers and celebrities in the business opportunity industry want is for start-ups to buy into their formats and formulas for running a business of your own.

Rather than set up your own business from scratch why not copy a proven, successful business model or programme instead? It's a persuasive and usually, winning argument, as shown by the hundreds of thousands flocking to #startup shows, business exhibitions, conferences and arenas each year looking for a ready-made business opportunity.

Tony and I both loathe and despise the money machine that is regurgitated 'guru speak' charged at a phenomenally obscene amount of money.

We can't prevent most people believing popular sayings about enterprise and entrepreneurship. These sayings have gone down into history as fact and are now ingrained. The saying Tony hates the most is:

"*You are the average of the 5 people you associate most with*".

This sounds right and there's always some truth in a fiction. Implied in this motivational quote is that you shouldn't associate with poor people, 'losers', and 'negative people'. Instead, choose and only associate with wealthy, successful and positive 'winners'.

The saying, and there are many variations of it, has its origins in the of 'law of attraction' writers, who promote how to get rich through their books, talks, academies and business opportunities, including MLM.

The fact is that we haven't found one successful entrepreneur that Tony has interviewed, that has discarded their best friends and family members and chosen wealthy successful, positive entrepreneurs to spend their time with. Yet sadly, we have met many debt ridden and depressed MLM leaders who have tried to follow this advice. They've left their past network of family and friends behind and now only associate with richer, more successful MLM leaders and are faking it until they make it with the trappings of success - car, house and spouse.

The superstar 'So you want to be a millionaire?' line up of the last 120 years of William Wattles, Napoleon Hill, Robert Schuller (Minister), Norman Vincent Peale (Donald Trump's Minister), Jim Rohn, Tony Robbins and Rhonda Byrne (the Secret) want you to-believe these 'law of attraction', 'secrets of success'.

They repeated the truth, in a slightly different way, from their predecessor and probably believe it themselves. It makes them money.

Tony much prefers the essential truth and cracking tip for business owners from Tina Boden. It is:

"*Don't work with tossers*".

It doesn't mean discarding friends and family but does mean getting rid of employees, suppliers and customers that make you unhappy. After all, freedom to choose who we work with is the main reason we start our own businesses.

As the fabulous JK Rowling recently retweeted about how untruths become truths: "*...if a patent forgery... is believed by so many people, the task of the historian is no longer to discover a forgery. The forgery is being believed. This fact is more important than the circumstance that it is a forgery." Hannah Arendt, the Origins of Totalitarianism*

With the help of observations of three famous entrepreneurs Tony has had the pleasure of knowing, he explained why he thinks it is better, for most people, to start their own business from scratch rather than buy into a ready-made business format or programme.

He was reminded of the vulnerability of those looking for a business of their own when watching two recent BBC documentaries, *"Hun this could be your opportunity to get rich' and 'Ellie Undercover on Multi-Level Marketing'* exposing the damage, financial and mental, that multi-level marketing can cause.

These documentaries showed the uplines

(independent distributors/business owners) of these large American Corporations, usually with supplements, weight loss and cosmetics product lines, seemingly targeting young, stay at home, Mums with a 'business of their own'.

Mumsnet has banned *MLM* adverts. In the documentaries some very large, global and glossy MLM companies such as *Forever Living*, *Valentus* plus the Utah based companies, *Nu Skin* and *Younique* were mentioned.

The one he disliked the most is *Herbalife* and he wondered if it wasn't mentioned because it is colossal and hugely influential in establishment circles, Herbalife is the second largest MLM company in the world. Herbalife is on the shirts of top football teams around the world and is supported by A-list celebrities and all the greatest American, motivational speakers including the late *Jim Rohn*. None of this, in my opinion, means Herbalife sells great business opportunities.

Tony makes it clear that he is a fan of much of the carefully self-regulated, franchise industry ($552 billion worldwide providing 9.1 million jobs). The power of the brand (e.g. Subway, Prontaprint and Recognition Express) with the relative lack of risk of failure does lead to a regular, almost guaranteed, income from the format. Franchise organisations make it clear that, like any business, it'll take at least 3 years hard work to get the income level you need. Although the new owner investment can be high in the top end franchises like McDonald's (est. min. £200,000) we've never heard of a McDonald's franchise failing - have you?

The concern with franchises is that many people with the same start-up investment and the right help around them can build better and more fulfilling businesses which they can adapt quickly to other opportunities which arise, changing market needs and personal circumstances. Many franchise owners, after a few years running their businesses, get disappointed with the return from their investment of time and money. Rather than being proud and happy in a business of their own, they feel as if they've just swapped one job for another.

There are many well-known and trusted brands among direct selling companies, even with an MLM structure. Some are great if it's a side hustle and you primarily get involved to sell the products and make an extra part-time income. I've never heard complaints about *Avon*, *Oriflame* or *Ann Summers* overpromising on the business opportunity - have you? Many direct selling companies are a good place to learn how to sell and earn a little extra income - just don't be sucked into the full time, a business of your own entrapment.

I mentioned Mike Winnet earlier in the book, he's a self-proclaimed "*Anti-motivational Speaker*" and is dedicated to getting the word out about "Contrapreneurs". These are the people creating the 'FREE' events, your chance to meet the top names in marketing, pay per click, motivational speaking and to learn how to change your life.

You only have to watch one of Mike's YouTube

videos to see how he exposes the 'Guru' events, highlighting the ploys used to get you there, get you doing as you're told, all ready for the moment that they ask you to put your hand in your pocket. Suddenly you're walking out of the room having shelled out hundreds or in some cases thousands of pounds for something you had no intention of buying when you went in. Their language is horrifyingly brilliant.

I chatted to Mike recently, he was very candid about what he'd wanted from life and how he was determined to get there. Mike knew that he wanted to build a company, one that he could sell and make a profit. He had a three-year timescale and a figure in his head that he wanted to sell for, he was smart and worked for what he thought was achievable. Prior to starting up his company though, he worked in start-ups for six years, he learned his craft and relied on the experience of his bosses as mentors.

Of being in a start-up he says:

"*There is a risk involved, you may work for less money and the company may not be secure or may have a high chance of failure, but I put myself through six years of learning before I even felt confident enough to start out on my own and I think that business owners need to realise that; realise that you have to have some experience in business before you can really succeed.*"

We talked about start-up funding and Mike says:

"*There are two ways, I had originally intended to work on the business part time until it could eventually replace my salary, however in the end I stripped back everything, cut all of my expenses and outgoings until I had six months' salary in the bank. This meant that I could have a real go at it, not make rushed decisions as I knew I had the time to build the business right."*

Mike's suggestion, when it comes to finding advice is either do as he did and work in the industry you want to be in or, if you're interested in something like investing, read a book by someone such as Warren Buffett, he says:

"*There are so many books out there, good books, unfortunately learning that way that takes time and effort and people want to be spoon fed, they go looking for a short cut. If this is your mindset then you're probably not going to be successful, you have to be able to see that you're not going to be a millionaire in ninety or hundred and twenty days and be sceptical of anyone who is suggesting that. The people that are genuinely successful now have put in years and years of hard work; they've had failures as well as successes. These are the people that understand business and the ones to learn from.*"

Talking about business mentors, a subject as you know, close to Tony's heart, Mike is adamant about the kind of business mentor you actually need. He has a video online about this, how many of the 'mentors' you see selling to a room are following someone else's script and have probably only been in business themselves six months. These are not the people you want supporting you when you start out.

Mike goes on to tell me "*I have two people that saw something in me, they made me believe I could go on to do more than I was doing at the time; one was in fact my boss. This was in 2008 and he told me I should go on and run my own business even though I was making money for him in his! I spoke to him a lot whilst I was in my early days, every six months I would take him out for a meal, and we would sit down to chat. I would tell him my ideas, the problems I had, and he gave me real advice as he was a 'time served' businessman.*"

I really like that expression 'time served'; it encapsulates everything we've been saying about mentors and the importance of working without someone who has walked through the pitfalls and traps and come out the other side.

Mike goes on to tell me how important it's been for him to have someone as a sounding board, more importantly though, having an altruistic mentor, someone who is there genuinely for you, because they want to help you, not because you're paying them or because they want to use your successes as their soundbites. I seriously urge you to look up Mike before you ever attend another conference. The flash car they are in front of is hired for the week, the income they say they earn has no costs of business deducted.

Some are so heavily in debt they're only 4 weeks away from bankruptcy. Mike has invested a great deal of time and money going out of his way to expose some of the most popular and most ridiculous claims he's seen on the internet, those set out to fool vulnerable people. He has actually tested out the claims and speaks from experience, so that you don't fall foul of them.

Watch **"The Contrepreneur Formula"** on YouTube. Mike has gone into great detail to show you exactly how these events word, the language used and fakery behind them.

All his films on the scams are great but this is beautifully put together and it explains clearly how it's done through the big motivational 'change your life' speaker events.

It's the same process that leading distributors in MLM use to recruit and sell their non-company motivational products, bootcamps, mastermind groups and events.

A recession, a financial crash, a national disaster or a pandemic are ideal. Desperate people who need morecash fast.

We saw loads of referrals happening from very famous people about how they are getting involved in ways to make passive income or semi-passive income during lockdown.

This is nearly always MLM in some way or another but will be with a digital or virtual 'product' or membership. It will be called referral marketing or networking of some kind.

One of the biggest problems with this industry, in both mine and Tony's opinion, is that once someone's been conned, they're too embarrassed to tell people and so the events keep happening. No one wants to admit that they've lost thousands of pounds following a formula 'guaranteed to succeed' only to fail. There was a BBC documentary on Samuel Leeds and an investigation into the Property Investors, which had led to Danny Butcher taking his own life. This is available to watch on YouTube. It shows just how easy it is to get further and further into debt, believing that your "*opportunity to make it big*" it just about to happen. Again, if you have the time, watch Mike's interview with Samuel Leeds.

These events are happening month after month, you will most likely have seen them or may even have been to them, I know I have. It takes a cool head not to be swept away by the hype and not to buy into the "*only available now*" and "*we only have a few places*" offers shovelled out.

It's one of those topics that makes me climb up onto my soapbox and in fact one of the things that Tony and I talk about at length. Between us, we've done an awful lot of research, we've attended events, watched videos and read the blogs and at no point are we convinced by the so called 'Gurus' that are making an obscene amount of money. Tony Robbins said, "*I am not your guru*" and really you should listen to him, that's the only endorsement you'll get in this book to follow his advice!

If you feel you need support, then speak to someone who has been where you are now, they'll most likely give you the best advice you can get and they'll give it you for free. If you don't have anyone to ask or you're really desperate for pearls of 'Guru' wisdom, buy a book, it won't break the bank nor will it get you so hyped and brainwashed that you'll part with your hard-earned cash or worse make you get your credit card out…

That's not to say that there aren't good motivational speakers and business leaders, someone else I mentioned previously is Brad Burton. Brad is "*The UK's #1 Motivational Business Speaker*" a title that Brad himself decided he wanted to be and so set about making it happen. Few of you may be surprised to see Tony supporting a motivational speaker but his relationship with Brad is one based on mutual trust and respect.

Now Brad can be a difficult man to track down but as soon as he heard about Tony's book, he was more than happy to have a chat with me. He's always delightfully down to earth and speaks freely. Brad will tell you that he was in debt when he started out and that he worked as a pizza delivery man whilst building up 4N. If you've never networked before then you may find 4N is a good place to start. I was a member for about 8 years when I started out and still have some fantastic business contacts and friends from those days. It's a relaxed vibe that welcomes you over a decent breakfast.

In the beginning though, times were hard for Brad, but as Tony says, you work hard, side hustle and get the right advice from the right people.

I asked Brad, what was it about certain people in his

industry that annoyed him, and he said:

"*Some speakers sell certainties and they behave as though there is some kind of hidden vault full of secrets, ones that by attending their events you can obtain the key. I can honestly say, having asked the top, successful people, what do they believe is the biggest "secret" in their industry and they'll often tell me 'there are no secrets'. You can't skip the steps, there are no shortcuts, and yet we're 'sold' that you can. It's all bullshit and yet people want to believe that you can, that there is a shortcut and there is a secret, this is what these certainty salespeople sell. People do not want the honesty that the people like myself and Tony bring, it's not palatable. They would rather hear that you can go on a course, spend £10,000 and before you know it, the millionaire lifestyle is coming your way.*"

Brad has always been a disrupter, whether it was in networking or motivational speaking, his next goal is, like Mike, to take on the "Personal Development" world.

Brad gives me a brilliant quote where he says:

"*Believing that because it's so expensive it works. The reason that it costs £18K is that it works - people take out loans for this, it's like a modern-day f*cking Jack and the Bean Stalk, swapping three cars for some beans.*"

It's clearly as much a passion for Brad as it is for us, getting quite animated Brad says

"*People sell these dreams, you can have a million-pound portfolio with no money, it's a myth but people don't want to hear it. I've been as close to quitting so many times in the fifteen years I've been doing this, but each time I've come back knowing something about myself and about business, there is no shortcut and the people that are peddling this, in my opinion are disgusting."*

We chatted about what it really means to be rich in business. Brad echo's Tony's words on what it means to be a Happipreneur, he continues;

"*Can you go to your kids' sports day? Can you stay in bed until 11am? We are sold this myth that every kid wants to be in a private jet. I'm from a working-class family, I have a lovely home in a lovely village and that's my dream, I don't want or need a 60-foot swimming pool but this is the nonsense that perpetuated, that you're following someone else's dream. This is something that Tony is spot on about, go find your dream, find what makes you successful."*

As you'd expect, Brad is asked to speak at a lot of events, some with well-known speakers, but he has turned them down. One of the reasons he tells me is this;

"*I turned down a gig because I don't want to be associated with some of the names on the bill, one thing that I will always stand by is this - the problem of selling yourself out for money, is that the selling out lasts forever but the money doesn't. You Google your favourite entrepreneur with the word scam after it and see what comes up, I know that no scams are associated with my name and that's the way I want it to stay.*

I've built my reputation on being honourable."

There are very few speakers out there that are like Brad, saying it as it is and keeping it real. He advises that if you are looking for someone to follow or whose advice you'd listen to, simply make sure that it's real, if they're telling you they're a success find out how they got there.

Please take this advice from us, creating a 'vision board' and giving yourself something to aim for is a good thing, but it will not make it happen.

The only way to succeed in business is to roll up your sleeves, put in the hours and graft. If you want something fast, then you really want the wrong thing.

Why were Tony's father, his father's brother and his business partner, Clare's father, all highly successful business owners? Why do some business owner-led enterprises fly high for decades and others struggle to get off the ground? Why does wealth not equate to happiness? Why are some people happier and more successful, in their terms, being employed rather than in a business of their own? Why is 'do what you love and are good at' the foundation of life as a Happipreneur?

The true stories in this book, help answer those questions for business owners, entrepreneurs and entrepreneurs in the post coronavirus pandemic world. When we started writing this book, we didn't know that business life as we know it would be turned upside down by the pandemic. We do believe that it shows all advice about business and life is only relevant to a moment in time and in the context of the thoughts and actions of the person being advised.

Most generic business and advice, even from the highest-paid gurus is not as useful as advice from a business owner in your sector who has dealt with and is dealing with the challenges and opportunities you face.

Tony and I are lifelong researchers, readers and learners. We share professional and practical experience in marketing. Winning and keeping customers is the number one skill that needs to be present in a business. It's self-evident that a business will not succeed in the long term unless it can do this well or 'beautifully' as Schumacher and Sirolli say.

Number two priority skill is managing cash flow and UK business owners would be greatly helped in this by avoiding borrowing to cover cashflow problems and if Tony's two decades and counting campaigns to reduce costs of utilities, broadband, regulatory compliance and #PayIn30Days was successful.

Is it sheer happenstance, chance rather than design, that Tony is in a unique position in the UK to answer these questions about enterprise? He has had access to more research and interviewed more business owners, many famous and successful, than anyone else. Above all, he has been immersed in enterprise since a very early age, founded his own businesses over three decades and made it his mission to do all he could to help new business owners survive and thrive.

In the summer of 2018, I saw Tony's one-man

‘Micro is Magic’ Show at an Art Gallery in Hull as part of Global Entrepreneurship Week. Originally called the Micro Myths and Magic Show’ he toured with it for two years, for expenses only. The audience in Hull was primarily young people thinking of starting a business, starting a business and in their first year of running a business. Tony tailored his show to each audience, so in Ilfracombe, it was to established business owners and in Chesterfield, it was to people thinking of starting a business, mostly on Universal Credit.

Exploding the myths around entrepreneurship is what everyone remembers about the show. One myth that struck with me is that there is an ideal type of high growth entrepreneur. These are the ones that our Government and lenders usually back. These are young people in small enterprises, hi-tech, often from universities as spin-outs, venture capital or angel-backed and growing steadily through their early years of trading.

Tony says that most high growth business owners have learned about their sector and the customers in the sector from their jobs. His father did that in the timber trade, Clare‘s father did that in commercial property and Sir Jim Ratcliffe did that in chemical engineering. Most businesses that grow substantially do so because the business owner is very good at what they do and love their business.

They don’t have a steady growth profile. Usually, they have ups and downs. They understand the sector and the customers, but they change rapidly what is right to offer their customers depending on the economy, environment and technology.

The 'ups' are usually from spotting an opportunity and making a deal. Many grow by acquisition, whether this is of another business, a new income stream, a property or a major contract. It's not formal education-related at all.

The reason Tony would say to any young person starting a business in the next few months, to do something you're good at and enjoy, bootstrap don't borrow, test trade first, build multiple income streams and ask for help from a business owner who understands your customers is LEARNING BY DOING. It's a fast learning experience. You need to know you've got enough paying customers before you can borrow. You need to be in business for a while before you have the skills and contacts which allow you to make deals to grow.

For example, Tony knows little about his father's background and how he made the necessary contacts from his box salesman days and personal life, including his first marriage. In order to become a shareholder and Managing Director of a Box Mill, he would have needed to be very good at what he did and have some productive relationships in place.

Tony does know that his father had made the deals throughout the sector BEFORE he started his own home-based business. That's why it was so successful so fast. Unlike Tony, he didn't start his own business until success was assured. He had big customers lined up and he convinced other box mills that he could do a better job for them than their current salesforce. He just wouldn't have had the know-how, skills or contacts to do that as a youngster.

Helping people of all ages from the young to the old, from the poor to the rich, get the know-how, skills and contacts to succeed in their own business is what many of the organisations Tony has founded or supported are all about.

Q&A Time

Q: What is your legacy?

A: Three incredibly bright children, thanks to Eileen, and their own application to learning and being useful. Hopefully, there are also many memories for family and friends of some great fun we had and the laughter we shared.

I'm aware that over the last thirty-five years I've done a lot of writing, TV, radio, videos and podcasts so whether I like it or not, some of my thoughts on life and enterprise may survive a year or two after I die. What is more useful are the videos of all the independent business owners I've interviewed.

Q: Would you have liked a career in broadcasting?

A: Yes, and in the last 20 years I could have done it really well, but not before. Radio I love but, like my stage talks, I get incredibly nervous in TV studios. In the last few years, I've done some more corporate TV videos and BBC Big Breakfast and I did OK. The reason I did OK was that I didn't have a pre-formulated answer in my head and I listened to the question. Listening, questioning and summarising are the must-have skills for most professional careers.

When I was doing a lot of influencing and negotiating training. I started to improve my own questioning and listening skills. So much so that Clare and Eileen have said I listen to what they say far more often now. The trouble was that all media training, particularly when you're going to be grilled by an antagonistic interviewer, as I was at Amway, means you're only half-listening to the question as you feverishly work on getting your 'must point' across.

You'll notice that Boris Johnson in the last General election refused to do any of the TV interviews or debates which wouldn't allow him to just use 'must points' and 'Get Brexit Done'.

I've had and failed at two auditions for presenting pilot TV small business shows because of nerves, I always failed cricket trials too, for the same reason. But I'd have loved to have a crack at presenting a show or documentary series on TV. When asked in later life, after my sporting and theatre ambitions were thwarted, what job I'd most like to have I always answered 'a sports writer and commentator'.

Q: Why were you so bad at listening?

A: I'm always thinking of the next thing to do or something that makes me laugh. I shouldn't have read Albert Camus at such a young age as although my outside appearance may suggest I'm serious and thoughtful, my mind tells me life is absurd.

Then there were many years of drinking with my best man, Digby. As we both had diametrically opposite political and social views, we maintained our friendship over a lifetime by not listening to a word the other said.

When we got to my house in Hessle after a night out, my Mum would bring a tray with cheese, biscuits and whisky and then we'd take it in turns to drink, eat and talk while the other was sleeping. I was even surprised at his funeral to hear that he'd founded a Freemason's lodge - I wouldn't even join a golf club!

"You have the ability, if you use it, to choose healthy instead of unhealthy thinking, feeling and acting"

Albert Ellis

XII
A Happipreneur

Tony believes that the years since 2010 have been the best of his life as a #Happipreneur but all the years since he set up his own business with Clare in 1986 have been happy.

He absolutely loved the lockdown during the pandemic as it gave him more time to campaign for micro-business owners and more time to be creative. He felt so lucky to be with Eileen, Carl, Alan and Sinead in sunny Scarborough and still able to communicate with his best friend, Clare, every week.

He says he's lucky to have had great teachers in books by Albert Ellis, EF Schumacher, Derren Brown, Oliver Burkeman, Barbara Ehrenreich and in business life from Clare Francis and Tina Boden. Clare and Tina taught him how to put friends and family first and be useful to others - all while running a business.

For example, he's made a big effort to stay in touch and see his oldest friends every year and he now raises money for charity by running half marathons and marathons each summer. He'd always donated money to charity but it was Clare and Tina's example of charity fundraising that made him realise he should do far more and not take the easy route.

"*Do what you love and are good at*" is the number one reason Tony gives as to why some people may consider being a #Happipreneur. The full list is:

1. Do what you love and are good at
2. Control your own destiny
3. Put friends and family first
4. Be useful to others
5. Avoid debt - make ends meet
6. Be enterprising
7. Enjoy hard work
8. Learn how to handle grief, setbacks and putdowns
9. Love life
10. LOVE BEING HAPPY

A #Happipreneur can be self-employed or employed. Tony points out that starting and running your own business is not the only way to happiness, fulfilment and putting family and friends first.

There are many people that achieve all of the above by being in jobs they love and they're great at what they do. Similarly, many people that have inherited or made a lot of money achieve happiness and fulfilment by investing in other people's enterprises.

Tony has chosen the route to happiness and fulfilment through starting and running his own businesses and that's why he can talk about #Happipreneurship with credibility. Not working for the man was the only way he found to control his own destiny.

Happipreneurship doesn't preclude being rich, having a job or being competitive.

Get to the top in your job and other lucrative income-earning opportunities will appear. All the members of Boris Johnson's cabinet are millionaires and as BJ says a Minister's salary is 'peanuts' and he couldn't live off it. But they know the route to being wealthy for the rest of their life is by getting to that *employed position* as a Government Minister.

Highly paid jobs can also be the springboard to a more enterprising future. How did Tony Blair, after leaving politics, start his own business with employees in place and £20 million in sales on day one? How did Sir Jim Ratcliffe and Warren Buffet become multi-billionaires?

Tony has on his desk photos of his Mum and Dad. His Dad's photo stands on a miniature wooden pallet which was presented to him at a Timber Trades Awards night. It's a constant reminder to Tony that running his father's business is not what he would have loved or could do well. He may have made money, but he wouldn't have been a #Happipreneur.

Conversely, his father loved designing and selling boxes and pallets. He did it from a young age until he died. Although he made the most money from the small number of years, he had his own business and he clearly didn't enjoy selling and negotiating on the phone as much as he did face to face. He was happiest 'on the road' in a job.

Tony enjoys the company of his rich and competitivefriends. He's not jealous of their wealth and he remains competitive himself.

Nick Keyte is one of his closest friends. They met at Middlesex Polytechnic and formed their own cricket team, which Tony captained, and Nick was Vice-Captain in the mid-seventies. They both left that team to join Mill Hill Village and then both went onto play and captain Great Houghton cricket team for many years. Nick still plays cricket today. Tony was Nick's best man. In business Tony has contracted with Nick and Nick has contracted with Tony.

Nick's garden in Solihull backed onto the prestigious Solihull Cricket Club and Nick's Solihull team against Tony's Great Houghton Team became an annual fixture for seven years.

It was a friendly, but a highly competitive match, as this programme note written by Tony says, "*Despite snooker away days, Lords Taverners' dinners, many tours and the abuse Keyte levelled at the Robbo captaincy in the last 20 years, they survive as friends to this day, ready to applaud whoever the victor may be - like hell.*"

Tony says Nick is fairly obsessed with figures - runs at cricket and money. As well as their shared love of sport, Nick and Tony have Human Resource Management careers in common.

Nick started his own computer recruitment businesswith a partner shortly after finishing his postgraduate qualifications. By any measure, Nick would have been regarded as a successful entrepreneur. Mitchell Keyte Computer Recruitment was one of the leaders in the country. Nick and Mitch were wealthy and they owned the building housing their offices.

At the eight consecutive Lords Taverners‘ Gala Dinners at the Metropole Hotel, which Tony attended, Nick and Mitch always won the charity auction for a Bill Tidy cartoon painting. They could pay many thousands for that privilege.

But into his forties, Nick gave up their business and went into employment as an HR Director and Vice President of some major companies including Johnson Controls and Bombardier. It’s the reverse story of Tony’s - Tony was in HR Management and employed until he was 34 and has been running his own businesses ever since.

Tony has gone from riches to rags and Nick has gone from riches to more riches. The point of this story is that #Happipreneurs can be competitive, ambitious and rich and they can achieve fulfilment and happiness in a job as much as in their own business.

The starting point is doing what you love and are very good at. Nick moves from company to company and Directorship to Directorship at mouth-watering salary and perks.

He is very independent in his jobs which involve restructuring complex organisations. He is controlling his own destiny even though he is in a job. He is happy and fulfilled and enjoys the top executive lifestyle. He has continued playing all his major sports - cricket, rugby and golf for much longer than Tony did. The media would regard Nick as both an entrepreneur and a top leader.

Nick's troubleshooting jobs seem similar in their challenge and independence to Tony's happiest job as Industrial Relations Manager at NCR Limited. Tony and Nick have similar HR qualifications and executive-level track records. They have similar egos and both preferred leading rather than being led. Tony believes he could do Nick's jobs.

But the reason Tony wouldn't be happy, whereas Nick is, tells you everything about the subject of this book - the Happipreneur and Why #MicroBizMatters?

Tony hated hiring and firing, pulling rank, managing egos and status needs, large company politics, profiteering and, especially, making people redundant. All are necessary requirements for the top jobs in big company HR and Nick is happy in his work.

EF Schumacher wrote "*Small is Beautiful - economics as if people mattered*" and Tony has spent over 20 years promoting #MicroBizMatters - enterprise as if people mattered.

Q & A Time

Q - Who would you suggest was one of the earliest entrepreneurs?

A: You'll love this.

There are many different types of writer; freelance journalists, scriptwriters, fiction - many genres, non-fiction, including travel, sport, business, magazines, blogs, speeches, podcasts, magazines, social media content - playwrights and songwriters.

Charles Dickens was many of these types of writers and, if the technology had been available, would have been an actor, film director, TV star, TED Talker, a major social media influencer, documentary writer, global investigative journalist, blogger and podcaster. As well as being one of the greatest writers of all time he was one of the greatest entrepreneurs ever in the creative arts.

Bob Dylan, a Nobel Prize winner for literature, is a modern day equivalent and Dylan is, despite his lyrics, a happy entrepreneur. For most of his adult life Charles Dickens pursued his passions but always so that he could make money. He made a difference to the world through his social commentary, campaigns, charitable enterprises, editorship and investigative journalism but never lost his adoring public from every walk of life. Politicians read Dickens and knew they had to act on what he wrote.

What made Dickens so successful, like Dylan, was that

he was a great entertainer - maybe the greatest. Dylan's never-ending tour of gigs is as exhausting but as essential to his continued success as Dickens' 100-night reading tours in theatres. Most successful entrepreneurs, in all sectors, realise they must be engaged with their audience, almost in the same way as an entertainer. They will develop multiple income streams from the audience they are engaged with.

For example, compare two of my all-time five favourite writers, because I loved the satire in their later work, Charles Dickens and Herman Melville. Herman's first two novels were very successful, so much so that he was able to buy a very nice property for his family and work as a full-time, self-employed, writer. He peaked too early. He had no more successful novels, collections of short stories and poetry in his lifetime.

My favourite, now regarded as classic, Melville novels and novellas such as Moby Dick, The Confidence Man, Bartleby the Scrivener, Benito Cereno and Billy Budd (published posthumously) made him so little money that he had to get a job. He worked as a full-time civil servant, in Customs, for over twenty years before retiring.

Melville kept promising his publishers more romantic travel tales like his first two novels, but he never delivered. Unlike Dickens, who always delivered, it is likely that Melville either didn't really know his audience or, more likely, didn't want to write what his audience would buy.

Compare Melville with Dickens. Compare Melville with *Brad Burton* - writer of motivational business books, or *Gary Vaynerchuk* the Brad Burton equivalent in the US and Globally.

Whatever the changes to the world of publishing (books or music) or changes to the algorithms on Facebook, Twitter or LinkedIn it is a fact that Dickens, Dylan, Burton and Vaynerchuk remain fully engaged with their audience who continue to buy their books and flock to see them perform.

In fact, no creative entrepreneur has ever done 'engagement' better than Dickens. How did he do it? Why does it work just as well today?

Aged 29, a Londoner, Charles Dickens was given the freedom of the city of Edinburgh. This took place in the summer of 1841. He went to the theatre, after one of the many large - (hundreds ate, and hundreds watched them eat from the balconies) - and lavish dinners in his honour. The audience, warned by the newspapers that 'Boz' would be present, crammed in to see him. As he entered the orchestra struck up 'Charley is my darling'.

His extraordinary popularity in the UK and USA increased year by year through to his death at 58. No organisation, company, publisher, agent, manager or publicist could have achieved this level of audience engagement for Charles Dickens. Charles Dickens, the entrepreneur-writer achieved it by his own actions to build his own brand around his unique personality and talents.

The brand loyalty for an individual usually lasts longer and is stronger than a company, product or service. Charlie Mullins OBE is Pimlico Plumbers. Kanya

King CBE is the MOBO Awards and Antony Chesworth is EKM. *Stormzy* is Stormzy. Boz was Charles Dickens.

Like most entrepreneurs I've met who have made their name out of doing something remarkably well - Chris Percival as a para medic, Antony Chesworth building online shops, Charlie Mullins out of plumbing - formal education played a very minor part in their learning. Dickens was almost totally self-taught in everything he excelled at. He read voraciously and loved learning how to perform.

The imaginative world, such as '*The Arabian Nights'* and '*Don Quixote'* was important to him. As stated earlier, my favourite satirical novel, by Dickens is '*Hard Times'* and in it he suggests individual 'fancy' (imagination and creativity) is the way to personal fulfilment and happiness whereas, process, facts (data), automation, factories and commerce are the way to greed, bullying, corruption and misery. Individual enterprise is most often good and institutional production is most often bad.

I don't know whether Schumacher read Dickens, but I know he would have approved. Schumacher made it clear that politicians and shareholders pre-occupation with increasing GDP and productivity were only likely to create stressed out, unhappy workers.

Dicken's genius was to teach himself how to write from the imagination and create characters which have never been surpassed in literature. Some of these characters are like you and me. By putting them in situations we have not experienced - a debtor's prison; a court of law; a gang of thieves; a revolution; a textile factory - we are forced to consider the rights and wrongs of their treatment by the state. Fiction led to social reform and, even, the family Christmas as we now know it.

His success as an entrepreneur, like most entrepreneurs, was based, not on positive attitude or mindset, but on street-smart understanding of what he could make and sell within the realities of affordable costs and positive cashflow. Positive cash flow was a motivating force for the workaholic Dickens as he was haunted by the Debtors' prison which his father was sent to. His mother and siblings joined his father in the prison, but he was banished, as a 12-year-old, to work in a blacking factory and pay his way.

Today's equivalent to the debtor's prison is credit scoring. It is easier to escape the constraints of prison than it is to escape a low credit score in this digital-by-default world.

Dickens was renowned for immense physical energy and perseverance. Dickens taught himself how to write and do shorthand which led to apprentice journalist jobs, latterly as a parliamentary reporter. But he wanted to be successful in the imaginary world. He nearly became an actor and wrote many short stories which he submitted and had rejected before, after years of trying, at 22, a short comic fictional sketch was accepted by a magazine.

Six more sketches followed, and the magazine took him on in a job. Dickens continued to write street sketches of London and started to build his own brand whilst in a job by using the pseudonym 'Boz'. The illustrator he used for most of his life took the pseudonym of 'Phiz' to go with 'Boz'.

Dickens was fully independent by the age of 23 and built his brand further by his flamboyant dress. He was renowned for his blue cloak with velvet facings and brightly coloured, fancy waistcoats.

He learned, rather like test trading and crowd funding combined, that he could publish a novel in monthly numbers of a magazine and build the audience by getting feedback from the readers as the tension mounted and the public asked for more about certain characters.

Dickens, like most entrepreneurs, took on more work than he could handle once having promised three novels to three different publishers while writing a stage play and a libretto for an opera. Like most entrepreneurs he eventually found a way to control his own destiny and not be controlled as much by his customers (publishers).

He founded, created and edited his own weekly and monthly magazines. As soon as he could he took the Boz mania' on tour to the USA and Canada.

Eventually he was making more money from touring with his 'readings' (£33,000 in 1866-1868 when £300 a year was a good salary) than his prolific, financially successful and critically acclaimed novel writing. All achieved through mass entertainment with no need for mindset mayhem or hot coals walking - Tony Robbins eat your heart out.

Carrying on with my literacy theme, as I'm on a roll

here, I'd also suggest the Bronte sisters.

A few years ago there was a fabulous BBC two hours drama on the *Bronte* family. If you saw it then I'll wager you were impressed with the three sisters' unity and assertiveness just as much as their cumulative genius.

For example, Charlotte's riposte to her publisher's disbelief that she could have written 'Jane Eyre'; "*What makes you doubt it, Mr. Smith? My accent? My gender? My size?*".

What delighted me the most was that readers and listeners that have bought my satire 'Freedom from Bosses Forever' or attended my conference talks on the same subject, will now understand why I suggest the Bronte sisters are role models.

They are role models as great writers AND for all those that want to earn a living from their own business. Give me their kind of entrepreneurship any day of the week, especially over the 'get rich by hearing my story' and 'see how much money I've hustled for my idea' brigade.

Like many of us, the motivating force for their enterprise was independence rather than wealth. They had to earn a living. Their experiences as governesses and teachers had shown there was little security or happiness in those jobs, yet these were virtually the only jobs open to them. The three sisters wanted no more bosses and, as they were carers, they needed to work from home.

Charlotte, Emily and Anne tried to open their own

small private school and although their marketing material and pricing were good their location and credibility wasn't. As their brother and father's health deteriorated the urgency to make ends meet through their own enterprise increased. They agreed on a joint venture to become published authors - all for one and one for all.

Because of Emily and Anne's early deaths, soon after their brother's, Charlotte was the only one of the three sisters to fully taste monetary success and not for long as their father outlived them all. Yet these brilliant sisters lived long enough to see their aim, of being published authors, achieved.

What an achievement it was! Today they would have been called disruptors. Book publishers just didn't accept manuscripts from Yorkshire women. They not only broke the mould for novels, they made a sizeable crack in the glass ceiling too.

Every authentic entrepreneur I've met, who start and successfully run their own business, has the Bronte sisters' high level of self-awareness and hard work. They were bang up to date with the 'technology', limited though it was, of the publishing industry and what publishers thought readers would buy.

They were brilliant at creating and promoting their personal brand to gain entry to the market - Acton (Anne), Currer (Charlotte) and Ellis (Emily) Bell would be assumed to be three brothers, by prospective publishers, not three sisters.

So wrong but being market led is nearly always better than pushing your own agenda especially when you are your brand. When JK Rowling‘s agent eventually found a publisher for ‘Harry Potter’, they decided it would aid sales if the audience for the boy wizard didn’t know it was a woman author. They suggested to Joanne Rowling that she used the initials of her two forenames. As she only had one forename, she added the ‘K’ for Kathleen - her mother’s name.

The Bronte sisters played to their strengths and passions which gave them the necessary persistence to keep going in the face of terrible, debilitating domestic circumstances and rejection of their art. Like Dickens, they were afraid of debt and the debtors’ prison, so happily did not borrow. They wanted to create something out of nothing that they could be proud of. That is true entrepreneurship.

Above all, they knew what they were doing, and what they could be remarkable in doing, to capture a slice of the market for novels. They’d written hundreds of poems and little books throughout their short lifetimes. They read widely both to learn their craft and understand readers’ demand. They knew Emily’s writing was remarkable, genius even, so they needed to lead with her difference. They test traded and proved that poetry could enhance their credibility but would not earn them a living.

It had to be a novel writing joint enterprise and Emily would need to write a novel too. They swapped ideas on the novels they could write and what readers would like. They researched publishers and drew up a hit list. They expected rejection of their handwritten manuscripts - a tiresome, time-consuming business - and moved immediately to the next on the list. When eventually, of the three novels from the three Bells, two were accepted they took some pragmatic decisions without diluting their original aims.

Charlotte could have stopped the whole venture as her novel, 'The Professor' was the one rejected. Instead, she was encouraged by the criticism and set about writing a new novel – '*Jane Eyre'*. They were principled and, in the face of being ripped off, stood up for their rights immediately as demonstrated by Anne and Charlotte's 17-hour overnight journey to London to confront their publisher and reveal their identity.

So, here we have three great writers and together they made three great entrepreneurs. Hard work; self-awareness; (my 4Ps) passion; persistence; promotion and partnership are all displayed in the brilliant Bronte sisters' enterprise.

"All really important innovations and changes normally start from tiny minorities of people who do use their creative freedom"

EF Schumacher

XIII
Not an Entrepreneur… but a Happipreneur

Tony firmly believes that it's crazy to slow down as you get older since you're running out of time you need to do everything faster. So, don't expect him to disappear from Twitter, LinkedIn, Facebook, Instagram and Pinterest with his campaigns to support micro-business owners.

I spoke to him in February 2020 and his week ahead included a board meeting of Yorkshire in Business, a trip to Birmingham to meet the new Small Business Commissioner on #PayIn30days and then a flight to Malta on his own where he was planning to stay for a month to rewrite his psychological thriller, 'Loose Cannon' into 'Maltese Venom'.

As you know, things came to a head in March with the Coronavirus and he was forced to fly home. In typical Tony style he went straight into campaigning for the self-employed to get government help and whilst he did a tremendous job, true to form felt as though it wasn't enough. The fact that thousands of people are now getting a pay out that originally they didn't think they'd see and that finally all of the small business organisations came together to be heard as one, is testament to how hard he worked in such a short period of time and how strong his voice can be.

I asked Tony what went through his mind when he heard the announcement about business owners having to claim SSP and he told me, he doesn't want people to have to apply for SSP or Universal Credit, they're not sick nor out of work. They should be receiving grants, and this is what he's been campaigning for. At least 3 million business owners have missed out of grant support. At the time of writing he fears that even if they succeed with the #ForgottenLimited, #Wenta and #justiceforthenewselfemployed campaigns, it will be too little too late for most.

What's worse, of course, is digital taxation and the way grants have been managed through HMRC and PAYE, whoever is left standing will pay the Government back through the nose - increased taxes and social taxes including to pay for pensions and healthcare etc. The third with loans will see their businesses and livelihoods strangled too. #PayIn30Days will go on the back burner too as BigCos resume their bullying.

Tony tells me, he'll be campaigning until he dies but hopes there'll be a few more wins along the way to make it more fulfilling.

'In the eight days Tony was in Malta, three weeks before the UK's partial lockdown, he saw how superbly their Government handled the coronavirus crisis. They closed down their borders, even though they were swabbing, temperature testing and quarantining all passengers by sea and air. They made immediate grants available to all business owners closing every cafe, hotel, bar and shop.

They followed the South Korea model of lockdown with tracking and tracing. They only had 6 deaths in total. On June 3rd the UK had 354 deaths and the whole of Europe, all 27 countries, had fewer deaths than the UK. Malta had no deaths and no infections. 70% of small and micro-business owners in Malta are totally satisfied with how their Government has handled the pandemic and their vitally important tourism industry is starting up again for countries that have low or no infection rates.

Tony makes the point that how Governments treat small and micro-business owners is a choice. The USA and UK always support large companies first, but this is not the case in most other countries around the world. Tony is totally convinced that the need of the economy and large companies cost the USA and UK thousands of unnecessary deaths. Tony's #PayIn30Days campaign is unique to the UK because most countries ensure it already happens.

Tony has teamed up with Ian Cass, the Chief Executive of the Forum of Private Business. Tony tells me that Ian is "*the only maverick of the CEOs willing to take on Government.*"

In a recent blog Ian talks about how Government has let down micro-businesses owners during the Coronavirus lockdown, he says:

"*They start with big business first before moving on*

to small business issues, small and micro-businesses account for over 99% of the UK economy and any decisions on the economy and business should start with them.

"The problem with Government is they treat small and micro-businesses like boiled down Big Companies. We're not - we're better and more important. We innovate more, create more new jobs and opportunities, create more growth, are more flexible, collaborative and are vital to communities and society.'

Having met Ian myself at the 2019 Micro-business Matters event in Hull, I have seen his passion and dedication first-hand. I chatted to him at the event and he told me that Tony is seen as a bit of a loose cannon within government and that despite being, in their eyes idealistic, Tony is completely on the right track to ensure that businesses are paid promptly.

The original founder of the Forum of Private Business, Stan Mendham, was a massive help in Tony founding SFEDI and he met him many times even after he retired from FPB. He gave Tony a great piece of advice which was;

'Don't worry about mission statements, objectives, strategy and plans just let's agree on principles they should last forever'.

It's interesting to see that both of these men echo many of the desires Tony has for micro-business owners and a more level playing field.

I spoke to Tony regularly through the coronavirus lockdowns in the UK, from March through to June

2020 and he was in full-on campaigning mode on behalf of the self-employed and micro-business owners. He remained a #Happipreneur through this trying time but was sad about the unnecessary deaths and the 'deliberately, too little, too late', income support for the 3 million micro-business owners and self-employed people left out of the Chancellor's 'packages'.

On his social media activity, I've seen him complaining about unnecessary deaths because the UK and USA had not followed the lead of South Korea, (like nearly every other country in the world did) and get massive support throughout the UK. His 'Too Old' twitter poem engaged with hundreds of thousands.

But it was the lack of success with his micro-business owner campaigning that hurt him the most. In his words;

'They starved millions so that they'd have to take out loans. The debt trap is exactly where they want millions in the UK. The big Tory donors and contractors like JCB got furloughing until they were able to return to work early. Bounce back loans for desperate micro-business owners got 130,000 applications on the first day in early May.

*Banks and loans never were the answer and never will be. But expect more f***ing loans, more stealth online taxation for health care and social care and more volunteer mentor schemes from the Banks and Government to help us 'bounce back' and grow. Most of the time I don't think they see any difference between self-employment and unemployment - it's our fault* *we're not wealthy enough to matter to them.*'

He was particularly disappointed with the national Small Business Membership organisations and the Small Business Commissioner during the 'stay at home' phase. Only Ian Cass, CEO of the Forum of Private Business supported the 3 major campaigns, which Tony spent most of his time promoting. He said he shouldn't have been surprised as most of these organisations are sponsored each year by different Banks and they have to be seen to 'welcome' everything the Government does in order to stay in the Government and BigCo Sponsors tent.

He felt that the injustice and poverty being created by the Government's small business policies would mean they'd join him in the campaigns. #MicroBizMatters Day is all about promoting all the business membership networks in the UK so that they ask their members to give a little time to help each other. He felt that Tina and he would have to rethink who they invited to their main live streaming event in future.

Lockdown was the ideal opportunity for Government to say to any large company they were paying 80% of wages, giving loans to or buying from "*Pay your small and micro suppliers, with outstanding bills, NOW and agree that you'll #PayIn30Days all your suppliers in the future.*"

Tony has the research to show that new micro-business owners provide the most new jobs, innovation, creativity, growth and support for communities. The Conservative Government have this information too, as they commissioned ex Dragon and millionaire entrepreneur, Doug Richard to research and write two reports on what support should be given to small businesses. Giving all start-ups and new business owners the best chance of success is the best way to grow the economy. Do not try to 'pick winners'. Tony could have written the report for free as he'd been advocating this for ten years before.

Unfortunately, Doug Richard got caught up in a court case about him having underage sex and little has been heard of him for the last ten years. Tony's family have noted that a lot of the people Tony has met and liked over the years - Sir Jimmy Saville and Sir Rolf Harris included - have turned out not to be heroes. I'm not sure that this is a reflection on Tony, just that he takes people at face value and perhaps naively, expects them to be as decent as he is.

Tony would have added one more important thing to Doug Richard's reports on what new micro-business owners contribute to the UK. This is that they provide happier and healthier workplaces.

Tony says the usual suspects always assume that companies with advanced HR processes and procedures are the best places to work but the research doesn't back this up. In fact, the USA is the 26th best country in the world to work and live and the UK is the 28th This is primarily because large shareholder-owned companies provide the most employment. and the least happiness. Seven out of ten big company employees don't like their jobs. Stress-related health problems are rampant in both countries. The average length of service of each employee is pitiful. This is exactly as Schumacher predicted.

The statistics are almost reversed in micro-businesses where on average employees are nearly twice as happy, stay employed for longer and have under half the amount of sickness absence. Schumacher answered the question 'Why #MicroBizMatters?' - because of their contribution to public welfare including employee welfare.

Tony says that the coronavirus tragedy in the UK shows how important employee happiness and welfare is. The majority of large organisations that kept working through the lockdown - NHS, Care home chains, construction sites, Amazon and major supermarkets are awful employers of front-line workers. The level of sickness-related absence, stress and unhappiness, and the strains in the civil service team supporting Ministers, was contributory to the poor decision making, massive death rate and suffering for the UK population during and after lockdown.

On returning from a locked-down Malta to the UK, Tony started lobbying for his school friend, Sir Jim Ratcliffe to be appointed to lead the UK effort to contain and reduce the number of infections. He is a scientist, a manufacturer, an accountant and a significant part of Ineos success is from it being the industry leader on health and safety. Above all, he would have brought to No 10 his management team, nearly all of which have been with him for over 20 years. They are a happy team - Sir Jim calls it '*collegiate*' and '*we don't tolerate big egos*'.

Tony is convinced that the happiest workplaces, even in the largest organisations, are created by business owners that have started their own business and had a micro-business, at least at the start. The HR processes won't be written down and many business owners lead by walking around and chatting rather than appraisal systems, goal setting sessions, strategy away days and the rest but it works. Why does it work.?

The top reason is most start-up micro-business owners are building their own business to last. Having happy staff means happy customers and suppliers and repeat business. Because you build your business to last, you recruit, train and look after your employees so that they will last with you. You may not be able to yet compete on salary with larger companies, but you'll win hands down on happiness, welfare and interesting, responsible and fulfilling work. As Freddie Herzberg said in the 70s *"you can't motivate someone doing a shit job"*.

Conversely, happy employees do not matter as much to managers on a career ladder. They may not be looking to stay in the company for more than three years themselves. Employees are a means to an end - to get them a promotion or whatever the next rung on the career ladder is. They'll only be interested in their team, not all the employees in the workplace.

The business owner at micro-level is interested in everyone and will use all their talents to the full. If they get beyond the micro size, the business owner will still have a set of beliefs and values about recruiting, training and looking after employees that all their leaders MUST follow.

Tony and Clare have studied this for decades. Their success as consultants to all sizes of the company was often measured from happiness surveys, job retention and reduced sickness absence. Remember Tony was also Investors in People Small Business Champion and has visited and interviewed hundreds of small and micro-business owners and their employees.

He's never been able to persuade Government to learn from micro-business owners on anything, but he has persuaded large companies to adopt the HR practices of business owner led organisations. As Dr Sirolli would say Government and most big company leaders are so patronising and paternalistic that they can't get their heads around anything but big is better and *'wealthier is cleverer'* (Tony's phrase).

Happy workplaces come from #Happipreneurs leading them. JK Rowling puts it well;

"*If someone asked for my recipe for happiness, step one would be finding out what you love doing the most in the world and step two would be finding someone to pay you to do it.*"

Proportionately, independent business owners invest a lot more money into creating happy workplaces than do the large companies led by 'parasites' (shareholders), as Schumacher termed it. The way they create their workplaces is usually unique to them and their values. Four examples of outstanding workplaces full of happy employees are four of the annual #MicroBiz-Matters Day venues - Portobello Business Centre, Pimlico Plumbers, EKM and Yorkshire in Business.

Two of these are business owner founded and led medium to large companies where the business owner has started the company and built it through the microphase - Antony Chesworth and Charlie Mullins OBE. Two are enterprise agencies and micro-enterprises where the leaders Jenn Crowther and Alex Gajic have experience of micro-businesses for over 15 years.

Tony and Clare had helped businesses develop happy workplaces for many years before they realised how important leadership was to the process. Tony believes that business owners become better leaders than their big company executive equivalents and he'd seen the proof of that with clients and colleagues such as Mike Reilly at Sonatest, Peter Kindersley at Dorling Kindersley, Lord Sugar at Amstrad, Julian Richer at Richer Sounds and Gordon Roddick at the Big Issue.

'*In Search of Happiness*', his phrase, had become as important to him as *'In Search of Excellence'* (Tom Peters). But it was only when he gave part of a SFEDI project on business owner leadership development to a company called Happy Computers that he realised how important transparency, trust, decision making and values are.

Happy Computers are led by Henry Stewart and Henry believes #MicroBizMatters and that Small is

Beautiful. He regularly writes on the benefits to Government of allowing small and micro-businesses to collaborate and deliver large scale government contracts, rather than the usual suspects always getting them - Capita, G4S, Atos, Serco, Maximus and the rest.

To walk into Henry Stewart‘s Happy Computers building - a training company - was an uplifting experience. It made learning a joy. It made going into work a joy. Until Tina and Tony's 3rd Annual #MicroBizMatters Day in January 2017 at Pimlico Plumbers, he'd never met such a happy group of staff and customers.

Some 20 years later, Henry Stewart is still running his businesses, but he also tries to make a difference to work life and leadership by hosting Conferences and speaking at events on his Happy Manifesto. What Tony loves about the Happy Manifesto is that it asks leaders to let people control their own destiny in the workplace and to support them rather than *"approve what they do*".

Most micro-business owners know the value of investing in happy and trusted employees is that all will be great when the business owner has to leave the workplace. They can take decisions, they can innovate, they can give outstanding customer care.

Tony interviewed a pub owner in the Highlands once who said they'd tripled their turnover by investing in their bar staff - building a happy team. The owner had decided to turn the pub into an entertainment venue but in order to fill it, he'd need to attract some of the best up and coming bands so that people would travel many miles to the gigs at his pub. This meant the pub owner going on the road to watch and sign up these up and coming bands. If he couldn't trust his team to have done an excellent job while he was away with customers, suppliers and in the community, he'd have ended up with no business at all.

Tony's two favourite principles of Henry Stewart's Happy Manifesto, which chime perfectly with his #Happipreneurship business philosophy are:

"Give freedom within clear guidelines. People want to know what's expected of them. But they want freedom to find the best way to achieve their goals."

and

"Love work. Get a life. The world and your job need you well rested, well-nourished and well supported."

So, what next?

As well as "*campaigning for micro-business owners until I snuff it*", Tony is looking forward to squeezing every minute of happiness he can pursuing his favourite activities with friends and family.

On the business side, these include his co-chairing Yorkshire in Business Limited, being Patron of the John Cracknell Youth Enterprise Bank, a judge for the Great British Entrepreneurs Awards and especially running as many annual #MicroBizMatters Days as his and Tina's limited funds allow.

On the personal side, enjoying time with friends and family comes first - lots more sport, ballet, theatre and gigs - accompanied by delicious food, red wine and real ales. Coming a close second is his writing and charity fundraising ambitions.

His excuse for going to Malta on his own again was to rewrite 'Loose Cannon' into 'Maltese Venom'. He also has his next satire about seagulls on the go (don't ask!).

He was inspired many years ago by Tina and Clare's charity fundraising efforts. His main charity is MacMillan Cancer Support in memory of five friends - Jude, Digby, Charles, Mandy and Elizabeth. Each summer he runs at least 4 half and full marathons and that means training runs every other day throughout the year. He loves it, particularly finishing his training runs at the seafront with a coffee and chocolate cake.

However, if he's out running, don't be surprised if he runs straight passed you and doesn't see you wave! Jenn Crowther tells me that she'll often see him out running and even if she has a glass of wine on the table in front of her, he'll still not see her… whether it's a marathon or his daily run, Tony is in the 'zone'.

Finally, he hopes to put together and tour with a new show, based around the Happipreneurship business philosophy. I hope to be with him in the show and on the tour. Whatever happens, ordinary it won't be.

Why not say hello to him online and join in on the next annual #MicroBizMatters Day (hint - it's always the second Friday of the New Year)?

Q &A Time

Q: You say that a #Happipreneur puts friends and family first but you had a totally happy year completely alone. How come?

A: Just gaining pleasure out of selfish thoughts and actions isn't totally fulfilling. Happipreneurs need to be useful as well. It's really difficult to be useful on your own. Even my Uncle Ron, Jude and now Clare who live on their own have devoted their lives to putting family and friends first.

Q: Do you think the happiest time you had with family and friends was when you were with Amway?

A: No - I enjoyed most of those five years but I've certainly enjoyed being in our own business much more. Eileen enjoyed the occasional fantastic trip - first-class on a plane and lovely hotel in nice resorts - but she was busy most of the time with Carl who needed a lot of attention, then Alan and Sinead were both born during my time at Amway. Her happiest years in Milton Keynes with the kids were still to come as were mine.

Q: But you made some great friends at Amway?

A: Yes, I did - in my team especially. Clare, of course, is my very best friend and became my business partner. Stewart McArthur was my boss until I succeeded him as CEO. We were fantastic friends at Amway and for many years after. We are both very competitive and loved playing and watching sport - rugby, football, cricket, tennis and snooker in particular. We also enjoyed taking the piss out of each other. He probably won the verbal insults battle as he introduced me once at an Amway rally as "*the only man I know who drives an ashtray*".

Q: Did you make friends with many of the distributor leaders?

A: No, that was impossible. It really is the biggest difference between all my other jobs and all the time I had running my own businesses. Half my time, in the latter years at Amway, was spent with people who weren't in the least friendly. The Diamonds and Double Diamonds were very time-consuming and apart from two couples out of twelve, they were constantly at you. They tried to get better deals from the company all the time. That may be understandable as they were entrepreneurs but it's a kind of entrepreneurship I don't like. Most of the time they were disrespectful to Amway employees. Even on Direct Distributor seminars abroad, which are not as intense or as luxurious as the trips with the Diamonds, it was often a real trial of our patience and professionalism.

Imagine over 200 of us on an Amway chartered plane going to a lovely resort in the sun, with loads of activities, entertainment, fine food and drink and yet the handful of Amway staff found it a difficult assignment.

I was only on two of these to the Algarve and Majorca. There were formal seminars in the mornings, but the afternoons and evenings were largely about 'networking' and fun - not for us though - it was work. One of the reasons I had a suite with a large lounge and fully stocked bar and a coffee machine, was that the Diamonds would make separate appointments to meet day and night. It was always about trying to change company rules, bonuses and products to their financial advantage.

Happipreneurs they were not. It was worse for our distributor services staff and sales managers, as it was very difficult for them to do their jobs because the Diamonds ignored their advice and wanted to see me. The Diamonds' loyalty was to their 'uplines' in the States and they'd been taught to keep the company's staff at arm's length. In fact, the leaders throughout the multilevel marketing industry have a very ambivalent attitude to people in jobs. I once saw a video of an event in the States, not Amway, where they had a fake grave on the stage and a leader was berating Joe Nobody who had a J.O.B. and had died poor because he'd not joined the MLM scheme.

Naturally, every member of staff was very professional, always positive and smiley, but I do think it ironic that these people with the positive mindset, who managed to get their distributor groups into a state of continual excitement, in public at least, were often some of the most negative, bullying and blackmailing individuals you could hope never to meet. I'm very grateful to the two Diamond couples that were OK with me. Friendship was out of the question and why having our own business has been great in comparison - Clare and I have made a lot of fabulous friends out of customers, suppliers and employees. Paul Crook, that brave supporter of start-ups in Africa, was our first employee and Clare and I still see him every year when he comes over.

Q: What was the worst thing about the major leaders at Amway?

A: I don't think that what I'd choose would be the same as most Amway staff. But the worst thing for me was a cluster of behaviours which Clare, Eileen, Jude and I just cannot stand. It was the husband's attitude in the husband-and-wife distributorship. At times it felt like being surrounded by white supremacists.

For example, when the couple spoke at rallies the wife would speak for up to fifteen minutes and then the husband would speak 45 minutes or longer. There was very little diversity or equality in Amway leading distributorships. It was what I don't like about the white male evangelical preachers too - and Amway was very wrapped up in this kind of preaching. That's no good for me.

Even though it's not politically correct I believe in positive discrimination to promote equality. When we put together the first SFEDI team in London there was me on a contract and Donna, Julie and Stefan all on salary - two black people, two white people, two women and two men.

Q: What do you think we've achieved by writing this book?

A: I come from a boxing family, so I'll answer by saying I hope we've pulled no punches and we may even have delivered one or two knockout blows to those that rip-off micro-business owners in the UK. For example,

I don't believe in generic business advice as being particularly useful unlike sector and functional advice, like your social media marketing. But I do think that as two people that have built their own businesses and interviewed thousands of business owners that we've provided some good guidelines for others, especially start-ups.

We've also passed on what we've learned from some great teachers and authors about how to make ends meet and live a happy life. You never know #Happipreneurship may catch on now. I think we've achieved everything we set out to do if every reader feels we've explained what it's like to be a #Happipreneur and why #MicroBizMatters. It has been great fun - thanks, Taryn.

Q: How would you sum things up Tony?

A: The main reason I've been consistently happy since 2010, is because I've done as Albert Ellis and others suggest. The only thing we can control is our own thoughts and actions. We can even practice how we react in horrible situations. I enjoyed every minute of lockdown and felt so lucky that I was with Eileen, Carl, Alan and Sinead. My moods and sulkiness have been far less since I've lived to be a #Happipreneur nearly every minute of every day. It's about realising how lucky we are and as David Hockney said recently, *"I love life*".

EF Schumacher puts it all into perspective, but Albert Ellis, the psychologist, expressed it best when he said "*masturbation is good but musturbation is bad."* Musturbation describes the three things that hold us back:

I *must* do well. You *must* treat me well and the world *must* be easy. Just brilliant advice for everyone by Albert Ellis. I know that the for the rest of my life I'll be battling against a government that doesn't believe #MicroBizMatters, but I'll still enjoy every single day.

*"Any intelligent fool can
invent further complications,
but it takes a genius to retain
or recapture simplicity"*

EF Schumacher

XIV
Observational Q&A

When you get to know Tony, it's clear to see that he has inherited his father's desire to be liked and in brief moments there are hints of the vulnerable child looking for approval. Therefore, does his integrity stem from a place of wanting to please as opposed to a genuine altruism?

One of the most intriguing conversations I had with Tony was in regard to him being an entrepreneur.

When I asked him about being one, he was quite firm in his belief that he wasn't.

His reasoning behind this was that in his mind an entrepreneur works hard to improve his or her own life, status or business, whereas Tony's sole purpose has been to improve others.

The Cambridge dictionary defines an entrepreneur as:

"Someone who makes money by starting their own business, especially when this involves seeing a new opportunity and taking risks."

So, in one way, he most definitely is. Leaving Amway and setting up in business was most definitely a risk, not having a client pool or knowing whether it would be a success took a leap of faith. Also having worked tirelessly to be heard and to make change, to me is the mark of an entrepreneur, perhaps not in a conventional way but here is a man that trailblazes.

Q1 - Do you feel that Tony is an entrepreneur?

Clare Francis

"I agree with Tony's definition, most entrepreneurs are driven to make a success of their own business and hopefully will help others by the product or service they offer. Tony however has always been a social enterprise which at times has annoyed me as I have wanted him to be a bit more focused on making money for his business because it would help him in the long run help others. If he had been more focused in the early days on making his own business more financially stable, then he could lean more towards being philanthropic."

Tina Boden

"I would say that he's not, I understand why Tony would say no, we both feel that the term has now been skewed, I don't like using the term for myself, even though I know I am one, so yes I can see why Tony would say that. Tony sees himself less likely to consider taking a financial risk that he feels an entrepreneur would take."

Nigel Hudson

"I'd label him 'essence of enterprise' if it didn't sound too much like a naff perfume (especially if you catch him at the end of one of his charity half marathons).

Tony has repeatedly identified needs and built organisations to meet those needs. All of the substance without any of the BS."

Paul Lancaster

"I would say that Tony is entrepreneurial not an entrepreneur as he uses what he's got to make things happen. Tony is very much purpose before profit, knows what he's talking about and inspires people to listen and get involved."

Brad Burton

"I think, simply that Tony is someone who is making a difference, it's not about a label it's simply what he's doing."

Jenn Crowther

"I think Tony is a leader. He has been an entrepreneur in the past, but he's now evolved from that. I know this based on his own business success, he totally was an entrepreneur, but he's surpassed that and gone to the next level."

So, in that respect the answers are quite divided. I'll leave you to make up your own mind, however it's clear that entrepreneur or not, he certainly has a skill in raising his head above the parapet and getting people to listen to him.

This then led me onto the future and whether those I spoke to felt his campaigns were worthwhile and attainable.

Q2 - Do you feel that Tony is naïve in his current endeavours?

Clare Francis

"He has such a driving need to have achieved something in his life, he will definitely make some of these things happen. The #PayIn30Days for instance, he will achieve this, he has taught himself how to network and get out there with people. Therefore, he's got to know some tremendously influential people now on the back of this and I believe that he really will achieve something.

It may be he needs to narrow down his focus, for instance have other people run the MicroBizMatters Day to allow more time for him to put his energy to the projects that will raise money for his business and in turn allow him to keep on campaigning."

Tina Boden

"No, I don't think he's naïve, I think he's determined and like me he fears that he's fighting a losing battle, but he won't give in. This isn't naïvety on his part but a narrowmindedness of the powers that are not understanding the smaller businesses. He's doing what he believes in and not backing down from what's important."

Nigel Hudson

"Tony is a very positive person, unlike me, he looks at things from a marketer's perspective which makes us different. I'm very evidenced based and rational whereas Tony is intuitive and emotion which makes us chalk and cheese, although a good combination.

Tony is a good example of someone with passion and enthusiasm who connects with people and thereby influences them.

He has the potential to succeed at whatever he sets out to do because of the force of his personality and enthusiasm. The positivity you get from him encourages people to get on board."

Tim Campbell OBE

"Not naive, the world needs more optimists and he is the archetypal optimist. Has the ability to bring people together for a good cause. He's one of the good guys.

He is a model that people could replicate if they want

to have a more wholesome conversation in business and personally.

Is it achievable, to get microbusiness championed? - Yes, it is."

Brad Burton

"You have to start somewhere. If someone doesn't make a start you won't see change. I think that what Tony is doing is admirable, it looks like he's pushing back the waves King Canute style and more people need to join this campaign and support what is the backbone of this country. We need to stop being treated like second class citizens and the way you do that is to stop acting like a second-class citizen.

Personally, I now expect 100% upfront. I'm confident enough to walk away from big companies and this is what I would say. If a big company won't pay me up-front, I'll say, no problem, it can't go in the diary. More and more business owners need to be prepared to walk away."

Jenn Crowther

"Totally not, he's definitely not naïve, he's more aware than anyone I know of, he just comes across as a little bit scatty sometimes! This is just who he is and believe me, he knows this stuff."

Q3 - My next question was based purely on the eccentricity of the man in the red hat. How is Tony viewed?

Clare Francis

"I think that initially Tony is underestimated, without a doubt. He has a phenomenal memory and he is very, very bright, but yes, I can understand why he has adopted the persona and it's been very successful I think, but initially, particularly younger people might think 'Who the heck is this berk?!'

So, with some people it can work against him, although once they get to know him, he is then introduced as a personality, on balance it works quite well for him.

It does make it easy for people to underestimate him, which when you think about it, it's a clever way of doing things really, if you're approached by someone very intense and serious, often the response is less enthusiastic. Whereas when you meet Tony, you're gradually swayed to his views without actually realising you got there."

Tina Boden

"I refer to him as my quirky business partner. He is eccentric. People underestimate his knowledge and his ability. He has always been too giving and so people try to take from him."

Nigel Hudson

"He's evolved to be more eccentric over time and he's gone down a path where he doesn't much care what government think of him. It may not be the best way to influence government but there doesn't seem to be any other ways that work including being formal.

Being himself and doing what he feels like doing - helping others his way rather than thinking about government approval.

#Payin30Days, going about it the opposite way, rather than approaching government to help, he's mobilising huge numbers of micro-business owners to use their backing to sway government's hand. Moving from working inside the tent to outside the tent. I think he's regressed to the teenage way of 'I don't give a damn; I'm going to do it anyway."

Brad Burton

"All day long, it's beautiful, they think "Who's this dickhead?" It's a strategy that works for both of us. I know that I look like a drug dealer and so people underestimate me, they do the same with Tony. With his feather in his cap you can't miss him, I'll have been on stage and see the feather poking up and know he's in audience. In business you've got to stand up, so Tony in a line-up of one hundred business owners will stand out. He's marketing even when he's not marketing. Most 'normal' people wouldn't do that, they want to

be vanilla, so when it comes to speakers and business

owners, how many are daft enough to wear a red hat? One.

He's created a field of one. In business you need to stand out."

Jenn Crowther

"I think he is viewed as his own brand; he's done what he set out to achieve, which is create an identity for himself. You can't miss him, you know who he is, he stands out of the crowd, he does this on purpose, and it works."

Q4 - What is the key Takeaway you'd like people to know about Tony?

Tina Boden

"*He's a very caring man. From a woman's perspective of being in business in a man's world, I have the utmost love and respect for Tony, for the love and respect he has for being in business with a woman and for what he believes that women can do in a business world."*

Nigel Hudson

"Tony is all about basics - fundamental lessons are

what you need to go back to and applying them in a peculiar situation. Finding innovative ways of applying them in unusual circumstances. Right now we're in a different environment but Tony's lessons are even more true today.

Being of value to others is a great way to evaluate your own sense of self and it has a way of coming back to you."

Paul Lancaster

"Tony knows what he's talking about and I wish that more people would listen to him. He's very funny and engaging, and always ahead of the game."

Brad Burton

*"He's always been supportive of me, particularly when I was starting out on the circuit, I'd bump into him and he'd be encouraging but more important, brutally honest. There would be a time when I'd died on stage and he'd say to me afterwards "Tough crowd" but if I said "no I was sh*t" he'd look me in the eye and say "Yeah you were". That's what I liked, I love that he is totally honest, but some people would rather not hear that.*

If you want someone to lie to you, go to some of these motivational speakers, want someone to tell you the truth... go to the 'Dickhead' in the red feathered hat."

Jenn Crowther

"The key takeaway is how genuine he is. He has every business person's best at heart. I have never seen anybody go out there and be so passionate about something and just follow that. Tony is what you see, it's all genuine."

Tim Campbell OBE

"Tony is a great catalyst for the movement, and I regret not having had more time to spend around him.

One of my key mantras to live by is that friendship is very cheap, but one of the best things you can have, and by cheap, I mean that maintaining it doesn't take a lot.

That's the kind of guy Tony is."

I don't think that I could put it better myself.

"The art of love is largely the art of persistence"

Albert Ellis

XV
2021 - Riding The Waves Of A Pandemic

In December 2019, my mum and dad came back to the UK, from a Christmas break in Spain, they were shockingly poorly but we put it down to winter travel. A week or so later a virus out of China was all over the news, nothing we expected to affect us here in the UK, but, troubling all the same. Over the coming weeks we were blindsided by restrictions, miscommunication and the beginning of a (to date) two year nightmare. As I write this, it's December 2021, we're currently all waiting for the next round of constraints to be placed upon us, without any confidence that those in charge actually a) know what they're doing and more worryingly b) don't give an actual toss about anyone but themselves.

Throughout this book you'll have seen the positivity we feel toward business and how hard Tony, in particular, has worked to champion it. This positivity has been sorely tested, it's a crisis of global proportions and the gulf between those getting on and getting government assistance and those struggling to continue day by day, is also of global proportions.

Initially, I was proud to see how many micro-business owners appeared to rise up and turn the situation to their advantage. I won't use the word pivot, because that actually implies a smooth movement or turning around, we business owners didn't do that, we scrambled, stumbled and clawed our way to making our business work in new and unfamiliar territory. But many of us managed to do it, becoming solely online traders, learning new technology, adapting to the impersonal way of holding meetings through our computers. Many added new skills or services and some changed their business completely.

In 2020 there were 5.7 million businesses in the UK. 96% of these were micro-businesses. In 2021 business numbers have dropped by a heart wrenching 8.6% BUT, micro-businesses persevered, and were the only category to actually show a growth in numbers.

It was empowering to watch, compared with the monolithic corporations floundering and ponderously making their changes; six months in and many of these giants were clearly unable to make progress, weighed down by layers of meetings and managerial approvals, complaints were soaring as were the length of their call handing and customer services telephone lines. Thus, began the call for government help.

Watching supermarkets and power companies go cap in hand, whilst making profits from those on the breadline was truly sickening. But nothing prepared us for the impact of so many falling under the radar and being ineligible for any form of help or support.

I'm going to let Tony talk speak on behalf of the #ExcludedUK whom he's currently championing and explain why it's so important to us to help those who have gone without for so long.

For me, one of the positives of lockdown was seeing people come together, no, not just the Thursday night clapping or neighbours helping neighbours (although, long may that community spirit continue) actually business owners working together and collaborating. I actually found that I had more time to network simply because there was no travel time involved; I met new people and found some amazing businesses that I previously didn't know existed. Through the powers of Zoom & Teams (just to name a couple) business owners reached out and were able to thrive.

In my marketing business, I discovered that there were two mindsets, those that instinctively pulled back and cut all, what they perceived to be, unnecessary costs and those that realised they need to market and be seen. I'm not going to lie, it was a sickening time, worrying that each morning when I checked my emails that another client would have decided to pause their campaigns. Fortunately, this didn't happen, but I know that in part, it's down to the frank conversations I had with clients, explaining the importance of retaining their current online presence. Understanding that during the lean months you need to market harder is a hard sell, but it's a factual one.

On the publishing side, I knew I had to do something drastic, and so I reached out to potential clients that had been considering writing a book and offered ghostwriting services, after all, there was more time for this.

Luckily, this was taken up and I spent twelve months almost working myself into the ground, at the end of lockdown though, my businesses had endured and so had I (just about!).

Would I do it again? Yes, in a heartbeat. Am I more prepared now? Without a doubt. Have I learnt from the experience? Tremendously. That's one of the things about being a micro-business owner, you have the opportunity to learn so much about yourself as your business grows. I'm putting in place changes to my business structure, so that I can ensure future growth and security, based on the observations I've made from the last twelve months.

This is something, as a business owner you come to understand, if I hadn't loved what I did, it would have been easy to cave in and let the business go. Because I'm passionate about both marketing & publishing then it was never a question that I would give it my everything.

This is the true ethos of being a Happipreneur – even in the toughest, darkest days, you get through and your persevere because you know it's where your heart lies and you 'know' you can make it through.

Speaking to Brad Burton about the pandemic he said "*After 2 years or so... The game board has been cleared. Businesses that were on the edge pre-pandemic have gone. Older Business models torpedo'd. My once 5,000 meeting per year real business Networking org. 4Networking... is now a hybrid / online model. There really has never been a better time to make a name for yourself, a life for your family and start that business you keep talking about starting!*"

Similarly, and echoing my own perspective, Tina Boden considers the pandemic to have been a '*good thing*' in terms of her own business. In conversation she said,

"*After the initial fears and worry that most of us had, I actually realised that this was a time that would enable me to change how I offered my services and reflect on what I wanted to do going forward. Lockdown meant that I was unable to see clients face to face and those that, prior the pandemic were reluctant to work remotely, now embraced it and have continued to do so. This means that I am now in a position to work from wherever I am, so the future for me is now more positive. I think that, most importantly, it gave micro-business owners a chance to stop and review how their businesses were working and what they no longer needed to do. We're often so busy 'doing' that we don't get the opportunity to take time out. This was much needed for so many of us and I think has created better and stronger business people.*"

I mentioned earlier that there had been an increase in micro-businesses in the last twelve months, many of these have been created out of necessity, farm shops, cake makers and handmade goods are all on the increase. Consumers heard and embraced the message of buying local. It was great to see Facebook Pages listing all the places you could buy fresh goods and how independent stores evolved to meet customer demand and still follow restrictions. But can these businesses continue? Tina summed up some of the fears that we may have;

"*Furlough gave people time to build businesses whilst still having their bills paid, if you've read the book, you'll see that we advocate for side hustles and not giving up the day job or getting into debt to build a business. However, what made a business successful during lockdown may not be sustainable in the long-term. Only time will show how many of these new start-ups have prevailed.*"

For many becoming self-employed was a necessity, more and more companies issued redundancies and cut hours and this also led to the increase in start-ups. With the right mind-set and support, these businesses could thrive, unfortunately the support hasn't been there. Tony & I watched in horror as the backbone of the economy was ignored and mistreated. Exclusions punished those starting their business or in the first year of trading and offered them no way to get financial support.

Nigel Hudson observes that, "*Covid looks to have had a mixed impact on business start-up.*

It's been suggested, including by the Financial Times, that one of the factors boosting the numbers of new start-ups has been online retailing. Certainly, it looks like all things online are going to be even more important in the future. I thought Zoom was an ice lolly until the modern plague came along! As with any technological shift, we can expect this to have helped some and hindered others.

More anecdotally, I've seen things getting tougher. During the pandemic it looks like a lot of people on furlough and the like tried their hand at an online side hustle for a bit of extra cash. Their unsustainably low prices (if you wanted to make a living) undermined some established businesses and heightened competition for newbies.

My conclusion is that anyone starting a business today should really understand and apply Tony's tips and pay even greater attention to the digital dimensions of winning and keeping customers."

Jenn Crowther, Chief Executive of Yorkshire in Business adds that in her opinion,

"The pandemic hasn't put off businesses growing, what it has done is take away any insecurity of diversifying or expanding, this is because the whole world has suffered from insecurity so there's been less to lose. Individuals who have faced adversity head on and shown resilience are the ones that have adapted and grown into more sustainable businesses.

It has been a difficult time for individuals working solely, self-belief and motivation have been the challenge, but many have sought out pillars of support from various avenues, which have meant that they are no longer alone and this can be key to keeping strong and determined in business. It has been so important to go back to the roots of why a person started their business in the first place and to find the love they had at first, to reignite this passion and to set a clear path ahead.

There has been a clear divide in business over the last two years, with many established businesses being

given financial support, which has resulted in their long-term survival and key to future successes. In comparison those who are newly self-employed in last three years have found themselves financially worse off and have either had to live off debt or give up business altogether, which, unless more support is provided, we could see the results of in five-seven years; this is the lifespan of many businesses so, in years to come, we may see lesser job opportunities and a decline in business services and products."

Will the future be a bright one for micro-business? Optimistically, Tony, Brad, Tina, Nigel, Jenn and I say yes, there are going to be opportunities not to be missed, and providing people take the advice offered here and start out from the right position; then we see no reason why it can't be there for the taking.

There is a lot of work to be done to alleviate fear and uncertainty; the pandemic does not appear to be going away anytime soon and we have to adjust our own mindset to overcome the challenges we're yet to face. It's not the same situation by any stretch of the imagination, but I like to think that we, as micro-business owners are working together with the same community spirit that those in the 1940's had post war. The drive to support, promote and collaborate with others is humbling, this is what will, in the long term make us rise and level the playing field. If we, in our millions band together, as Tony has been advocating for years, then we will beat a corrupt and broken system designed to hold us down.

Are you ready? I know I am.

Pandemic Q&A

Q: You've been very vocal about the way in which so many business owners have not been supported, in your opinion, what should have been done?

A: I've been very vocal for nearly twenty years, about Government policies that have adversely and progressively hindered the chances of start-ups, freelancers, self-employed people and micro-business owners ability to survive and thrive. Apart from the USA, I know of no other country which treats as 'deadweight' over 95% of its business owners while giving £billions of Government funding and support to small, medium and, particularly, large businesses.

All business owners want is a more level playing field so that they can make ends meet. The government should not have found 16 separate, often, conflicting, excuses excluding over 3 million business owners from Covid support schemes. Having decided on the furlough scheme for income support to employees and another scheme for the self-employed they should have ensured that every one of the 3 million received payments for the time their businesses was unable to trade because of Government restrictions.

They could have done this by using the 2018/19 tax returns and after January 2021 the 2019/2020 tax returns for the later Covid trading restrictions. Loans were never the answer as that just increases the already business-killing burden of debt which has been increasing year by year since 2010.

They could have also improved the ability of 95% of business owners ability to survive and thrive by not funding, buying from or contracting with large organisations which do not #Payin30Days or less - that would have got £26 billion cash flowing over twice as fast to 5.7 million micro-business owners.

As when it suits them, the USA and UK can find hundreds of billions to spend on financial sector crashes, overseas wars to be fought and drugs to be bought the Government could have helped all citizens, including 70% of business owners working from home, by subsidising our insane utilities and broadband costs during the pandemic.

It's the one million, hardworking taxpayers that have had to use food banks for the first time and the 3 million, and increasing, kids in poverty in the UK, that is a direct result of these Government policies. This is why I'll always be vocal about mercilessly discriminatory Government policies, including Government income support. I'm hated for it, but someone has to stand up to them. Fortunately, Gina Miller, Martin Lewis, Greg Wright and the Metro Mayors, led by Andy Burnham, and a small number of my friends and colleagues have similar views and are vocal too.

Speaking to Sonali Joshi who is Founder/Director of ExcludedUK CIC's, she echoed my thoughts and summed it up perfectly,

"*What was entirely lacking from the UK Government's response, was fair and adequate financial support for all UK taxpayers in need to see them through the pandemic. However, the disparities that have resulted and increased as time has passed are significant and the impacts on those left without adequate support, due to the hard-edge cut-offs to the criteria for support, have been quite phenomenal and ultimately devastating. The UK Government should have offered fair and equal support to all UK taxpayers in need, leaving no one behind - what we were all led to believe after the Chancellor initially announced the schemes in March 2020. And even if not at the outset, due to the speed of implementation of the schemes, as has so often been pointed out by the Chancellor and Government ministers, they had ample time to address the situation once the gaps in support and their harsh impacts on affected individuals came to light.*"

Q: 2020 was predicted to see a rise in new start-ups, whilst the actual figures remain shrouded, this would appear to be the case but equally many shut their doors. What advice would you give a new start-up during the pandemic?

A: 2020 and 2021 will be record years for start-ups with up to a million new start-ups each year. A small number of limited companies will have shut their doors but most self-employed people have to carry on despite the lack of earnings from their self-employment. Even those that had to find jobs will continue to run their business on a part-time basis. For many freelancers, there are few other work options unless they completely change careers. For example, in the creative sector, we see musicians, camera operators and stage crews taking on other types of employment, even awful jobs with Amazon, but they will return to their self employed career when live entertainment returns, as it surely will. I'm biased but the whole purpose of our 'Happipreneurship' philosophy and my 'Who Wants To Be A Happipreneur?' show is to say that starting and running your own business can be the most fabulous way of life.

Just don't listen to the government, the banks, the academics, the gurus, the contrepreneurs, salespeople and the self-improvement industry. Instead, listen to people in your sector or with your skillset that are happily making ends meet in their own business.

We've covered it all in this and other books we've written. You've got a better than 8 of 10 chance of still trading in 3 years time if you :-

1) Bootstrap don't borrow - until you've got enough paying customers to know you can pay back.
2) Test trade first - preferably while still in a job or with other income streams.
3) Ask for help from a business owner who understands your customers.
4) Build multiple income streams - don't put all your eggs in one basket.
5) Enjoy doing something you are good at.

Q: What is your greatest concern for up and coming businesses in the next five years?

A: That the Contrepreneurs and the UK Establishment outgun the Happipreneurs and all who want to make ends meet through a happy, enterprising work-life. There are great business support organisations like Yorkshire in Business and the John Cracknell Youth Enterprise Bank, which I'm respectively Chair and Patron of, which I know will be around for the next 5 years so the future is bright for many up and coming business owners.

All the work campaigning for recognition of 'Why #MicroBizMatters?" is paying off too as I recently attended a talk by the current Small Business Commissioner, Liz Barclay where she almost reiterated every single campaign we have mounted in support of micro business owners such as #PayIn30Days or less, #NotAnSME #Indie25ER (buying from indie business owners) and #MicroBizMatters.

The UK is one of the richest and yet unhappiest countries in the world. It will remain so until we have a government that recognises that Small is Beautiful - economics as if people matter - is worth a try. I'm certain that there are enough enterprising people can create the jobs, innovation, local economic growth and community support that we need to be a much happier and healthier society. Voters will ensure the Government has to consider the welfare, lives and livelihoods of the many and not just the rich few. Maximising shareholder value economics is a disaster.

Q: What is #ExcludedUK and why is it so important to you, that you're putting yourself through a gruelling 70 shows in your 70th year?

A: When you're well into the third act of your life, I think you're entitled to say and do what the hell you want. What I want to do for the rest of my life is raise funds for those much less fortunate than I am. The easiest way for me to do this is to perform the **'Who Wants To Be A Happipreneur?'** Shows and sell this book to raise funds for #ExcludedUK Boost grants. I'm also running 70 x 7 miles or more for Macmillan Cancer Support to include my 8th consecutive Great North Run (half marathon) and 4th marathon (Yorkshire).

The travel and the personal costs incurred are somewhat 'gruelling' but the show itself is everything I've ever wanted to do as a writer, speaker and business owner. We have so much fun at the shows. The aim is to entertain, provoke thoughts and action and above all ensure everyone attending feels more cheerful about their enterprising future at the end of the show than they did at the beginning.

Why am I devoting the rest of my life to raising funds for the #ExcludedUK Boost Grants? The answer is that I've seen how much a small grant with community support helps enterprising people to restart their lives and livelihoods. The estimated 3.8 million individuals and businesses excluded from the CJRS and SEISS schemes have already faced nearly two years without adequate and fair support. Despite, all #ExcludedUK's efforts since it formed as a grassroots community interest company - totally volunteer-led - in May 2020, alongside many other campaign groups, high-profile individuals and the business community, the calls for fair and adequate support have been to no avail. The government are not going to reverse their punitive decisions, but we can get help to those that were excluded.

The 30 suicides to date have hit our community hard and no more suicides is our aim.

#ExcludedUK has been inundated with testimonies from individuals and businesses who were excluded from support and who have been trying to get back on their feet and hoping to claw back some of their losses. Yet, as we speak, they still face cancellation after cancellation across sectors – events, retail, creative industries, hospitality, fitness, beauty, alternative therapies and travel are some of the worst affected. The sparse gyms. cancelled classes, empty shops, deserted market stalls and petless dog walkers, kennels and catteries are in every town. These are enterprising people so they will find a way to make ends meet but those in the worst positions need a helping hand.

A small grant can help them on their way to developing a new income stream, renting a chair in a hairdresser, paying for heating, food or broadband. It can give hope. It will take a generation to repair the damage but I can certainly make a start by raising funds to help them. Most of them were happipreneurs and they can be happipreneurs once again. It's a lot of fun for me too.

PART TWO

THE SMALL IS BEAUTIFUL ROLL OF HONOUR

Introduction To Roll of Honour

This 'Small is Beautiful' Roll of Honour can be signed by organisations of any size. Please email TonyRobinsonOBE@gmail.com the name of your organisation and the name of someone in control of the organisation who will uphold the values.

EF Schumacher predicted in 1973 that many large corporations would never say 'enough' and would exploit employees and suppliers, engender inequality and destroy our communities and the planet.

Happily, there are a small number of large corporations and many medium-sized businesses which along with most small and micro-business owners do believe in Schumacher's 'Small is Beautiful' values.

It is important that we recognise these organisations and choose to do business with them.

By preferring to buy from those on this 'Small is Beautiful' Roll of Honour we send a message to the exploiters and bullies. Eventually, we will convince most sector leading organisations that it is good for their business and good for our communities to subscribe to our 'Small is Beautiful' values.

These values include:

1. #PayIn30Days ALL suppliers ALL the time
2. Promoting equality and diversity
3. A fair day's pay for a fair day's work

4. Protecting our environment and communities

5. Unlimited growth is pathological

6. Small can make a difference and should be supported.

We first published the Small is Beautiful Roll of Honour (includes the #MicroBizMatters Hall of Fame) on our 5th Annual #MicroBizMatters - 2021 will be our 7th. It is continually updated online and a printed version is available at the main event of each Annual #MicroBizMatters Day. More details at:

http://TonyRobinsonOBE.com and please download the Small is Beautiful logo to display online and offline.

Thank you.

Our annual social media Day of Recognition, Action and Learning reaches over one million business owners - giving time to help each other. We call this the #PowerOfPlenty.

This Small is Beautiful Roll of Honour lists the businesses and people supporting EF Schumacher's and #MicroBizMatters' values.

We should all promote and buy from organisations on the Roll of Honour.

Small is Beautiful Roll of Honour

#FirstTMaster (Martin Mullen)

4 Social Good - Creator of Social Enterprises (Saundra Glenn)

Adrian Ashton (Adrian Ashton)

Adrenaline Content Marketing

(Susan Scarre)

Always Wear Red and ANGELFYSH

(Michael Owen & Lisa Forster Owen)

Ariadne Associates (Simon Jones)

ASAPay (Lorraine W)

Ashdown Audio Visual (Ian Chisnall)

AutismAble CIC (Andrew Forster)

Awards International (Don Hales)

B2B Marketing Global Ltd (Catrina Clulow)

Big Ian Donaghy (Ian Donaghy)

Bizradio.co.uk (Paul Andrews)

Blue Oyster Leading Edge Solutions Ltd

(Peter Jones)

Boomerang Consultancy, Boomerang Property & Boomerang Healthcare (Paul Tute)

Bridge Road Consultants Ltd (Debra Levitt)

British Independent Retailers Association

(Andrew Goodacre)

Bus and Bird Arts (Clare Taylor)

Business Achievers (Ron Immink)

Business Writers Limited (Huw Sayer)

Cambridge Social Media (Lenka Koppova)

CDCS Wirral (David Hall)

Cell Pack Solutions Ltd (Eddie Czestochowski)

Clearwave Enterprise Solutions

(Elliott Chandler)

Clowne Enterprise (Paul Davies)

Cocoonfxmedia Ltd & Lichfield & Tamworth Chamber of Commerce (James Blackman)

Copa Fizz (Gillian Bartlett)

Creative Leopard (Amy Archer)

Crook Consults (Paul Crook)

Deals4Worcestershire (Sy Hawkes)

Diginnomica (Dennis Howlett)

Digirank Ltd (Karen Pearce)

E Factor Group Ltd (Mark Webb)

EKM (Antony Chesworth)

ELECOMM LIMITED (John Hamilton)

Electrician - Electrical Safety for the Hearts and Ohms (Ian Simpson)

Empowering Change (Eve V Earley)

Enigma-Graphics (Roger Crackett)

Enterprise Nation (Emma Jones MBE)

Essential Business (Julie Stanford)

Essential Communications (Sam Rudland)

Esther Lawson IPA Group (Esther Lawson)

Famous Publicity Ltd (Tina Fotherby)

Far North (Ian Farrar)

Farillio (Merlie Calvert)

FCM Publishing & Chronos Publishing

(Taryn Lee Johnston)

Fondatrice Happy Therapy (Emma Meston)

FreeAgent (Ed Molyneux)

GymWolf PT (Ian David Worthington)

Holonomics Education

(Simon Robinson & Maria Auxiliadora Moraes Amiden Robinson)

Hottclix.co.uk (Jaqjit Sandhu)

Imvelo Ltd (Tamma Carel)

International Association of Bookkeepers

(Janet Jack)

International Copywriters Association

(Quentin Pain)

IRIS Solutions (Averill MacGillivray) assisting with **Lovestorm Cakeaway** (Leilani Storm, 14)

Itchy Fingers Design (Amanda Lucas)

John Cracknell Youth Enterprise Bank

(Charles Cracknell)

John Cracknell Youth Enterprise Bank

(Charles Cracknell)

Keystone St Neots (Hayley Williams)

Laredofineart.com & Laredoparis.com & Thedevelopmentspace.com (Claire Rose)

Leapfrog Mountain (Jackie Jenks OBE)

Linda Huckle Training & The Athena Network - Blackwater Valley Region (Linda Huckle)

Market Accents (Noreen Cesareo)

Micro-business Awards 2020 (Ruairi Devlin)

Mind Fit Ltd & YP2Grow (Neville Gaunt)

MINT Business Club (Nicola Jayne Little)

Minutehack.com (Dan Matthews)

Morgan Walsh Consultancy (Gary Howell)

Mums Bake Cakes (Paula Wilkinson)

N&R Accountancy Services (Richard Holland)

North Yorkshire Law (Natalie Foster)

Paid (Tom Howsam)

PANDA - Performing Arts Network & Development Agency (Anne Marie Crowther)

Peter Richardson Estates (Peter Richardson)

Poppy Design Studio (Simon Cox)

Print Inc & Design (Angela Windsor)

Problem Solving Company Ltd

(Janice B Gordon)

Purpol Marketing (Denise O'Leary)

RaeRae's Vegan Dessert Sauces

(Avaiyia Rae, 10)

Realise Development (Mike Chitty)

rradar (Gary Gallen)

Sadie Skipworth Social Media (Sadie Skipworth)

Salbor Ltd (Fran Boorman)

Sarah's Style of Art (Sarah Louise Milburn)

Shop Local Club Card

(Marcus Naidoo & Sam Naidoo)

ShopAppy.com (Dr Jackie Mulligan)

Simply Great Britain (Emily Whitehead)

Small Business Solutions (Albert Wright)

Small Business Web Services & The Biz Helpers Podcast (Ian Wilson)

Somerton Environmental Ltd

(Rebecca Bomers)

Successful Women Academy & The Athena Network - Central London region (AnYes van Rhijn**)**

Supa Designs (Patrick Healy)

Swakeleys Properties Limited (Clare Francis)

Swarm Apprenticeships & Norwich Mustard (Robert Ashton)

Techie Fairy (Chris Carlton)

The Digital Gene Sharon (Sinclair Williams)

The Exploration Habit Ltd (Alan Arnett)

The Forum of Private Business (Ian Cass)

The New Forest Tartan Company

(Kate Collison)

The Organisation for Business Empowerment Ltd (Elsa Caleb)

The Positive Pen (Janet Doran)

The Talent Finders (Nathan Konstantino)

Think Design Manchester Ltd (Paul Grogan)

Toucan Diversity (Anne-Marie Asgari)

TryLife Interactive Film Series (Paul Irwin)

Tweeting Goddess & Women's Inspire Network (Samantha Kelly)

Unique Wakefield (Sarah Firth)

Upkeep Training (Sarah Bentley)

Urban River (Carl Buckley)

Wagstaff Recruitment (Ruth Foster)

Wenta (Jennifer Condon)

Xero (Gary Turner)

Yorkshire in Business Limited (Jenn Crowther)

Zarywacz and Business Action

(Robert Zarywacz)

Inspire Scotland (Michael Doolin)

#MicroBizMatters Hall of Fame

Co-Founders:

Tina Boden & Tony Robinson OBE

Adrian Ashton

Alex Gajic

Alison Chesworth

Allen Pluck

Antony Chesworth

Catrina Clulow

Charles Cracknell

Charlie Mullins OBE *(our Tsar)*

Chris Percival

Clare Francis

Dan Martin

Dawn Whiteley MBE

Dee Maria Olajide

Dinah Bennett OBE

Ed Goodman

Elaine Clark

Elsa Caleb

Eve Lodge

Gaynor Carr

Henry Stewart

Ian Cass

James Blackman

Janet Jack

Janice B Gordon

Jo Harrison

Julia Emelogu

Kanya King CBE *(our inspiration)*

Karl Plunkett

Kate Hardcastle MBE

Kit Hargreaves

Laura Henry

Lorraine Allman

Marianne Whitfield

Martin Kirby

Martin Mullen

Michelle Dorrell

Mike Notarantonio

Mike Peates

Millie Notarantonio

Naomi Timperley

Neal Boden

Nigel Hudson

Patricia van den Akker

Paul Crook

Paul Lancaster

Penny Power OBE

Rhian Kempadoo-Millar

Ron Immink

Sadie Skipworth

Simon Cox

Sinead Robinson

Sway

Thomas Arran

Tim Campbell MBE

Tina Fotherby

Tom Evans

Tripp Braden

Zia Mallick

In memory of:

Stefan Topfer

Roanne Dods

Valerie Dwyer

Special Thanks

I'd like to take this opportunity to thank everyone that took the time to speak to me and share their thoughts on the man that is Tony.

So many of you have been generous of your time, often on more than one occasion.

It has helped me bring to life the man in the red hat.

Thank you all.

Song For BJ - Don’t Think Twice, It’s Our Lives

Well, it ain’t no use to hide and lie, BJ

We know Dom’s game by now

And it ain’t no use to hide and lie, BJ

Too many dead, anyhow

When your masters call for their pot of gold

Don’t say you spent it killing the old

You’re the reason our blood runs cold

Don’t think twice, it’s all life

And it ain’t no use herding the poor, BJ

They don’t listen anymore

And it ain’t no use purging the sick, BJ

Your doctors gonna lock the door

When they tug your strings to shine their shoes

You best be giving ‘em women and booze

You killed our livelihoods and we got nothing to lose

Don't think twice, it's all life

And it ain't no use sending 'em home, BJ
A home they never knew
And it ain't no use calling them names, BJ
Just cos they don't look like you
So when they come a-knocking to hand over the keys
You'd better learn to kneel, say sorry and please
We just know that we CAN'T BREATHE
Don't think twice, it's our lives

#YouTube video here:
https://lnkd.in/eUQ2ZW2

Thx to Bob Dylan - my amended words

Verse 1 is for #EveryLifeMatters,
2 #MicroBizMatters
3 #BlackLivesMatter.

Reading List

It would be remiss of me not to list Tony's other titles here as well as some of the books he is passionate about.

1. How to Start a Business & Ignite Your Life: A Simple Guide to Combining Business Wisdom with Passion by **Ernesto Sirolli**
2. Small is Beautiful - economics as if people mattered by **EF Schumacher**
3. How to stubbornly refuse to make yourself miserable about anything, yes anything by **Albert Ellis**
4. Happy - Why more or less everything is absolutely fine by **Derren Brown**
5. The Lean Startup by **Eric Ries**
6. #MicroBizMatters Start Up Guide by Tony Robinson OBE with **Nigel Hudson & Peter Drury**
7. Bog-Standard Business: How I Took the Plunge and Became the Millionaire Plumber by **Charlie Mullins OBE**
8. The Mom Test (How to talk to customers and learn if your business is a good idea when everyone is lying to you) by **Rob Fitzpatrick**
9. Get Off Your Arse by **Brad Burton**

10. The Antidote - happiness for people who can't stand positive thinking by **Oliver Burkeman**
11. Smile or Die - how positive thinking fooled America and the world by **Barbara Ehrenreich**
12. Be Useful by **Jos Burton**
13. Rockstar Retirement Programme by **Dominic Watson**
14. Business Evolution: Creating Growth in a Rapidly Changing World by **Janice B Gordon**
15. Business is Personal by **Penny Power OBE**
16. Winner: How to Win Business Awards by **Denise O'Leary**
17. In Search of Excellence by **Tom Peters and Robert H Waterman** and Liberation Management by **Tom Peters**
18. Power and Greed - a short history of the world by **Phillipe Gigantes**
19. The Plague and The Outsider by **Albert Camus**
20. Hard Times by **Charles Dickens**
21. Bartleby the Scrivener by **Herman Melville**
22. Freedom from Bosses Forever and Soculitherz on TV - 20 Feisty Enterprise Tips by **Tony Robinson OBE**
23. Loose Cannon by **Tony Robinson OBE**
24. A Perfect Little Gift by **Tony Robinson OBE**

Blog: The American Dream Turned Nightmare by **David Brear**

YouTube Videos:

'Bullshit' TV series by **Penn and Teller**.

Talks on Scepticism by **Penn Juliette and James Randi**.

The Contrepreneur series of videos by **Mike Winnet**.

Website:

Start-up and micro-business owner tips, guides, videos, podcasts, #MicroBizMatters Day interviews and blogs are at www.tonyrobinsonOBE.com - everything is free with no signups or pop-ups and no contact details are required.

Chronos Publishing

Life Stories

We sincerely hope you enjoyed this book.

If you'd like to know more about our forthcoming titles, authors and special events, or to be notified of early releases then follow us:
on Facebook @ChronosPublishing
on Twitter @ChronosPublish
or come find us on the web at:
www.chronospublishing.com
We love what we do and we'd like you to be part of a thriving community of people who enjoy books and the very best reading experiences.

Taryn Johnston
Creative Director
FCM Media Group

A Perfect Little Gift
Tony Robinson OBE

A selection of poetry and prose from 50 years of writing.

A unique, observational view of life in a quirky and sometimes whimsical manner.

Here Tony gives us a brief glimpse into his mind and the humour that shapes his life as he shares his deepest thoughts, loves and fears.

Looking at life, death and love in his own special way, Tony has captured his own personal journey and those who have inspired him to write in this summary of half a century.

Coming 2022

Top Ten Tips For Starting Your Own Business
Tony Robinson OBE & Nigel Hudson

Tony's Ten Terrific Tips" is for anyone looking to start-up and earn a living by working for themselves, such as a sole trader, self-employed person or a micro business owner.

It's based on experience – three decades of starting and running our own businesses and helping other people do likewise.

Simple and short – based on 10 essential tips

Practical help - to apply the tips to your business and extra real-life guidance

Coming 2022

Index

A

B

C

D

E

F

G

H

I

J

K

L

M

N

S

T

U

V

W

X

Y

Z